The Prophetic Existence

The Prophetic Existence

ANDRE NEHER

Translated from the French by WILLIAM WOLF

South Brunswick and New York: A. S. Barnes and Co.
London: Thomas Yoseloff Ltd

A. S. Barnes and Co., Inc.

Cranbury, New Jersey 08512

Thomas Yoseloff Ltd

108 New Bond Street

London W1Y OQX, England

SBN: 498 06627 4

Printed in the United States of America

Contents

Introduction

The term "prophecy" does not adequately describe the idea which this book wishes to analyze. We can hardly separate the concept of prophecy from that of anticipation. In common usage, the prophet is a man who *fore*sees and *fore*tells. We place the entire accent on the prefix. The *seeing* and the *telling* seem to be secondary; they appear to be but forms of the substance of prophecy, which aims at the discovery, the unveiling, and the announcement of the future. On the other side, the prophecy whose essence we wish to make clear is not necessarily bound up with anticipation. Its vision does not have to be tied with the future, but has a value of its own, a value for that moment. Its telling is not a foretelling but it exists immediately in the moment of the word. In that prophecy the vision and the word are in search of a discovery. But what they unveil is not the future. It is rather the absolute. Prophecy answers the nostalgia of a knowledge—not of the knowledge of tomorrow but that of God. In our book prophecy will be studied as a category of revelation. Prophetic experience occupies a place among all attempts —real or illusory, historical or mythical—to connect the divine with the human. In some way or other it implies a relation between eternity and time, a dialogue between God and man.

We need hardly point out that this dialogue is not necessarily pursued in words. Sometimes God's voice is —silence. Nor is that dialogue always visible. God's appearance is sometimes—darkness. This does not matter, as long as that silence and that darkness reveal God, even if the revelation only probes a mystery.

7

We must rather specify that prophecy is not satisfied with a revelation which remains intimate and hidden, whether it is lucid or mysterious. It does not simply discover the divine voice or its silence in exterior nature or its manifestations, nor in interior nature with its emotions. It is neither contemplation nor prayer. Going beyond the frame of a personal communion, the prophetic experience permeates man in order to give itself to others. This distinguishes prophecy from other forms of revelation, and the prophet from other religious people. Prophetic revelation is not limited to a reception, to an acceptance, or an interpretation. It calls for a transmission. The prophet takes part in the transcendent, not only in order to communicate with it intimately, but in order to share with it the effort to face the extraordinary. Two joint acts therefore constitute prophecy—revelation and communication. The prophet receives his revelation, which brings him in touch with the appearance of the transcendent, with the same intensity as any other religious person. But once chosen by God, he is also made to face the nontranscendent. He conquers time and stands in *history*.

When the prophets describe their psychological experience they liken it to playing the part of an organ, an instrument. Through them the infinite tries to penetrate the finite; eternity clears a path towards time. At first sight it is not so much the content of the prophetic message that matters but rather the manner in which the prophet is filled with that message. This is done in a struggling, organizing, and instrumental way. We are dealing with metaphysical time. Physical time is being transformed. Prophecy is not just the place of a revelation but rather the work of all revealed experience. Prophecy transforms the absolute into relative terms. Through the prism of prophecy divine time is reflected in various historical times.

Once prophetism is defined in this manner, we arrive

at an entire scale of extraordinary rich attitudes. As history testifies, they vary according to the religious systems with which they are connected; they are spaced out through the ages, from the primitive eras when uniform concepts were worked out by groups, to modern societies where every individual forms his own spiritual dimension. Prophetism covers the entire vast field of human experience, from magic to mysticism. These two boundaries, which are commonly conceived of as the base and the apex, the impure and the pure, a rough sketch and the final realization, point to the diversity of the intermediary elements. But once we become aware of extreme—though by no means exclusive—attitudes, we discover a deep relationship between all forms of prophetism. We cannot accept the strict discrimination between magic and mysticism.[1] Rather, we find a unity between the scattered manifestations of prophetism, and we might even be tempted to formulate an analysis of prophetism in general terms, which would be valid for all the climates of prophetic thinking.

But since we shall not yield to this temptation, the object of this book is confined to one particular prophetism which is strictly limited in history—*Biblical prophetism*. In order to underline this important restriction, I will often make use of the Hebrew terms *navi* or *n'vuah* for prophet and prophecy, respectively, rather than the equivalent English terms, since in the Bible and in the thinking of Biblical man—i.e., in Jewish thinking[2]—the original terms designate persons and notions whose irreducible essence this book wishes to point out, although it cannot be denied that those terms are somehow related to the general phenomenon of prophetism. In doing so, we do not relinquish from the very beginning a formulation in general terms, since Biblical prophetism is like a mirror of universal prophetism, but a mirror through which the reflections are put together in an unexpected and new light.

In fact, the Bible appears to be a veritable *compendium* of prophetism. We find there every effort to establish and to realize a relation between God and man, from vulgar efforts to the most sublime. At least in its lower forms, Biblical prophetism has a share in the universal phenomenon of magic; it knows ecstatic inspiration and mysticism; it even submits to the rational and institutional divination of the cults. It has messages for the smallest and the greatest event—whether it is a question of finding some asses or the ultimate pacification of a torn universe. It is a revolution and an eschatology. Seen by themselves, each one of those aspects stands in close relationship with parallels which comparative history has discovered in other civilizations. But the Bible is the only document where those opposite aspects are deeply connected with each other and placed within a common perspective. It is the same One God, always known by the same name, and from beginning to end He reveals Himself to man and yearns for communion with him. In other places, transitory and one-time contacts are made between certain gods and certain men, and the quality of the prophetism established in this way depends on the nature of those gods and the character of the people. In the Bible, the most diverse and even contradictory prophetic experiences are organized in the great notion of the same God who speaks to the same men all through history.

Step by step, the Bible describes a history of prophetism, where the actors are not pale legendary figures but beings of flesh and blood; not merely "types" of a caste or profession, but individuals with names, characters, and physiognomies of their own.

From the epoch of the Patriarchs, men like Abraham, Isaac, Jacob, and Joseph are more than nomad chieftains. They are in constant touch with God, who conveys to them His will, His orders, His blessings, and His revelations. We are not surprised to find that Abraham is called a *navi,* which, in Biblical terminology, implies prophecy.

Later, the supreme prophet appears, Moses — the leader of that great movement which took the Israelites out of Egypt and led them to the borders of Canaan. In spite of his unequaled qualities as a prophet, Moses was not the only one of his time. Eldad and Medad were also prophets, and Moses wished that the entire people of God were prophets.[3] Another contemporary of Moses was Balaam, the Midianite prophet,[4] whose example, according to the Bible, proves that authentic prophetic revelation was not restricted to the Hebrews.

All through the centuries that followed the establishment of the Israelites in Canaan the political power was in the hands of prophets. For the so-called judges were in reality prophets, and some of them were even explicitly given that title. When the country was ruled by kings, the prophets became the arbitrators of power. An uninterrupted chain leads from the prophetic brotherhoods of the times of Samuel, the last judge, to those of Elijah and Elisha in the ninth century. The great political crises— the establishment of the dynasties of Saul and David, the post-Solomon schism, the overthrow of the dynasties of the Northern kingdom—all originate in those prophetic circles in which we find persons of below average inspiration together with particularly strong ones, like Samuel, Gad, Nathan, Ahijah, Elijah, Elisha, and Michayu.

The series of literary prophets starts with the eighth century. The Bible does not merely speak of them but makes them speak and transmits to us their messages, their *books.*[5] Amos, Hosea and Jonah in the eighth century as well as Micah, Isaiah, Joel, Obadiah, Nahum, Habakkuk, and Zephaniah in the seventh are contemporaries of the last years of Samaria and of the reprieve of the kingdom of Judah. In the sixth century Jeremiah, Ezekiel, and

Daniel live during the great catastrophe, the fall of Jerusalem and the Egyptian or Babylonian exile. Towards
the end of that period, up to the middle of the fifth century, Haggai and Zachariah help with the reconstruction
of Jerusalem and the reinauguration of the Temple. Malachi is the last canonical prophet, and his message coincides with the restoration of the new Jewish state under
Ezra and Nehemiah.

A long but uninterrupted interval leads from Abraham
to Malachi. Biblical prophecy is always a dialogue between God and man. This dialogue has a rhythm all of its
own. When we read the Bible attentively, we can easily
discover the originality of that *Biblical time,* always directed towards the future.

In its canonical form the Biblical concept of time is
linear and purposeful, creating and alive. The world has
a beginning and an end, which have been written down on
the first and last pages of the sacred text. The first page
of the Biblical canon is the story of the Creation (Genesis
1); that introduction to the world is a "beginning," and
Creation is the starting point of history. The last prophecy
of the Old Testament, that of Malachi, is still to be found
at the end of the collection of the Prophets, and his words
are those of the last of the canonical prophets. Time is
fulfilled by the coming of God (Malachi 3:23f.), and
this is also the dénouement of creation. Between that
beginning and that end time unfolds with a continuity
which may be compared to a chain each of whose links, in
spite of their similarity, marks a new step in the progression. The Bible gives us the impression of a continuity
whose constituent elements are of a great variety and are
spread out over many centuries. Not only is such an impression superficial, but it is also absurd to assume the
existence of a last "redactor" who would have given a
general *meaning* to fragments that originally did not have
any. For the direction of Biblical time is not formal but

substantial. It is embedded in the very nature of Biblical
things, in the movement of history as it is told by the Biblical author. Before being integrated with the rest, every
part carried within itself a mark which corresponded
with the meaning of the general idea and which determined its insertion in a whole where it then occupied its
precise place. Neither could that place have been anywhere else, nor could the direction have been reversed.

Nevertheless the reader becomes well aware of the
time of the adoption of each of these sections. Biblical
evolution is not introduced with one stroke, nor through
the will of one single person, within a well-prepared
frame. Step by step, people of different types had lived
through it in widely separated epochs. Neither those
people nor those epochs knew their morrows; but they
did give birth to that future, which was the product of long
journeys, uncertainties, and errors. At every one of those
moments Biblical thought could find its original expression only at the price of conflict with contradictory thought
forms. He who studies a certain Biblical period for its
meaningfulness must always remain aware of the fact
that much effort was put in by those who themselves did
not yet know of that very meaning and actually had to
fight for its recognition. If, therefore, the canonical concept of Biblical time is valid and authentic, and even exclusively so, we still must admit that the Bible knows of
other concepts of time. These are the remainder of the
spiritual work of Biblical generations, the contemporaries
of civilizations which influenced them and who, in their
attempt to understand time, had to make use of certain
methods. Biblical time is thus a complex one: it comprises
not only the spiritual temptations which the world offered
to the ancient Hebrews but also the original directions
which those same Hebrews gave to their own concept of
the world. Anticipating our conclusions we can say that
the establishment of a definite order and the attribution

of a genuinely Hebrew meaning to the progression of Biblical time was, step by step, the work of the *prophets,* and that Biblical time is characterized by a constant effort to reach the *prophetic* standard.

However, we must make it quite clear that all this refers only to the *canonical* dimension, and that the *critical* method does not agree with those statements and views, but rather presents us with another perspective than that of a straight line from Abraham to Malachi. The problems created by the critical reconstitution of Biblical prophecy play a major role in Wellhausen's system, which even today receives a great deal of acclaim.

According to Wellhausen Biblical prophetism appears in full view only in the eighth century. The authentic type of Hebrew prophecy arises with those prophets who are called *great* or *literary.* The first of these is Amos. Before that time there was hardly anything but obscurity, and only the eighth century brought clarity, the cause for this being that the "great" prophets left us written testimony of their messages. It is true that these texts themselves present many problems, and a discussion is called for in order to determine which sections of the canonical books stem from the prophet himself and which from his editor, in order to eliminate later additions, changes, and interpolations. But in spite of the importance of such critical work which sometimes discovers in the book of an eighth- or seventh-century prophet certain layers which force us to go down as far as the fourth or the third century, in spite of such uncertainties, it is unanimously admitted that the prophet's "book" carries the authentic essence of the prophet, that such and such parts of the book constitute the original message of the prophet, reflect his true thought, and describe the milieu in which he lived. From the eighth century on we have a considerable minimum of established facts, thanks to which it is possible to reconstruct and to understand the history of the Hebrew prophets. As far as the literary prophets are concerned, we can therefore attempt an analysis of the essence of prophecy, all the while remaining loyal to an historic understanding of the phenomenon.

However, the inflexibility of Wellhausen's system has for some time come under scrutiny. The great prophets did not appear in the eighth century out of the blue sky. They are the sons of their fathers, the children of a tradition, men of their time and their milieu. Even when they proclaim they are radically different from those prophets who preceded them, their conduct, if not their inspiration, shows that they are definitely under the influence of their predecessors. Those Biblical "prophets" who antedate the eighth century are, to a certain degree, as authentic as those of the eighth century, no matter how difficult it may be to establish that degree. But that difficulty must not preclude the investigation of the matter. Although our analysis is addressed to the great prophets, this does not mean that our studies limit themselves to them. What it does mean is that we start with them. Their appearance coincides with the clarity of history; for whatever follows is intelligible and whatever preceded them is obscure. We must begin from the clear line in order to explore in two directions—going down to the very end of Biblical times and going up to its origins.

Many historians have made use of this method, which, while going up in history, has led them to those periods which Wellhausen's system had all but barred to research (Rowley, Kittel, Cassuto, Jacob, Haldar, Buber, Kaufmann, von Rad).[6] Much light has been shed on regions which heretofore had been condemned. Some scholars authenticate the prophecies of Elijah, others those of the prophets who were connected with the court of David and Solomon, others again the Nazarite prophecies of the Judges. Some scholars go back as far as Moses, others even to the Patriarchs. All of these phenomena apparently contain various degrees of profound and continuous tendencies which can be discovered among the great prophets too. For these do not offer a *new* form of prophecy but rather a more *accessible* one. In clear and contemporary documents the great prophets realize and establish what preceding prophets had worked out, although no trace of it may have come down to us.

In limiting Biblical prophetism to literary prophets, the critical method formulates not so much a demand for a break in the canonical scheme as one for additional studies. Whereas the amount of documents to be researched remains the same, their distribution and interpretations are different. While in the canonical perspective the originality of Biblical prophecies is affirmed at once, the critical method *isolates* Hebrew prophetism, sets it aside from other prophetisms of ancient times, especially from those of the Orient whose influences might have affected Hebrew prophecies or the studies of which offer interesting parallels. This also holds true of certain modern prophecies, since their interpretation is likely to change the range of Hebrew prophetism. This is especially the case with Christian prophetism in all thought systems which do not make allowance for a break between the Old and the New Testament.

However, such comparisons touch only the first steps of our inquiry. Canon and history come together when we wish to understand Hebrew prophetism in its essential expression: namely, time.

For we must ask ourselves how Biblical tradition can be put in order, and how we can, step by step, give a really Hebraic sense to the progression of Biblical time.[7] Within the framework of Hebrew religion we distinguish usually between a popular and a higher level. It is assumed that on the popular level we find encounters and reconciliations, mutual influences of neighboring religions and the rise, in Hebrew thought, of mythical and ritual forms which characterized all Semites and were perhaps even shared by all of mankind. On the higher stage, so it is said, an elite was on the alert, who protected Hebraism from all adulterations and degeneration. This is an alluring theory which allows us to see the originality of Biblical history in the continuity of its *great men*. It is, however, based on a very naïve idealism which does not take into account the variations of ethics. The distinction between those two levels can only be maintained by introducing into the Bible our own scale of values or, at least, that of the nineteenth century, which associated the moral calling with *genius*. But this is not the standard of the Bible, whose text does not attribute great affirmations to *great* men but rather to *obedient* ones. Biblical men of rank are not represented as innovators of a moral postulate but as servants of the Biblical God.

The Biblical prophets, too, are servants. It is just their inspiration which is a witness to their obedience, which does not free them but rather brings them closer to God's word. In order to understand them in their essence, we must therefore first place them within the milieu of the other Hebrews, to whom they were closely tied in a world of their own, namely, that of service and of the *Covenant*. Prophetic thought arises out of the Hebraic tradition. But to the prophets that tradition was not only a matter of thought but of life. They fought for its maintenance and for its triumph. Within the Covenant they were not only the servants but the witnesses of the absolute.

Thus we put the subject matter of our investigation into shape. Out of ancient prophetisms and the time forms which explain them arises its very opposite: Biblical time, which offers Hebraic thought a new dimension and a new world. All the Hebrews refer to the tradition of that thought. But the prophets test it in life. The essence of Biblical prophetism lies in this dramatic passage from tradition to existence.

Notes

1. See M. Pradines, *L'esprit de la religion,* Paris 1941, p. 12.
2. The reader will find in this book a *Jewish* formulation of prophecy. This means that he will find here again a tradition of thinking which is nevertheless not uniform at all and calls for frequent and important choices. As a matter of fact, within Jewish thinking there exist two mutually exclusive tendencies. One of these sees in prophecy an ahistorical, largely human attitude, conditioned by ethics, but, in the last instance, subordinated to the metaphysical will of the divinity. Such a description uses the style of psychology or ethics. (Philo, *De vita Mosis,* II, 68f.; Maimonides, *Guide of the Perplexed,* II, 32–48.) The other view sees in prophecy an historical phenomenon, which is tied to Biblical time and space and expresses the development of Biblical existence as written down by the prophets (Babylonian Talmud Baba bathra 14b and Med katan 25a. Josephus, *Contra Appionem* I, 7, also Judah Hallevi, *Kuzari,* IV, 16f.) We have here decided in favor of the *finite* view of Biblical prophecy and not for the *infinite* perspective. Our language will therefore be historical and metaphysical rather than psychological or ethical. In the nineteenth century Jewish concern with prophecy was mainly a social one (Darmesteter, *Les prophètes d'Israel;* Hermann Cohen, *Das soziale Ideal bei Plato und den Propheten,* and *Der Prophetismus und die Soziologie,* both in: *Juedische Schriften,* 1924, vol. I and II, resp.) In the twentieth century, Franz Rosenzweig *(The Star of Redemption),* Martin Buber *(Prophetic Faith)* and Abraham Heschel *(The Prophets)* have again brought metaphysics to bear on the problem. Our own approach comes close to Heschel's. Further on we shall indicate where we differ from him.
3. Numbers 11:26, 29.
4. Numbers, 22–24.
5. However, in that scriptural period we also have great prophets, whose message has not been committed to writing: a first Zacharia (II Chr., 24:22; Huldah. II Kings 22:14; Uriah. Jeremiah 26:20).
6. H. H. Rowley. *The Doctrine of Election,* London 1948; Rudolph Kittel, *Geschichte des Volkes Israel,* Stuttgart 1923; Cassuto, *From Adam to Noah; From Noah to Abraham* (Hebrew) Jerusalem 1950f.; Edmond Jacob, *La tradition historique en Israel,* Montpellier 1942; A. Haldar, *Associations of Cultic Prophets among the Ancient Semites,* Upsala 1945. Buber, *op. cit.* Yehezkel Kaufmann: *The Religion of Israel from its Beginnings to the Babylonian Exile.* Chicago, 1959. Gerhard von Rad: *Theologie des Alten Testaments.* Munich, 1958–1960.
7. See P. Ricoeur: *Revue d'Histoire et de Philosophie Religieuses,* 1953, pp. 296ff.

The Prophetic Existence

PART I
The Non-Biblical Prophetisms

1

Geographical Distribution

I.

The literature of ancient Egypt is characterized by an intimate relationship between prophecy and folklore. Divination is not only called upon in hieratic, diplomatic, and religious texts, but it is the very stuff of many popular stories that form the most picturesque and original element of ancient Egyptian literature, which is replete with predictions and foretellings of all kinds. In most of those stories prophets seem like magicians. They are stereotypes who use a simple but well-tested divinatory technique. In such books prophecy does not go beyond the bounds of magic.

But certain texts do present an exception, and there the prophets have another dimension than that of magicians. They have a well-described personality, a vigorous independence, a foreboding of things which go beyond the rather restricted and familiar horizon of folklore. Their message is not woven with the threads of anecdotes and little stories but rather moves on the plane of history.

Such is the prophet Nefer-Rohu, a contemporary of Amenemhet I, who flourished about the year 2000 B.C.[1] and was the founder of the twelfth dynasty. A native of Heliopolis, Nefer-Rohu is "a man with a mighty arm, a scribe who knows how to use his fingers, a powerful man, wealthier than any of his peers." He is an expert in the art of "speaking of the past and the future." Perhaps he

23

received that double faculty from his approach as a scribe, but also from the religious functions which he exercised at Bubaste, for "he belongs to Bast," one of the goddesses of the Delta. Without a doubt this means that he was the *man of a goddess,* a prophet-priest attached to the cult or the temple of a god.

This is also the case with the prophet Ipuwer, a contemporary of the Pharaohs of the twelfth dynasty.[2] Of his functions we know only that he was a *Sage* and perhaps an important official of the royal treasury. But the *Admonitions* which he addressed to the old Pharaoh show how strong a personality he was. He acquitted himself of his task as an informer with much dignity and realism, and he told his sovereign all he knew about the anarchy which raged in the Empire. He predicted the restoration and the return to order with the complete force of a visionary.

The common feature of the prophecies of Nefer-Rohu and of Ipuwer is the sobriety of their inspiration. At least in the fragments of the texts that have come down to us neither of them uses technical methods in order to attain an inspiration; they are no magicians. Neither of them uses psychological stimuli, nor do they betray an exaltation of their senses; their inspirations are not of the ecstatic kind. We meet here a type of intuitive prophecy which is so pure that it has not been considered prophetic at all. One might say that we have here a special type of wisdon literature, where predictions are a form of the rhetorical style.[3] Nevertheless Nefer-Rohu declares himself to be "concerned with the future of the country, attentive to what might happen, desirous of having a sage make a libation in his name, when seeing that what he had foretold had come true." Thus his prediction is not merely a literary one but the concern of his personality; he expects a fulfillment. Moreover, Ipuwer places a grave conviction in his announcements and, towards the end, expresses a profoundly prophetic sentiment: the pain of having to announce the disaster, "for not knowing it would be agreeable to the heart."[4]

Generally speaking, the somber and realistic accent of those texts reminds us particularly of certain pages of the Bible which are authentically prophetic.

> He said: Come on, my heart, and cry for the land that thou hast left.

> No rest—behold thou must face it; arise against what cometh . . . .

> The whole country is going to the ruins; no rest! The land is lost, and nobody cares, no one to talk to, no one who cries! . . .

> I show thee the land in desolation and misery; what has never happened before has come true. People will take up arms, and the land will rebel. They will fashion arrows of copper, and with blood they will beg for bread. Laughter will become unnatural, death is nothing to cry about . . . man will be persecuted by his own heart . . . .

> If someone speaks, one makes him shut up, and one answers him by brandishing a stick . . . .

> The sun forsakes man . . . one does not know when it is noon nor when it is dark . . . .

> I show thee the land in desolation and in misery . . . .

> (Prophecy of Nefer-Rohu)

> This is how it is: pestilence stalks the land, blood everywhere . . . .

> This is how it is: the land turns like a potter's wheel; a robber takes possession of the treasury . . . .

> This is how it is: laughter has disappeared, and sadness, mixed with mourning, is rampant in the land . . . .

> This is how it is: the great and the small say: Would that I were dead. The infants say: If I had only not been born . . . .

> Behold: the fire groweth, it riseth against the enemies of the land . . . .

> Behold: He who has been buried like a Horus is now placed in a coffin. What had been covered by a pyramid will be emptied out . . . .

> Behold: The mighty ones will have no news about their subjects; everything will be ruined . . . the Delta weeps . . . .

>   (Admonitions of Ipuwer)

Each one of these tragic predictions is complemented by an optimistic picture of the future. The antithesis is quite constant, and the coherence of the style betrays a plan where threats are balanced by promises, bad luck by good luck, and all that in an uninterrupted and dramatic succession:

> A king will come from the South. His name is Ameni, and he is the son of a Nubian woman and a native of Upper Egypt. Taking the white and the red crown, he will unite the mighty double pshent. He will cheer up the two lords [Horus and Set] with what they love . . . .

> Be glad, men of his epoch! That child of a man will acquire eternal fame. Those who wish to do harm and think of hatred will lose their courage in fright of him.

The Asians will fall by his sword, the Lybians will fall by his fire. The enemies will be defeated by his attack, the rebels by his might. The royal serpent on his forehead will pacify the revolutionaries . . . .

Then will the Wall of the Prince be built. It will prevent the Asians from descending into Egypt in order to beg for water, as is their wont, and to give their cattle to drink . . . .

Justice will find its place again, and injustice will be expelled. He who will see it and serve the king will be happy . . . .

(Prophecy of Nefer-Rohu)

How beautiful it will be when the ships will sail again . . . .

How beautiful it will be when human hands will build pyramids, dig ponds, and, to the glory of the gods, plant trees . . . .

How beautiful it will be when people will be drunk with a happy heart . . . .

How beautiful it will be when the mouth will be full with laughter and the dignitaries will be there to observe the happiness . . . .

(Admonitions of Ipuwer)

In the association of shadow and light the most original aspect of ancient Egyptian prophecy reveals itself: it has a clearly eschatological character. One must not read more into the texts than what they actually offer. For example, one should not follow Hugo Gressmann[5] and discover the reflection of scholarly speculations on primitive chaos, the destruction and a paradise-like renewal of the world. The plan is much more limited. Egyptian eschatology is not universal but rather political or, to be even more precise, dynastic. The belief in the divine character of the king led to the recognition of the ideal king in every new sovereign, and the optimistic description of the future corresponds really to a eulogy of the actual Pharaoh and to the hope which his subjects have in his regard, which in turn is the natural outcome of their religious beliefs. The pessimistic account and the description of the disaster include a criticism of the preceding dynasty. Thus prophecy serves national and dynastic politics.

But even after this limitation has been given recognition, Egyptian eschatology still has a certain value in the history of prophetic themes. The Bible, too, knows of dynastic prophetism, and even during the lifetime of its founder the dynasty of David most probably received prophetic approval. Certain prophecies contemporary with David—those by Nathan above all[6]—show the desire to recognize in the new sovereign the ideal type of king of Israel. Consequently, the Messianic aspiration, which was centered around the dynasty of David, could develop on facts of that kind. Among David's successors Hezekiah indisputably enjoyed a Messianic halo, and the trust placed in him has found a vibrant echo in the prophecies of Isaiah.[7] In addition, and independently of its contents, Egyptian eschatology presents in its form a characteristic scheme, with its alternating of bad luck and good luck, a rhythm which reminds us of the dialectics of the eschatology of the Hebrew prophets. Here we meet with a problem of influence, since Egyptian thought is very old and has had the time to influence Hebraic thought during the numerous periods of contact between Israel and Egypt.

But does that problem arise because of a secondary detail? The prophecy of Nefer-Rohu ends with a reference to justice and injustice. Thus the plan is not merely political; a moral note also shines through. The dialectic of bad luck and good luck turns, just as with the Hebrew prophets, into that of good and evil, which in turn are seen on the general level of social justice. Although this note is a very faint one in Egypt in the properly prophetic literature, it is not quite isolated in the whole of Egyptian thought. A long text is devoted to the *Lamentations of the Peasant*[8] who had become the victim of a greedy official and an unjust administration. Thus Egypt has not only given us, from very ancient times, eschatological prophecies but probably also—and this is an important contribution to the history of ancient prophetism—a social predication, a prophetism addressed to conscience.

II.

Contrary to Egypt, ancient Mesopotamia presents us, in the realm of prophecy, with a mere minimum of information. The civilizations which have followed one another in that region (Sumerian, Babylonian, Assyrian, and Chaldean) have left countless traces of magic and divination, but nothing, or hardly anything, is on a higher level that would permit the use of the word prophecy or prophet.

However, it is possible that certain expressions on the list of Babylonian soothsayers have a purely prophetic meaning. Even if the *ashipu,* the *baru,* and the *shailu* are only variations of soothsayer or exorcist, the *mahhu* is most probably an ecstatic prophet. Without using the techniques of divination he communicates the opinion of the divinity to which he is attached. The Temple of Ishtar in Arbela knows of such prophets, whose functions are mainly cultic, and through whose mouths Ishtar expresses her oracles to others. The *mahhu* therefore does not address himself to the divinity but is rather possessed of it. The phenomenon is not magic but rather mystic. It is true that the texts are neither numerous nor characteristic.

Their artificial form makes us believe that the magic formulas and incantations are merely implied. Whatever the case may be, we should point out that that entire prophetic priesthood has a very functional aspect. G. Conteneau[9] put it thus: "Babylonian cult is truly a state institution . . . . If we take into consideration those cases that have to do with divination, its functions through the medium of religious officials, the existence of a whole body of royal soothsayers about whom we have reports, we realize that we have here an organism as important as the finance or war department. This organization replaces our own advisory staff, an institution on which all state decisions depend—like questions of peace or war—an institution from which the history of Assyria and Babylonia receives its very moving power." The prophetism of the *mahhu* is no exception to this general rule, for he, too, is a kind of official in an organization which has the king as its head. Mesopotamia seems to have been the territory of *institutional* prophetism, and Biblical history too, proves its temporary existence within the very State of Israel.

The mention of Mesopotamia calls for a special consideration of the information which we have recently received through the royal archives of Mari.[10] On the whole, those documents from the time of Hammurabi furnish us with a glimpse of the Babylonian civilization at the beginning of the second millennium, and confirm what we have always known about the institutional role of divination. Again and again the officials tell the king that they have carefully "read the omens."

> Say this to my lord: Thus speaks Mukannisum, thy servant. I have done thy bidding concerning the matter of Addu with which thou hast entrusted me. The seers have looked at four sheep. I am sending their report to my lord. A complete report which my lord has sent me . . . . (Mukannisum's letter to the King of Mari, Zimri-Lim, Archives Royales, II, 139.)

Say this to my lord: Thus speaks Kibri-Dagan, thy servant. All is well with Dagan and Iakrub-El. All is well with the city of Terqua and its environs. Something else. Coming back to what my lord had written to me before concerning the house where the priestess of Dagan is to live, I have asked the oracles. The oracle has been in favor of the house of the former priestess. The god has replied in the affirmative, and I have put that house in order and I am supervising the arrangements. The priestess whom my lord will take to Dagan can live there. (Letter of Kibri-Dagan to Zimri-Lim, Archives Royales, III, 42)

Say this to my lord: Thus speaks Kibri-Dagan, thy servant: I have consulted the oracles concerning the well-being of Kunshi-matum, and oracle is favorable. May my lord have peace of mind. (*Ibid.*, 63)

We are dealing here with minor details of day-to-day life, which interest nobody but the king. The question of the new residence for the priestess of Dagan is taken up once more in another letter (III, 84) and a new consultation of the omens had become necessary. Kunshimatum's state of health is mentioned in detail in a brief bulletin (III, 64).

But in most cases the intervention of the oracles is sought in connection with important state affairs, like wars or negotiations:

. . . At the head of my lord's men marches Ilushu-Nasir the soothsayer, my lord's servant, and with the Babylonians marches a soothsayer from that country. Those six hundred men will stay in Shabazim. The soothsayers will reconcile the oracles. According to favorable oracles one hundred and fifty men will leave, and one hundred fifty men will come in . . . .

This letter (II, 22) is a war episode, where Hammurabi's troops join those of Zimri-Lim. The officer of the

King of Mari gives an account of the operations and underlines the importance of the soothsayers of the two armies and their oracles. In a long report of another officer (II,39) it is pointed out that the defense of a certain garrison was handled according to the indications of the oracles.

From an otherwise rather mutilated letter we conclude that every district was entitled to one soothsayer, and these, as religious administrators, were appointed by the king. The respect accorded to them by the royal governors is evident from a letter written by Kibri-Dagan, the governor of the district of Terqa, to King Zimri-Lim:

> · . . As for myself, I leave no stone unturned to have oracles taken on behalf of the well-being of the district . . . . (Archives Royales, III, 41.)

Thus we see that the administrative organization of divination was greatly advanced in the kingdom of Mari, and this was quite in line with the customs of Mesopotamia as a whole. But the interest of certain tablets of Mari lies in the fact that they throw some light on the manner in which those oracles were consulted and delivered. For unlike other Mesopotamian texts we observe here clearly that neither the proceedings of that divination nor the personalities of the presiding seers relied entirely on magic. In the texts of Mari, the *mahhu,* that seer who already in the texts of Arbela is different from the soothsayers is a true messenger of the divinity, a man *called,* who arises suddenly, and has a message, which can have been given to him only by the word of God:

> · . . Say this to my lord: Thus speaks Kibri-Dagan, thy servant: All is well with Dagan and Ikrub-Il. All is well with the city of Terqa and the district. Something else. On the day that I sent my lord my tablet the mahhu of Dagan came and announced as follows:

"God has commanded: hasten to write to the king that a funeral meal shall be consecrated to the manes of Iahdun-Lim." This is what the mahhu said, and I am writing it to my lord. May my lord do what seems good to him! . . . (Archives Royales III, 40)

. . . Say this to my lord: [Thus speaks] Kibri-Dagan, thy [servant]. All is well with Dagan and Ikrub-Il. All is well with the city of Terqa and the district. I am doing my share in having the barley harvested and winnowed. [Something else.] Concerning the new door which is to be built, the mahhu [has come], then . . . When I sent this tablet of mine to my lord the *mahhu* came again and said. . . . He declared categorically: . . . ye cannot build that door . . . will take place. Ye will not succeed! This is what the mahhu has said . . . . (Archives Royales III, 78)

. . . from Dagan . . . in these terms: concerning the sacrifice, Dagan wrote to me: "Write to the lord on the fourteenth of the next month that the sacrifice [to the dead?] shall be brought. This sacrifice must in no wise be omitted." This is what that man has said. So I have now written to my lord. May my lord think of it and do as he pleases . . . . (Archives Royales II, 90, fragment)

We are not here concerned with the object of the oracles, for these—sacrifices in honor of a dead king or the construction of a door—are minor matters. What does interest us is the personality of these "men of Dagan," who transmit God's own words, often in the form of a letter. The revelation is given without signs or omens, and is not the outcome of divining inferences. These men have religious or mystical experiences which remind us in certain aspects of Biblical prophetism in its purest forms. Sometimes the style of the oracle has a surprisingly Biblical tone. This is especially so in a letter in which an official of Zimri-Lim transmits to the king two oracles of the god Adad:

> . . . Concerning the men . . . had this to say: Hand over the men and the cows! My master before the kings . . . has commanded to hand over the men under these terms: "No more revolutions!"
>
> Through oracles the lord of Kallassu has spoken in these terms: "Am I not Adad, the lord of Kallassu, who has raised him on my knees and who has led him to the throne of the house of his father? After having led him to the throne of the house of his father I have also given him a residence. Now, as I have led him to the throne of the house of his father, I could take Nihlatum out of his hands. If he does not make delivery I am the master of the throne, of the territory, and the city, and whatever I have given I can take away. If, on the other hand, he will fulfill my wish, I shall give him thrones upon thrones, houses upon houses, territories upon territories, cities upon cities, and I shall give him the land from East to West."
>
> This is the reply of those who always consult the oracles. Now the respondent of Adad, the lord of Kallassu, supervises the region from Alhtum to Nihlatum. May my master know this!
>
> Earlier, when I lived at Mari, I sent to my master whatever the respondents had said. Now that I live in another country, do I not write to my master all that I hear and what I am told? If in the future any trouble should arise, will my master not express himself in these terms: "Why did you not write to me what the respondent has told you, since he supervises your region?" Therefore have I written it to my master. May my master know it!"

In these oracles the claims of the divinity are rather limited. They have no moral character and deal solely with the delivery of certain victims. But they are supported by formulas which betray a really prophetic conception of the kingship of Mari. The god bases his claims on the fact of an *election*: it is he who has raised the sovereign, who has given him a throne and a residence. He backs those claims by recalling the *contract* which ties the sovereign to the divinity. Thus the blessings and the warnings follow automatically the king's obedience or disobedience. Now the ideas of election and of contract are an integral part of what one might call Biblical theology. Thus the prophecies of Mari are interesting to Biblical prophecy for two reasons: just like the prophets of the Bible those of Mari appear intuitively inspired, and furthermore, they associate the ideas of the election and the covenant with divine intervention.[11]

These findings are of the utmost importance for the historian of Biblical prophetism. After all, the civilization of Mari is not completely alien to the Hebrew one. The Aramaean tribes installed at Mari at the times with which the archives of Zimri-Lim are dealing, and which are frequently mentioned in the letters, are the ancestors of the Hebraic tribes. One of them may be identical with the clan of the Terahites, and Mari was doubtlessly a stage in the migration which is mentioned in the Bible (Genesis 11:31), and which led the Terahites from Ur to Haran, and then the Terahite Abraham from Haran into Canaan. At this stage of our knowledge it is as yet impossible to define the exact connection between Mari and the Bible. Nevertheless the texts are clear enough to allow for the assumption of such a tie. Unlike the case of Egypt and Babylonia, the problem is not one of *influences* but of *sources*. In Mari we begin to discover the origins of Biblical prophetism. Without a doubt the *prophetism* of Mari constitutes the *prehistory* of Biblical prophetism.

III.

Even though Egypt and Babylonia sometimes prove the existence of prophetism, which was on a higher level than those of mantics, it is still of a moderate type. We have intuition without exaltation. *Asia Minor* is most probably the cradle of much stronger mystical prophecies which were to spread out for a long time in the most diverse countries. This is the prophetism of the *ecstasy* and the *enthusiasm*.

Phrygia is the center if not of the origin at least of the blossoming of that ecstatic prophetism, and also the center of the propagation which is felt for a long time and at great distances. Around the cults of Cibele and Attis there develops a frenetic and orgiastic religion which gives its faithful a power of vision the most apparent sign of which is a delirious state. This frenzy, which is sometimes provoked and entertained by exterior means—above all the absorption of strong drink or the rite of consuming raw meat—and which is often based on a simple spiritual communication with the divinity, transfigures people radically. Now they are possessed, and their state prepares them for hallucinatory visions or spoken prophecies, which are sometimes incomprehensible.

Phoenicia is one of the countries most strongly influenced by that Phrygian prophetism. From the tenth century on, which means after the invasion by the sea people and the breaking up of the Egyptian-Hittite coalition, and at the same time that Phoenicia arises as an independent empire, the Phoenician prophets are acquainted with ecstacies and frenzy in their particularly plastic and cruel forms. Their trance is attained through music and dancing, but also through bodily mutilations, nudism, and sexual excesses.

The description of these Phoenician prophets is given to

us mainly in the Bible,[12] where it deals with the servants of the Baal and the Astarte of Tyre, whose cult Jezebel had introduced in the Kingdom of Samaria in the ninth century. But before that Canaan had probably already been contaminated. The close relationship between the Phoenician and Canaanite civilizations easily explains the fact that ever since the Hebrews invaded Canaan, which is to say between the fifteenth and thirteenth centuries, the invaders met with the frenetic type of prophet, and at the time of Saul, the Hebrew prophetic brotherhoods resemble in certain aspects their Phoenician counterpart and perhaps gave rise to Canaanite prototypes. In any event, non-Biblical documents prove the existence of the phenomenon in Phoenicia long before the ninth century. Although we have but insufficient proof of this, the fact, if not the nature and extent of the phenomenon, cannot be denied.

In the twelfth century, an Egyptian official by the name of Wen-Amon undertook a journey to Phoenicia, where he wished to purchase some Lebanese wood for the construction of a boat for Amon-Ra, the king of the gods. Since he had no money, he offered instead the blessings of Amon himself, whose carefully guarded statue he had brought along. The story of his voyage is preserved in the Golenischeff Papyrus.[13] Because he was badly received at Dor and at Tyre, he landed at Byblos. But the King of Byblos was no friendlier than his colleagues. For nineteen days he refused to see the Egyptian and gave him to understand that he ought to leave the port of Byblos. However, a religious incident made the king change his mind:

. . . While the king brought a sacrifice to his gods, the god seized one of his young nobles and brought him to convulsions. He said: "Bring the god here. Bring the messenger of Amon who has him . . . Send him away!"

In the same night that the man was still having his convulsions, I found a ship bound for Egypt, I loaded all my things and waited for darkness to descend, for I said: When it will come, I shall take the god along so that no one can see him! The master of the port approached me and said: Stay till tomorrow, as the prince desires. I replied: Was it not you who told me every day: Leave my port! ... He turned around, went to tell the prince, and the prince sent word to the captain of the boat: Stay till tomorrow morning, as the prince desires! In the morning he took me up to the castle where he resides by the sea, while the sacrifice was being offered . . . .

Thus it was the gods of Byblos who inspired the prince with friendlier feelings. And they did this without being consulted, on the occasion of a sacrifice, through a prophet, whose "convulsions" properly underlined their ecstatic character.

We find the same situation in the texts of Ras-Shamra, from the fourteenth century.[14] An ecstasy is clearly mentioned, following the celebration of a cultic act:

Here! Give the gods to drink,
The hand of El the King will seize thee . . . .

This is the more interesting as the "possession," the entrance of the spirit of the god into that of the prophet, is termed "the hand that seized," an expression often found in the Bible. The funerary rites which are mentioned in the Ugaritic texts, with their often frenetic manifestations, are also accompanied by ecstasies, some of which lead to oracles.

The words used to designate the prophets of Ras-Shamra are not greatly characteristic. We find *noqed* (cultic prophet?), *ari-el* and *ish-el* (man of God), *choze* and *oded* (seer); each of these terms has an equivalent in the Bible.[15] It is hard to admit that all of these prophetic categories were ecstatic ones. The variety of functions corresponded to a variety of inspirations, and we may suggest that Phoenicia and Canaan also knew a more moderate prophetism besides a delirious one. This can be shown by some preliminary proofs. Ben-Hadad, King of Aram, and ten other kings besiege Hazrik in the principality of Hamat. The sovereign of Hamat, Zakir, consults his Baal:

> . . . And I lifted my hands towards Baal, and Baal answered me, and Baal . . . to me through seers and prophets: "Fear not, for I have made thee King, I shall be at thy side, and I shall deliver thee of all these kings . . . .[16]

The stele of Mesha contains two oracles which came from the god Kemosh. They are brief orders, directly transmitted to the King of Moab. The latter was probably a prophet himself, for on the stele he calls himself *noqed,* which is also found at Ras-Shamra. There is no reason why the prophecies of Hamat and Moab should be considered to be ecstatic ones. They are sober messages, transmitted without trance or frenzy. The countries of Aram and Moab are so close to Canaan that we may assume that there existed a temperate prophetism besides the exalted one.

IV.

The Mesha stele has led us to the beginning of the eighth century. This is the century when new and important centers of prophetism begin to show themselves, prophetisms which were to accompany Hebrew prophetism, and a quick study of which is necessary not only in the interest of comparative history but also because they themselves are interesting—namely, the prophetisms of Persia and Greece.

Persian prophetism presents itself in two distinct
forms.[17] The older one, which from the second millennium
on had been incorporated in Mazdaism, is orgiastic and
full of mysticism. The Mitra cult has an important place
here. There are many priests, prophets, and initiates who
are in no way different from the initiates of the Phrygian
ecstasies, since Mitra himself came from Phrygia and
had been imported into Persia. A younger form is that
of the Mazdaism of Zoroaster. The reform of Zoroaster,
which is assumed to have taken place in the seventh century, does not quite eliminate the ecstatic aspect, at least
as far as the personality of the reformer himself is concerned. Zoroaster is a prophet of the vision and the ecstasies, but also a *matran,* a mouthpiece. He does not get
his inspiration in a sacred rite but in direct contact with
the spirits, *spenta mainyu.* Thus, along with the conserva-
tion of the irrational element, we find here a very strong
anticultic reaction. The Hebrew prophets of the eighth
century had preceded him on this road of a "numinous"
spiritualism, which was to remain characteristic for modern mystical religions.

But Zoroaster's contribution to modern religious
thought is not only a formal one. Many historians hold
that it was through Persian channels that the apocalypse
invaded Judaism and then Christianity. Persian eschatology has indeed the appearance of a drama in three acts,
the rhythm of which illustrates the confrontation of cosmic good and evil. After having been *created,* the universe
exists in all its complexity. One day it will *return* to its
simplicity. What Egyptian eschatology had presented as a
possibility at two different times, a rotation, here becomes
a cosmic necessity. The future is contained in the actual
drama; it is its fruit and its necessary accomplishment.
We realize that Messianic expectations receive a new
meaning in this concept. In Egypt, it is only a change, for
better or worse, of a given situation, whereas in Persia

the Messiah is expected for absolute *salvation*. When the Apocalypse arises, it resolves the drama of God and the world. Thus Persian prophetism is apparently a universal prophetism, which one might be tempted to compare to a philosophy.

V.

Greek prophetism, on the other hand, is far from being a philosophy. Classical Greek literature is replete with allusions to people of very different character, people who fulfill a variety of functions, but alike in that they have a knowledge of events which escapes other people. Sometimes these are heroes of ancient legends (Orpheus, Museus, Bacchus, Epidmenides), sometimes semi-legendary persons, created or reshaped by poets and philosophers (Cassandra, Theresias); at other times again they are fortunetellers or wandering jugglers like the Bakides and the sybils; or, finally, they may be functionaries of a cult or a city. As they differ in their personalities, so do they in their functions. Some of them merely interpret correctly the will of the gods, others seem to have worked out real religious doctrines; or else they foretell the future, either in the form of short oracles or in the frame of elaborate visions. The same diversity is found in the means of expression—some of them convey simple answers without beating about the bush whereas others appeal first to poetic inspiration or to an ecstatic trance.

The Greek prophet is generally called *mantis,* which etymologically means one who is possessed. This fact immediately differentiates Hebrew prophetism from Greek. Whereas the latter appears to be a more and more exuberant development of magic trends, the former rejects more and more categorically any relation with magic and therefore comes closer to Greek philosophy than to Greek religion. The fact that Greek poets and philosophers be-

came more and more outspoken in their opposition to
prophetic phenomena shows that Greek prophecies had a
basically technical and magical character. By and by, ra-
tionalism revolted against the vulgarly irrational religious
manifestations, which could so easily be exploited for personal interests. This skepticism of the philosophers brings
to mind the more and more clearly expressed tendency of
the Hebrew prophets to escape the realm of magic.

In spite of this fundamental difference we must keep in
mind a number of analogies between Greek and Hebrew
prophetism. In the former, certain phenomena emerge
from the background of mantics, phenomena of different
shadings, which allow for a greater rapprochement with
Biblical prophetism.

Let us point out first that at the time the Bible was
being translated, the Greek Jews of the third century had
been forced into a confrontation of Hebrew and Greek
prophetism. They had to find a Greek word which could
properly express the Hebrew term *navi* and its synonyms
without betraying the meaning of Biblical prophetism.
Furthermore, it had to be placed opposite pagan prophetism within the framework of monotheistic apologetics
which the translators aimed at. Their choice fell on the
Greek word *prophetes,* which covers the Hebrew *navi* as
well as *ro'e* or *hoze,* although the last two are sometimes
rendered by *oron* or *bleton,* the *seer.* However, all three
stand, in the Hebrew Bible, for the authentic prophet in
his double function as the bearer of the word of God and a
visionary. Since the Greek translators distinguished between *navi* on the one hand and *ro'e* and *hoze* on the other,
we could have expected the word mantis in order to characterize the prophet-visionary as opposed to the prophet-
orator (Gr. *prophetes*). The Septuagint scrupulously
avoids the word *mantis* for the Biblical prophet, and uses
that term rather for the translation for the Hebrew *kos-
sem,* a magician. The difference between a *navi* and a *kos-*

sem is that between revelation and divination, and it is this very difference which the Septuagint introduced between the inspired prophet (Gr. *prophetes,* Hebr. *navi, ro'e, hoze*) and the soothsayer (Gr. *mantis,* Hebr. *kosem*). Even though the translators may not have had a systematic theory concerning prophetism which would be valid for the whole of the Bible,[18] they at least sensed that in the Greek language there was a fundamental difference between the contents of the terms *prophetes* and *mantis,* an important difference which, incidentally, antedated the period of the Septuagint. It was not the Hellenized Jews of the third century who created this distinction in order to better understand the difference between monotheistic and pagan prophetism. In order to designate two types of prophets, these Jews chose two different terms in classical Greek literature. But the word *prophetes* had a linguistic existence of its own, although it did not regain a living or even definite reality.[19]

On the other side, and in opposition to the rigid use which the Jewish-Greek writers made of this term, pagan Greek literature gives us different meanings of mantis, for they are not uniformly captured by mantic. Some of them are described as really inspired, who, beyond all magic necessities, are forced to see or to speak because a sacred intuition is revealed deep within the soul.

Sophocles gives his Theresias the appearance of a mantis and he is seen as such in the most primitive and magic forms. He eavesdrops upon the voices of the birds. Since he is blind, a boy must correctly interpret the sacrifices for him. But that mantis reaches also a much higher level of prophecy. He feels himself inspired by Apollo, and the bearer of a truth which he is bound to convey. In the way he addresses Oedipus or Creon he has the superb pride of an Elijah or a Jeremiah. Faced with the skepticism and the obduracy of the kings, he feels, just like the Biblical prophets, the agony of useless knowledge:

Oh, how terrible is knowledge, if the one who has
it does not benefit by it! I knew it well, but I had forgotten it, otherwise I would not have come here . . . .
Let me go home. You and I, we shall feel better there,
if you will only believe me . . . .

(*Oedipus Rex,* 316-321.)

In these scenes the mantis transcends divinatory technique. Blindness does not allow Theresias to practice
mantic, yet it does not prevent him from having an inner
and spiritual vision of the things which, in addition, turn
out to be true.

In an even more striking manner in Cassandra, Aeschylus describes a prophetess whose appearance is hardly
different from that of the great prophetic figures of the
Bible. Cassandra, too, is a mantis, but quite different from
the seers and the interpreters mentioned elsewhere by Aeschylus. The raising up of the terrible destiny of the
Atrides, to which Cassandra feels so tragically tied, reminds us of the great views into the future which Biblical
prophecy offers. We have no introductory magic opera-
tion. The seer is inspired by Apollo, and that comes on
suddenly and is self-explanatory. Cassandra senses the
whole burden of her vision and the suffering which comes
with the obligation of a prophet—to foretell evil times.[20]

We find with these persons subjects that occur again in
Biblical prophetism, above all others that of inspiration.
Theresias and Cassandra do not speak from a knowledge
received through magic or because of a divinatory capacity granted to them by Apollo once and for all, but
the divinity seizes them suddenly. Acting on the spur of
the moment, Apollo transfigures the personality of the
prophet. In this inner and unexpected illumination dwell
the dramatic elements of clairvoyance. A shock of this
kind can be found in the Phoenician forms of the prophecy,
as shown in the Golenischeff papyrus and the texts of

Ras-Shamra. But the Greek playwrights complete the description by adding the background of a tragic psychology.

Although not probable, it is still possible that the features which Aeschylus and Sophocles give their dramatic persons were based on the observation of contemporary poets and prophets. We do not know whether sixth- or fifth-century Greece had any manteis who were not plain magicians. But as early as the eighth century we do find another prophetic current which also reveals analogies with Biblical prophetism. This is the prophetism of the chresmologists.[21]

Does that term apply to a certain class of prophets rather than to particular individuals, and thus possibly include the sybils and the Bakkides? Now the Greek *chresmologis* is a common name whose meaning is quite clear. These "sayers of poems" were like other prophets in receiving their inspiration directly from the divinity and being immediately seized by ecstasies, or a "possession," without first turning to a divinatory technique. They lose that character beginning in the fifth century, after having shown it from the eighth to the sixth. From then on they are no longer inspired prophets but are merely publishers and interpreters of ancient inspired seers without the benefit of ecstasies or mysticism. But even after having lost the character of "prophets" they retain a trait which also characterized the inspired chresmologists of earlier centuries, and which was typical for that special category of seers and interpreters. We refer to their *popular aspect.* This term carries many nuances, many of which remind us of the way things appear in Hebrew prophetism.

The chresmologists are *private people,* who exercise their prophetic talent in complete autonomy. Unlike so many other prophets, they are not functionaries of an organized political or religious power, nor are they any more members of a religious association. They must be

distinguished from many another group: from the Aulic
prophets, who, while having some influence upon their
sovereigns, still depended on his authority; from the
cultic prophets, who belonged to the cult of a certain divinity, were invested by it, and were connected with the
temple in which they served by particular rules of divination and interpretation; from the mystics, who were initiated by the kind of hermeneutics which is typical of a
brotherhood. They appear as individuals, and their techniques and inspiration seem to stem only from the pecu-
liarities of their temperament.

However, they are not only private men, but *men of the
people*. Their sphere is neither a royal court nor a temple
nor an assembly, but the street. One finds them wherever
there is an anonymous crowd, in public places or on the
highways. Their *plebeian* character is so apparent that we
sometimes observe a difference on the social level between
a mantis and a chresmologist. Whereas the former seems
to be the prophet of the aristocracy and the higher middle class, the latter is the one of the plain people. The
plebeian epochs of Greek history were favorable to the
development of chresmology.[22]

Perhaps the prophets of the poor were poor themselves.
Since they did not depend on a special place, they traveled
through the country. Thus they soon became beggars.
Their prophetism turned into a more or less lucrative
trade. Their most frequent function was to sell oracles.
The earlier types offered their own oracles, whereas their
followers offered those of their predecessors. The importance of the oracles depended on the misery of the clients.
Since their pay was small, the chresmologists dealt with
few subjects. But they were the only Greek prophets
who had a character of *actuality*. Other inspired visions
had to do with a distant future, and the closer the events
were in time, the more obscure were the prophecies. The
chresmologists, on the other hand, were forced by the

day-to-day cares of their clients to be concerned with actual problems. They had to take care of immediate problems and even then not in connection with some important person but rather with the swarming life of the people at large.

They did not have a social message but remained within the frame of daily concerns. However, it is interesting to point out a social message in eighth-century Greece, at the same time as the ministry of the Hebrew prophet Amos, that "herald of justice." Eduard Meyer has brought to our attention the analogy between the message of Amos and the works of Hesiod.[23] Although we must not speak of "Hesiod's religion," the religion described by him is quite different from the one we find in Homer's works. It is no longer a religion of aristocrats or citizens, a religion animated by great military or national purposes, but rather a popular religion, one for the peasants of Boeotia, with their concern for economy, work, with an often superstitious but always strict legality.[24] The central element of this religion of the common man is the need for justice, for the constantly renewed trust in Dike, the daughter of Zeus, who denounces before his throne the abuses to which she has become victim on earth. For that justice is only an ideal opposed by the brutal reality of the world, where injustice and violence rule. Personal experiences have turned Hesiod into the mouthpiece for justice. In the first part of his *Work and Days* he tells us how he has become the victim of the perfidious mentality of his brother Perseus. The feeling that he lives in a world filled with iniquities has led him to embrace a pessimism which permeates his entire religious philosophy, where the myth of the ages and of their progressive decay plays an important role. A further consequence was that he became suspicious of, and even inimical to, civilization. The gods are the guarantors of a right which is constantly trampled upon by human civilization. Everywhere in

Hesiod we find the idea of an inner corruption of civilization and of its extreme noxiousness. Some have found
this also in Amos and Hosea and generally with the Biblical prophets of the eighth century, and certain historians go so far as to see herein the essential prophetic
message of that period.[25] Thus we realize that the analogies between Hesiod's "religion" and that of the Hebrew prophets of the eighth century have to do with the
subject of justice on its most philosophical level.

Clearly a new rapprochement takes shape between
Greek and Hebrew prophetism. It is no longer merely a
question of method or psychology, but of the very content of the message which the prophets delivered. We
might even ask ourselves whether that convergence is not
an outcome of the popular origin which we find equally in
Greek chresmology and in Hebrew prophetism. Should,
among all the ancient prophetisms, Hebrew and Greek
callings have had the privilege of revealing to mankind
not only a religious future or destiny but also the principles of a just and equitable social existence?

Notes

1. All quotations are taken from the anthology *The Literature of the Ancient Egyptians* by Adolf Erman.

2. *Ibid.,* p. 130.

3. A. Lods, *Les prophètes d'Israel et les débuts du Judaism.* Paris 1935,
pp. 77ff. Charles-F. Jean. *Le milieu biblique avant Jésus-Christ,* Paris
1923, II pp. 145, 149.

4. The text is, however, not clear, and the translation therefore doubtful.

5. Hugo Gressmann, *Der Ursprung der israelitisch-juedischen Eschatolo-
gie,* Gottingen, 1905. See also his "Foreign Influences in Hebrew
Prophecy," JBS, 1925.

6. About the antiquity of Nathan's prophecy see Marcel Simon "La
prophétie de Nathan et le Temple," *Revue d'Histoire et de Philosophie
Religieuses,* 1952.

7. *Ibid.,* pp. 41ff.

8. Erman, *op. cit.*, p. 157

9. G. Conteneau, *La divination chez les Assyriens et les Babyloniens,* Paris 1940, p. 361.

10. A. Parrot, *Archives royales de Mari,* Paris 1950.

11. A. Lods, "Une tablette inédite de Mari," in *Studies in Old Testament Prophecy,* Edinburgh, 1950, p. 103.

12. Non-Biblical testimonies are late: Apuleus, Heliodorus, Lucian.

13. Erman. *op. cit.*, p. 225.

14. About the prophetism in the texts of Ras-Shamra see A. Lods, *Quelques remarques sur les poèmes mythologiques de Ras-Shamra et leurs rapports avec l'A.T.,* RHPR 1936, II, p. 122. A. Haldar, *Associations of Cultic Prophets Among the Ancient Semites,* Upsala 1945. pp. 79ff. Engnell. *Studies in Divine Kingship in the Ancient Near East.* 1943, p. 142.

15. See Haldar, *op. cit.* It is remarkable that so far no equivalent for the Hebrew word *navi* has been found in other Semitic texts.

16. Texts in Lidzbarski: *Ephemeris fuer semitische Epigraphik, III,* 1909–15, p. 3.

17. See Nyberg, *Die Religionen des Alten Iran,* Leipzig, 1938.

18. See Erich Fascher: *Prophetes,* Giessen, 1927, pp. 102ff.

19. Examples in Fascher, *op. cit.,* pp. 11ff.

20. Agamemnon, 1072–1330.

21. Bouche-Leclerq: *Histoire de la divination dans l'Antiquité,* II, pp. 92ff. Erwin Rohde: *Psyche,* transl. by Reymond, pp. 264ff. Martin P. Nilsson: *Geschichte der griechischen Religion,* 1941, I, pp. 578ff. Max Weber: *Gesammelte Aufsätze zur Religionssoziologie, III: Das antike Judentum,* Tuebingen, 1921, p. 284.

22. K. Koehler: *Der Prophet der Hebraer und die Mantik der Griechen in ihrem gegenseitigen Verhaeltnis.* Darmstadt, 1860, p. 24.

23. Eduard Meyer: *Hesiods Erga und das Gedicht von den fuenf Menshengeschlechtern.* 1910, p. 157.

24. See Gernet-Boulanger: *Le génie grec dans la religion.* 1932, pp. 110f. Nilsson, *op. cit.,* pp. 588f.

25. See A. Causse: *Du groupe ethnique à la communité religieuse.* Paris, 1937, pp. 94ff.

2
The Types

I.

The above balance sheet allows us to discern the great
lines of ancient prophetism. Four main streams, unequally
distributed in different countries of the Orient, define
prophetic experience.

The first of these, most widely spread out and perhaps
to be designated as the lowest and most impure, is the
magic current; as soon as one enters an ancient religious
civilization, one finds clear proof of this current. All
peoples have their own magicians and soothsayers. Mantic is the most widely imagined form of contact between
things divine and human. One might at first be tempted
to consider this to be a repository of the primitive community and to reduce its ethnic expressions to the general
scheme of the group mentality. Although this would be
a legitimate hypothesis, it must be complemented by another one: every people found a time and occasion for
modifying these schemes and clothing them with a character of their own. Besides its unchangeable function within every religious society, mantic had particular tasks
within such a society, as is attested to by the variety of
its manifestations in the empires of the Orient.

In Mesopotamia, the real domain of mantic, magic is
part of a bureaucracy; its interpreters are functionaries,
yet their presence is indispensable when it comes to a
political decision. If, therefore, the prophetic institution
has invaded all the sectors of the public life in Sumer and

Babylonia, it is because it could not exist without super-natural support. In order to justify its existence and its future, the Mesopotamian state never found great religious energy, or an institution which could be compared to the deification of the Egyptian Pharaoh. The Mesopotamian gods were neither men's masters nor their associates. Their indifference to human destiny did not stem from a divine hostility towards man but from a fatalism to which the gods themselves were subject and which preoccupied them to such a degree that they did not care about man at all. The sufferings of Mesopotamian gods, some of whom were considered to be mortal, created a religious climate of anxiety. Nobody was sure of the morrow in a state where the gods themselves could not escape the trap of hazards and catastrophes. Death was an object of fear, and it was deemed the inevitable and ultimate end. It was impossible to cross over, and afterlife was neither a belief nor a hope. The king offered no help at all in this dilemma. Although he was the son of the gods and appointed by them to serve them, his religious situation was quite weak, for he was entangled in the mortality of the gods, his parents, and his masters, and also in the inexorable fate of man; and a man he never ceased to be. Babylonian liturgy knew of no prayer or rite specially addressed to the king, who, like his own subjects, approached the gods only out of fear.[1] Whenever he did have to play a role in the official liturgy, it was to prove the frailty of his investiture. Thus, during the New Year festival he was, with the help of certain symbolic rites, temporarily dethroned, and therein he imitated the drama of his divine patron. In a religious society which was so ill prepared to face actual life and the future with confidence, mantic was bound to occupy a prominent place, as it was indeed called upon to furnish the kind of help and enlightenment which beliefs and institutions could not give. Every act in political life, the smallest as well as the most important undertaking, was preceded by magic consultation. The reply given by the divinity, or rather the response of which it was delivered by divinatory practices, was carefully registered. It was used not only for throwing light on the specific action at hand but on all similar actions which would one day have to be transacted under analogous circumstances. A real mantic diplomacy developed—the prophets were its officials, and its formulas and recipes were its code. The information received was faithfully communicated to the superior authorities. There was a certain hierarchy involved, and quite naturally the king became the supreme head. All consultations were centered around his person, but they found their way to his office through a whole net of agents, who were especially nominated for the functions of soothsayers. Mesopotamia could not arrive at anything but institutional mantic, the substitute for a strong idea in religious life. Therefore Mesopotamian "prophetism" also lacks breadth and fruitfulness. It could only be a vast enterprise of consultations and informations, and even the prophetism of Mari is no exception to that rule. For the prophetic texts of Mari, which exist in great numbers but are very poor spiritually, show that the Aramaeans who were installed at Mari could not see in prophetism anything that was not common to all of Mesopotamia, namely, the ability to know divine intentions which, their set of beliefs being what it was, remained shut up and inaccessible. It is possible that those Aramaeans who emigrated into Canaan (where they were called Hebrews) preserved in their cities and in their state something of that conjectural and institutional prophetism. But in spite of its origins, Hebrew prophetism cannot be reduced to that. The Hebrews worked out an absolutely new type of prophetism, since during their migration from Mesopotamia to Canaan their religious beliefs led to profound modifications.

The example of Egypt shows how mantic created on its

own level different institutions according to the various beliefs. The royal authority gave the Egyptian state the religious stability which was absent in Mesopotamia. Pharaoh was the incarnation of the divinity or, better still, of *maat*, which is the manifestation of Osiris as well as the word of Pharaoh, right and order, social justice, and cosmic harmony.[2] The belief in survival, which originally had been limited to the royal person but was subsequently extended to all of his subjects, eliminated the haunting fear of death. People banished that fear by appropriate rites and a simple recitation of a stereotyped list of sins.

In Egypt mantic did not occupy the important place it held in Mesopotamia. It manifested itself rather in the stubborn insistence on primitive beliefs, as they still exist in modern societies in various superstitions. It was connected with functions other than divination, and it played an important role, which was the outcome of the particularities of Egyptian religion. Religious stability in Egypt lived through a critical moment—the demise of the Pharaoh.[3] Until his successor had mounted the throne, the whole structure was threatened to its very foundations. Myths and rites brought on the transition and the re-establishment of the cosmic and social order. Mantic assumed then an exact and new function. Through the means of appropriate "prophecies" it did its share in minimizing the disturbance and in underlining its temporary character, by the double vision of a catastrophe and the restoration. Prophets of the rank of a Nefer-Rohu and Ipuwer evidently had magic functions, and if their prophecies could not influence the events, they could at least change attitudes. The antithetical arrangement of a saddening vision and a happy future allows the spirit of the listener to understand that even such a catastrophe has its limitations.

The dominant note of such a prophecy is neither its optimism nor its pessimism but its ritual value. In a system which was periodically interrupted by the death of the deified sovereign, prophecy contributed to the re-establishment of a continuity, side by side with numerous other rites. This Egyptian prophecy is really neither dynastic nor eschatologic. The political interests of the dynasty did not come first. What mattered was the meaning of royal functions in Egypt. Although the prophets were servants of the crown, it was a situation which they had not chosen for themselves. They shared it with all other Egyptians, because the religious structure placed on them, too, strictly defined duties. Egyptian eschatology could not be exclusively tied to prophetic revelation, simply because it impregnated Egyptian religious conscience on all levels. Belief in survival was so strong, the rites of passage seemed to work so well, that the future was secured; if not the immediate future in this life, so at least in afterlife. The end—the *eschaton*—with its assurance of the highest bliss through survival, was somehow taken into account at every moment of life on earth, and to announce it, no prophecy was called for. Eschatological expectations dealt with a future which all mortals were sure to attain at the time of passing on, and in a way that was absolutely certain.[4]

Thus we cannot be too careful when stating the problem of Egyptian influences on Hebrew prophetism. It will not do to point out that both Egypt and Israel knew dynastic and eschatological prophetisms, and that Israel necessarily found such schemes through contacts with its mighty neighbor. What has to be investigated is, what *meaning* the Hebrews gave to the royal function, because the importance of the Pharaonic power and not the existence of a dynasty explains, as we have seen, the Egyptian dynastic prophetism. Now there can be no greater difference than that between the Egyptian and the Hebrew concept of the king, and nothing more striking among all the peoples of the Orient than the religious significance of kingship with

the Hebrews.[5] In Egypt, the king was a god. In Israel,
God was the king. This simple difference, whose consequences are far-reaching for the structure of Hebrew society, requires a particular study of Hebrew dynastic
prophetism. The Egyptian model could not have created
Hebrew messianism, unless it had at the same time
changed the concept of kingship in Israel. Also, the eschatology of the Hebrew prophets of the eighth century is
based on a general concept of the world and human destiny, a concept which is entirely different from Egyptian
ideas. The Hebrew prophets had no assurance whatever
concerning the *end*. They had but two certainties to offer:
it was not given to rites to bring about or to change the
end; and obedience to God's will was all-powerful to realize that end. That obedience was called the *good* by the
prophets, and disobedience *evil*. In Hebrew eschatology
the dialectic of good and evil was of an ethical order, for
it gave man a choice. When good and evil appeared in
Egyptian prophecies, they were two instants of a succession, whereas in Israel they constituted an alternative.
This difference of structure destroys all inner analogy between the ethical eschatology of the Hebrews and the
magic eschatology of the Egyptians.

II.

Opposite the magic type of prophecy we have the current of a *social claim*. Just as the former seems to be attached to the lowest forms of human mentality, the latter appears to answer man's most ideal concerns. It has
nearly become a commonplace to state that it is found in
Biblical prophetism. But ought we not also to take into
consideration Greek chresmology, Greek social literature,
and Hesiod's thoughts, when we draw up a balance of the
prophetic contribution to the social history of the world?
Besides the Biblical prophets only the chresmologists

were men of the people. Everywhere else the prophets were related to the priests or the functionaries. Here they have a clearly plebeian or even proletarian character. Nevertheless there exist insurmountable differences between chresmology and Biblical prophecy, foremost of which is the fact of the anonymity of chresmology. We do not know a single chresmologist by name, through his tribulations or through his life. Whereas the life of the Biblical prophets is as interesting as their message, the chresmologists, as indicated by Bouche-Leclerq,[6] appear like a parade of phantoms. Just as with the great "prophets" of classical tragedies, we may well ask ourselves whether "those figures have not been put together by a mystical imagination." Biblical prophecy is part of a story, whereas Greek prophecy is perhaps, in its more important elements, the product of poets and exalted men. But even if we are to suppose that behind the chresmologists there stands a concrete reality, the message attributed to them is still entirely different from that of the Biblical prophets. Chresmology has not passed beyong the limits of the individual but is only concerned with personal cares. Unlike Biblical prophecy it did not know how to transcend the individual and arrive at the *people* beyond mere persons. Unlike Biblical prophecy, it did not know how to work out politics and ethics valid for the whole community. Still less did it know how to discover behind the community mankind as a whole. It is the original privilege of Biblical prophecy to have wished to prophesy not just for the benefit of certain people but for mankind.

However, there are other non-Biblical social claims. But what strikes us there is that we are not really dealing with prophetism. Neither the Egyptian author of *The Peasant's Complaints* nor Hesiod boasts of a prophetic inspiration. Their grievances and criticisms stem from purely human reflections and experiences. The gods are addressed only as witnesses or judges. They are not the ones who inspire the indignation and the revolt which the writers and poets feel deep in their souls.

It is not by accident that the texts of that group, as far as they have come down to us, are devoid of a sacred character. Throughout antiquity justice had been arrived at by the lay spirit, by reason. In Mesopotamia it was identical with a well-functioning administration. Whatever did not hurt local customs or general needs was considered just. The birth of justice was an act of coordination, of systematization, and of a just distribution. When the authority of the gods was called upon, it was done for secondary reasons. Hammurabi received his code from the hands of the god Shamash, but the spirit of his code is in no way indebted to that god, for it is quite secular, and moreover it is transmitted from hand to hand, without divine revelation. When Shamash gives man his laws, he is not a god any more but an abstract idea. In Egypt the establishment of justice led to a progressive weakening of the king's religious power. The more the myth of royal divinity lost its influence, the more social reforms arose. The participation of all citizens in the fate of survival, which had originally been reserved for the king only, led to the first equalities within Egyptian society, but at the same time they indicate a greater and greater decline in the sacred character of the state. In Egypt justice went hand in hand with the secularization of the regime. In Greece this was even more striking. For there the ideas of justice could develop only after rational philosophy had deprived mythical religion of a rather large part of its domain.

The secular character of these social claims led to another one, clearly discernible in the "prophetic" texts. The "prophets" of justice in Egypt and Greece are sages rather than prophets. To them, justice means a proper order in the cities, the safeguarding of property, of acquired goods, of social hierarchies. Hesiod is concerned with inheritance, and around this subject he works out that of justice.[7] The Egyptian writers concur with the notables, with people who are well off. Revolutionaries are considered dissenters and robbers, and it is these whom they take to task.[8]

The Bible, too, knows of that wisdom, *hokma,* which concerns itself with the order of the established regime. But the Bible does not identify it with prophecy. On the contrary: prophecy is opposed to *hokma* and presents a world view where values are just the opposite of those presented by *hokma.* In the eyes of prophecy, the established social order is the suspect par excellence. Contrary to what happened elsewhere in the ancient world, in Israel justice remained eminently religious. The prophets thought of it as being God's principal attribute, and only this religious perspective gives Hebrew social prophetism its true meaning. It would be a grave error of interpretation to consider Hebrew prophetism, within the realm of social claims, as the dawn of secular and emancipated thought. The Hebrew prophets expected justice from God only, no matter how unfathomable that was, how terrifying or strengthening, and in any case, irrational. That belief characterized their claims and set them apart from all other men of antiquity who reflected on justice. Only a justice conceived as transcendent could overthrow the social ideas to such an extent as to make out of poor, naked man—man without any possessions—the just man. Everywhere else social claims were a matter of political wisdom. Only in Israel, where we find religious inspiration, could it become one of the aspects of prophetism.

III.

The mystical current is as strong in prophetism as the magic one. Beginning in Egypt and Mesopotamia, it invaded Asia Minor, and in Persia and Greece it became one of the elements of a double religion, the mystery of Mitra side by side with Zend-Avesta, Dionysus side by side with Apollo. It was as obstinate as magic. Through the gnosis it was to herald and keep close to Christianity, where it grew and created the magnificent spiritual waves of medieval and modern mysticism. In this stream are to be found the origin and the end result of Hebrew prophetism. The first Hebrew prophets are the brethren of the Phoenician and Canaanite prophets, and their successors preserved somewhat that relationship, if only through the fact that certain forms of ecstasis and frenzy were maintained and by the parallels which the Bible establishes between the *navi*, the prophet, and the *meshugga*, the fool, the exalted one, a parallel which can still be felt at the time of Jeremiah. It was these *neviim* who were the forerunners of Christian mystics. This suggestion does not have to be made legitimate by a Christian typology of the Old Testament nor by a scheme of spiritual evolution of the kind made famous by Bergson.[9] All we need is a psychological comparison between Jeremiah and Ruysbroek, between Ezekiel and St. John of the Cross.

But these affinities cover up profound divergences. In this respect mysticism is like magic: in spite of superficial analogies each religion develops a mysticism of its own and in every society mystical prophetism has its particular function. It would be utterly wrong to consider the Hebrew prophets simple intermediaries between the inspired men of Phrygian frenzy and the exalted ones of Christian mysticism. They were not a steppingstone between primitive and more highly developed forms of mysticism. Their mysticism is one of a kind, because contrary to preceding and following mystical currents their mysticism is not connected with a mystery.

Outside Hebrew civilization, the mystical prophet is mainly a mystic, the initiator of a rite of salvation. It is true that in any form the sacred is a mysterious dimension, but the mystics are not, like the magicians and the sooth-sayers, the teachers of a global mystery. The sacred interests them only as a road towards salvation: a road which is narrow but necessary. This is the *mystery,* for the service of which the mystical prophets live, and which is concentrated in some rite or sometimes in an abstract symbolism, and which is entrusted to certain initiates who accept its disciplines and dangers. This mystery changes from region to region, and from one epoch to another. In Asia Minor it is the mystery of vegetation and fertility, the biological salvation of a soil and mankind subjected to the periodic cycle of death. In Egypt, Persia, and Greece it is the mystery of deification, the metaphysical salvation of men condemned to physical existence. In the gnosis, finally, it is the total, dazzling, definitive mystery, which Christianity has placed in the mystery of the Cross.

Therefore, when we come to Hebrew prophetism, we must not allow ourselves to be misled by appearances. Hebrew prophetism could not be mystic, because the religion to which it belonged ignored the mysteries. It is true that certain cultic demands, a certain tendency towards self-discipline—ecstasis or asceticism—could, during the long history of Hebrew prophetism, lead to mystic attitudes. Therefore we meet certain superficial and formal analogies between the earliest Hebrew prophets and those of Canaan, and again between the *navi* of the classical period and the Christian mystics. But neither the cult nor this discipline had anything to do with the mystery, and what may superficially appear to be mystic regarding the Hebrew prophets is not so in a deeper sense. The mysticism of the Hebrew prophets must be studied, but only with the all-important reservation that Hebrew religious thought was stubborn in its refusal to make salvation dependent on the mediation by a mystery.

IV.

He who rejects the mystery does not reject revelation. The Apocalypse, too, is a total and definitive revelation, but, contrary to the mystery, it does not wish to be enforced by a rite or a discipline. Its rise does not have to be caused, but it arrives at the proper time, through a process of maturation, the length of which sometimes stirs up impatience, but which is bound to come. We have seen that in Persian thinking eschatology is expressed in a drama in which the Apocalypse is the third act. We find the Apocalypse in the last documents of Hebrew prophetism which already belong to the period of the Exile or the Second Temple, and lead directly to Christianity. Some people wanted to discover in the Biblical Apocalypse (for instance in Daniel) an intermediate link between the Persian eschatology where it was supposedly born, and Christian eschatology which would be its crowning. It is hard to evaluate the importance of Persian influence. But it is certain that there was a Hebrew eschatology before the Exile, which means prior to any Persian influence, and thus nothing prevents us from considering the Biblical Apocalypse to be the natural development of that pre-Exilic Hebrew eschatology. The profound change in the Jewish outlook is not due to any contact with Persia but to an evolution which leads up to Christianity. In the last centuries before our era Jewish eschatology found a new direction, which we shall call Christic, as will be explained.

A prophecy becomes Christic when the prophets who reveal it are certain to be contemporaries of Christ the Savior and Messiah. A prophet who can say *"I have seen the Son of Man"* is no longer a prophet in the ancient sense of the eschatology. He no longer belongs to time. The end is with him or behind him. Such a prophetism was prevalent in Jewish society during the last centuries before the Christian era, and has found its most grandiose expression in Christianity. It appeared in the post-Christian society whenever a false Messiah arose. The first Christian communities knew numerous prophets, but the ecclesiastical organization reduced them by and by. Their chief meaning resided in the fact that they were contemporaries and witnesses of Christ. But time made them useless and even embarrassing. When their testimony became old it attracted suspicion. The same holds true of the Jewish community. Here too, prophetism has remained alive, and Jewish history is full of sudden appearances of inspired men—half prophets and full-fledged prophets. However, their prophecies were never canonized. This was, however, not the doing of an ecclesiastical system. The end of the prophetical canon is the line which separates authentic Biblical prophetism from that which was not, because the Jewish prophet had become Christic instead of eschatological. Here we have a valuable *terminus ante quem* for Jewish Biblical prophetism—it antedates Christ. Prophetic time excludes parousia. Only a coming can be expected, not a return. In the Hebrew sense of the term Hebrew prophetism stops exactly where Christianity begins.

The concept of *prophetic time* which we have mentioned does not involve only the eschatological type of prophecy. Magical, social, and mystical prophetisms, too, are based on certain exact concepts of *time*. Magic arises out of an intimacy with the time of rites and myths. Philosophies which are based on a concept of cyclical time favor speculations about social wisdom. Consciousness of a mystical time lends itself to frenzy and ecstasis. The prophets of magic, wisdom, and ecstasis live in different times which we shall have to analyze in order to understand the particular character of the time of Biblical prophecy. The Hebrew prophet differs from the Christian prophet by speaking in a precise dimension of time, but he also differs from ancient prophets through his radical refusal to accept ancient religious temporalities. Biblical prophecy reaches its authentic expression in the uniqueness of its concept of time.

Notes

1. See H. Frankfort, *La royauté et les dieux,* transl. by Marty-Krieger, Paris, 1951, pp. 289ff.
2. *Ibid.,* pp. 98ff.
3. *Ibid.,* pp. 152ff.
4. See Masson-Oursel, *La pensée en Orient,* 1951, p. 23.
5. This problem is expressed in excellent terms by Frankfort. *op. cit.,* pp. 426ff.
6. Bouche-Leclerq, *Histoire de la divination dans l'antiquité,* p. 93.
7. *Les Travaux et les Jours,* pp. 208ff.
8. See Erman, *op. cit.,* p. 135.
9. Henri Bergson, *Les deux sources de la morale et de la religion,* ch. III.

3

The Perspectives of Time

Ritual Time

At first, time was felt as the rhythm of *nature*—the succession of the seasons, the movement of the heavenly bodies, the hidden or apparent progress in vegetation, all reminding us of regular recurring cycles interrupted by natural phenomena such as eclipses, torrential rains, droughts, hurricanes, etc. Then it was felt in the rhythm of *man,* though not at first in the physiological and pyschological changes that affect the individual but rather in the collective movements of ethnic communities. Migrations and conquests swept people away in their journeys, the rhythms of which were considered as important as the periods of nature. The first chronologies take into account this double aspect—the cosmic and the human—of time, for they are based on computations relating to stars as well as to history. The beginnings of dynasties or cities and the date of a conquest appear in the calendars with the same importance as the revolutions of the sun, the moon, and the stars. But this agreement in the manner of counting time is symptomatic of the *problem* which the calendar tried to solve; namely, the problem of the *relationship between man and nature*. The vigorous antithesis man-nature, with all that it means in terms of conflicts and antagonisms, dwells in the very midst of time, for here is the meeting place for the rhythm of man and nature. But does that meeting necessarily lead to a conflict, or does it not rather offer hope for an appeasement?

This is the alternative which has haunted the spirit of ancient civilizations.

A variety of answers has been given, and we would have to study the history and the institutions of every particular nation in order to find out in which way each understood the relationship between man and nature in the dimension of time. The example of Egypt and Mesopotamia shows how two countries which were close to each other spiritually could interpret time in quite different manners. The soil and climate of Mesopotamia are subject to sudden changes. Neither the seasons nor agricultural products are guaranteed to follow regularly. There are frequent droughts and inundations, which play havoc with the calculations of peasants and those of the builders of cities. Babylonians and Chaldeans interpreted such catastrophes as victories of nature over man. The time in which such events display themselves is the scene of a muffled, tenacious, and at times triumphant hostility of nature versus man, who tries to free himself with the help of myths. The Babylonian account of the Deluge is largely one of such myths of compensation.

People realize that even a total victory of nature is not final. The supremacy of cosmic forces over man is limited. It lasts only until a certain moment, from which time on everything may begin all over again. The deluge can destroy everything, but humanity is reborn and begins its work again. That myth reabsorbs the catastrophical extent of the natural cataclysms which attacked the inhabitants of Mesopotamia. It makes them appear as the phases of a struggle which, even under the most disastrous conditions in which the vanquished live, never ends. Egypt does not know of such a myth, and this can easily be explained by pointing to the evenness of the Egyptian climate and the fertile permanence of its soil, which is irrigated by the Nile in unchangeable intervals. Agricultural existence did not give people the idea that man and nature live in a perpetual conflict, since things happened just the other way round: the development of time made the gifts of nature and the requirements of the farmers always coincide. Moreover, the geographic situation of Egypt made it easy for that country to find permanent satisfaction in limited conquests. The natural borders of Egypt are so well defined that every Pharaoh knew quite well just how far he could advance if he was to remain the absolute ruler over his country. Even if and when a raid took him beyond those natural borders of his country, a halt would not stop his ambitions; and when he returned to his capital, he became again what indeed he had never ceased being—the uncontested sovereign of an uncontested realm. This vivid feeling of a stable possession, of an assured installation in a well-defined territory, helped also in reconciling the Egyptian with nature, in the political development of time.

The personal power of the sovereign was the symbol of the solidarity of Egyptian man and nature. No myth was needed to illustrate this, and it could be endangered only by the weakening of the personal power of the Pharaoh, so that, for example, his death and the problems of succession to the throne revived in Egypt, too, the painful antagonism between man and nature; and in order to solve it one applied measures similar to those which were used in Mesopotamia. But in Egypt the moments of anxiety were an exception, whereas in Mesopotamia each day stirred up the feeling of a conflict. This was so because that country did not constitute a geographical whole and did not have natural borders in which a well-defined empire could install itself.[1] The security of its sovereign was illusory, and he was constantly obliged to incite his people to new adventures. Conquests remained indefinitely unfulfilled. In order to capture such a perpetual rhythm, together with other procedures, a myth arose; namely, that of the Tower of Babel, of the *house that joined earth to heaven*. The temples which arose on the plains of the Tigris and the Euphrates certify in their mythical symbolism that man can conquer space, and if he cannot reach the limits of a well-defined world, he has at least reached the heavens. A vertical equilibrium thus compensates for the horizontal discontinuity. It is once again remarkable that the myth of the Tower of Babel has no equivalent in Egypt. Thus we realize that, considering the proximity of Egypt and Mesopotamia, there is a great variety in the interpretation of time as a battlefield between man and nature. The same holds true for other nations in antiquity, although in many cases concerning them, historical investigation has not advanced sufficiently to furnish us with reliable data.

But in spite of all differences, ancient civilizations agree in their *cultic* approach to time. They introduce *ritual time* in religious life, and this shows man's anxiety vis-à-vis nature as well as the pacification of hostile elements which face each other in time.

The complicated rites which were staged by the priests and to which the entire nation from sovereign to slave subjected itself presented essentially a participation of man's life in the mysterious life of nature. In order to be realized, every rite calls for a certain time, and that ritual time has an exceptional character. If the duration of secular time is filled with obstacles and jeopardizes man's existence, ritual time fills and enriches man's life, provided that the rite is observed without any profanation. Mircea Eliade has shown in an excellent analysis that we are dealing here with a plenary and interdependent time which must relate to preceding and following times which are devoted to the same rite. No matter how much time elapses, a communication is established between one ritual moment and the next, and the same hierophanic duration runs through all the times which are dedicated to the same rite. The feeling of this continuity leads first to an appeasement. The vexations of secular life yield to security which at first is merely abstract, but which is then made concrete by the very content of the rite. For ritual times are not void; they do not suspend secular time without filling the interval with some thing, namely, the mythical and often actual meaning of the rite.

The rite is really an overture to mythical time. Every ritual time restores mythical time, which is the time of repetition and also that of possibility. "In *illo tempore,* the mythical epoch, everything is possible."[2] The examples quoted above, concerning the times of the Babylonian myths of the Deluge and of the Tower, are characteristic. They remind us of a fragment of mythical time, when everything was, or became again, possible—the conquest of space and man's recovery in the face of nature. Let us imagine that a ritual repeatedly reminded the Mesopotamians of the Deluge. This would mean the resurrection of human existence after a cosmic catastrophe, and it would bring that idea to life in the spirit of the participants as long as that rite lasted. We have no trace of such a ritual. But we do know that the sacred towers were the scenes of rites of ascension and of hierogamy, which allowed the faithful to participate in the mythical instant of the joining of heaven and earth, of the divinity and man. A summary study of the great ritual ceremonies of ancient peoples shows us the myth which those rites perpetuated by their very repetition, a myth which was made concrete either by the stories which the priests recounted or by a mimic liturgy which tied the participants even more closely to the reality of the myth. Now the dominating myth of ancient rituals is that of the meeting—sometimes harrowing, sometimes harmonious—of man and nature. One gets the impression that this myth has haunted the mind, and we have already noticed the origin of that painful anxiety. That origin is the experience of time. The minds that were tortured by time freed themselves by implanting it within a rite.

Some of the ritual scenarios may be regarded as an integral synthesis of the religious dispositions of the people who invented them. This is specifically the case with the liturgy of the New Year in Mesopotamia, the ritual of the royal succession in Egypt, and of the mourning of Tammuz in Phoenicia and Canaan, which are the more interesting because it has often been maintained that certain rites in the Bible were influenced by them. Now such rituals show in a striking manner what role time and its problems played in the mentality of the ancient Orient.

"The feast of the New Year can be considered as the most complete expression of Mesopotamian religiosity."[3] According to an unchangeable calendar it occurred in the spring, in the first days of the month of Nissan. At that time of the year, day after day was devoted to the episodes of a myth, the exterior meaning of which could be easily discerned. It dealt with the enthroning of the god Marduk, or rather with the restoration of his power after a temporary eclipse. This is a cosmogonic myth, a demonstration of the drama of the creation, which Mesopotamian literature presents as a work achieved by Marduk not without difficulties. But if we look deeper, we see that the myth testifies to man's perplexity in the face of nature's seasonal cycles. The New Year was not chosen arbitrarily. During Nissan vegetation rises from death to life. The rite does not merely have the function of aiding in this passing but, also of making it conscious. The meeting of the two epochs is felt like a shock. The old and the new year meet in a combat whose outcome would remain undecided if the rite were not to assure the triumph of the New Year. But during the twelve days' duration of the rite the conflict breaks out effectively in all kinds of liturgical scenes, each of which has to do with the central theme of the struggle between the old and the new, between death and rebirth.

The gods are the prime actors of the drama. Marduk is made prisoner by the forces of death; he is chained and held captive in a mountain. The other gods lament and mourn. But they recover soon. Boats which carry the gods of the principal cities of the plains converge on Babylon. Among them is Nabu, the son and avenger of Marduk. With the help of the other gods he liberates Marduk by force. The ritual ends with the victory of Marduk and the solemn banquet of the gods, who give him supreme power and who, together with him, determine the fate of man. So far we have a step-by-step presentation of the story of creation, where the same gods meet in the same battles. At every renewal of spring Mesopotamian liturgy revives for several days the haunting memories of the great cosmic adversities: order and disorder, the world and chaos, light and darkness, the gods and their enemies. All the painful jolts of the theogony, all the cruel phases of the theomachy, which marked the beginnings of the world, are restored. It is true that this is done in order to be overwhelmed by religious emotion, for the liturgy of the New Year is that of a festival; and the joy of order regained, of a re-created world, is the dominating feeling at the beginning of Nissan. Nevertheless the preliminary phases of the festival, which last many days, show that even if anxiety is eventually overcome, it is despite everything felt at first with great intensity.

On the other hand, the scenario does not interest the divinities any longer from a certain time on, but rather the people who become important actors in the liturgy. During the first days of the festival the people search for the lost god, and their restlessness becomes so impetuous that the city becomes a prey to tumults, and its inhabitants fight one another. Obviously that disorder in the streets is in imitation of the trouble that reigns simultaneously among the gods. But it is indispensable to the efficacy of the rite, and the people have their well-determined places in the chaotic period of the festival. Furthermore, at the very moment that the people yield to those raging ex-

cesses, the king must subject himself to a very characteristic ceremony of atonement. He must enter the sanctuary
of Marduk, which has been deprived of its royal emblems.
The high priest slaps his face and calls on him to make a
confession of innocence. Then he returns to the king the
symbols of his power and slaps him again. By this ceremony the king is reinstated, just like the god Marduk, but
this is done at the price of a temporary disappearance, of
a dispossession and a humiliation just as in actual death.

In this degradation of the king and the general tumult
there is a purposeful confusion and a suspension of all
rules. The social topsy-turvy constitutes a return to chaos,
only that now the heroes of the experience are not the gods
but human beings. It is they who are gripped in that cosmic drama during the days of the festival. The rupture
which is brought about by the renewal of the year in the
continuous cycle of nature reaches out for man and tears
him apart, so that, just like nature, he must die and fight
for his own survival. The rhythm of human existence and
even that of divine existence can from then on be in accord with the rhythm of nature—this is the meeting of
human time and cosmic time. This is the happy consequence of the festival of the New Year. But this happiness is dearly paid for. The ritualization of time appeases
the Mesopotamians at the price of a temporary but concrete experience of profound disturbances. The very foundations of society are undermined, the king is dethroned
and humiliated, and the people resort to rebellion and anarchy. The mythological connotations are tragic, because
man is forced to call on jealous and fierce gods who wish
to harm and destroy each other. Although that mortal
anxiety is eventually overcome, its obligatory appearance
during the festival shows the extent of the haunting experiences people lived through during the days of the
festival.

What the festival of the New Year realized annually

in Mesopotamia—the reestablishment of harmony between cosmic and human time—was done in Egypt in the
ceremonies of succession whenever a Pharaoh died. Frankfort[4] has shown that the divine incarnation of the Egyptian sovereign was by itself enough to assure the immer-
sion of Egyptian society in cosmic time. This problem
arose only with the disappearance of the Pharaoh. Then
a ritual was enacted, with incantations, ceremonies, but
also realistic dramatic plays, "mysteries," whose different acts remind us, in content if not in form, of the days
of the Mesopotamian festival. The mythological proto-
type of the event is simple: Horus accedes to the throne
of his father Osiris, who has been assassinated by Seth.
But this theme is utilized in different ways. We are here
interested in a double aspect. The passing from life to
death in itself presents an event to which the Egyptians
have attached a complicated and meaningful rite.

Pharaoh's death is hardly treated differently from that
of his subjects. True, there is more pomp in the ceremonies, and a greater profusion of symbols, but they can
be easily explained. They express the common Egpytian
nostalgia and hope for an eventful reintegration with the
life of nature. The fundamental discontinuity between
death and life, the hiatus between earthly and cosmic
survival, are ritually overcome by the ceremonies of the
transfiguration of the old sovereign and the advent and
crowning of the new one. But the passing of human time
into cosmic time is also shown in the aspects of a conflict,
which the ritual of succession has to master. The death
of Osiris is due to a murder, and the accession of Horus
can be achieved only by conflict with the allies of the as-
sassin Seth. That atmosphere of a crisis dominated certain
phases of the ritual ceremony of crowning, which signifi-
cantly enough, takes place at the New Year, when the Nile
begins to rise. It is to symbolize the crowning of the king
of Upper and Lower Egypt. The heads of these countries

intervene at a certain moment during the rites of crowning, for they represent hostile elements, just as, in the
mythological version, Horus and Seth have their allies and
their adversaries. Twice there is a simulation of a fight.
The conflict is eventually solved, at the very end of the
ceremony. The king dresses himself in a garment which
is endowed with exceptional powers, and this rite represents the mutual embarrassment of Horus and Osiris.
Seth is vanquished, and Horus occupies his throne.

All of these features—the very need for a rite of con-
ciliation and the preliminary symbols of the conflict—
testify, just as in Mesopotamia, to the vivid conscience
of a fatal rivalry of the times, at every moment of the
passing. The rite discovers that conscience and appeases
it. If the ritual symbols of the conflict are not as numerous
and dramatic in Egypt as in Mesopotamia, this is without
a doubt because the system of a coregency—real or imagined—dimishes the catastrophic effects of the death of
the Pharaoh. In political life the new sovereign has indeed already been installed. The harmony of the times
has been assured in advance, and the rites of crowning
serve only to remind people of it. In Mesopotamia, on the
other hand, the month of Nissan renews every year the
uncertainty of the morrow in agricultural existence. The
rite of the New Year assists effectively in the passing from
death to life and the resurrection of nature.

The Mesopotamian festival of the New Year and the
Egyptian rite of royal succession are eminently political
ceremonies, which are of interest to the destiny of the
state. Nevertheless we readily find features that do not
only relate to collective life but to the agrarian existence
of the inhabitants. The agrarian significance of Osiris becomes apparent in certain phases of the Egyptian ritual:
the inevitable death of Osiris, which is the indispensable
condition for the coming of Horus, is represented by the
threshing of the barley. The passing from death to life

thus covers an agrarian symbolism. The structural relation between the Babylonian New Year and the liturgy
of the passion of Dumuzi has also been pointed out. That
divinity disappeared, "died," to come to life again, and
the phases of his drama were sung in sacred hymns like
the following:[5]

> This lamentation is indeed for the wheat; the fields
> cannot bring it forth!
> This lamentation is indeed for the mighty river; it
> cannot bring forth its waters!
> This lamentation is indeed for the soil, it cannot
> bring forth grain!
> This lamentation is indeed for the marshes; they
> cannot bring forth fish!
> This lamentation is indeed for the vine; it cannot
> bring forth wine!
> This lamentation is indeed for the gardens; they
> cannot bring forth plants!
> This lamentation is indeed for the palace; it cannot
> bring forth life! . . .
>
> Where there was no longer any grass, they graze!
> Where there was no longer any water, they drink!
> Where there were no longer any stables, a stable is
> being built!
> Where there was no longer any shade of reeds, one
> rests under reeds.

These hymns convey the tears and the joys of a popu-
lation of farmers. They were sung in the Babylonian temples at the very same time when in the capital the ritual
of the New Year was being enacted—which in itself was
entirely constructed on the two themes of the disappearance and the rediscovery of Marduk. Apparently the rites
of passage of the New Year and the crowning of the Pharaoh were recent and political expressions of primitively
agrarian liturgies. For quite some time we have been well

aware of the relationship between the Babylonian Dumuzi, the Canaanite Tammuz, the Phoenician Adonis, and Osiris. A universal theme underlies the rituals of those dying and resurrected gods. But whereas in Egypt and in Mesopotamia that theme is only subsidiary, Phoenicia and Canaan maintained it in its primitive and even barbaric form. Fortunately, the mythology of Ras-Shamra completes and confirms the documentation which so far only the Bible and Greek historians had furnished. The central myths of the Ugaritic pantheon—with Baal, Anat, Aleyin, and Mot as their heroes—reflect an agrarian way of life without embellishment. The rational influence of the priests is hardly discernible for the rites preserve something of the spontaneous mentality of agrarian societies. One must never lose sight of this when examining that "religion of Baal" which the Hebrews encountered when they first came to Canaan. In its rough state this was a religion for farmers, for men entirely given to the rhythms of the time of the seasons and of vegetation.

Here the struggle to find a place for man in nature is more pathetic than elsewhere, as is shown by the rites. First the soil had to be mastered, and its fertility depended on all kinds of imponderabilities which were attributed to the *master* of the field, the Baal. He haunted the field, of which the farmer could only become the proprietor after having exorcised the Baal through rites of initiation or foundation. Then one had to master the cosmic Baals, who were the masters of the subterranean water, the rain from heaven, the vegetation, the winds, the dew, the plagues, etc. Each of these manifested his power at a precise moment of the season, and the rite had to intervene to increase or weaken his strength. The return of the seasons was ascribed to these divinities, whose wide ranges are proven by the great mythological cycles of Ras-Shamra and others. With these revivals correspond the rites of passion of Adonis, Tammuz, and Aleyin, which synthesize, at the zenith or the nadir of the seasons, countless lesser rites which were scattered all through the year.

Many ways were invented by the Canaanites and Phoenicians to support that struggle in all its phases. But two of these seem to be characteristic for the "religion of Baal" because they are combined with the very essence of every agrarian religion: human sacrifices and erotic rites.

Human sacrifices were extant in Canaan, Phoenicia, and the territories that depended on them, until recent times. As a matter of fact they had been introduced into the cult of Carthage, and the Bible notes their existence near Jerusalem up to the time of Jeremiah.[6] If the Melech of Tyre (moloch) permanently offered children up as sacrifices in his sanctuary, victims were also offered to him on other occasions, generally at the time of natural or military catastrophes.[7] But the old layers of Canaanite civilization show that the political significance of such sacrifices is of recent date. Originally an agrarian intention prevailed. As mentioned above, we are dealing with a sacrifice of foundation. It was extended to new houses after it had first applied to new fields, from which the Baal could be driven out only through a sacrificial rite.

The erotic aspect of the agrarian rites has to do with the relationship of the mystery of vegetation to that of human fertility. The time of human growth, reproduction, and decay is like a living answer to the time of vegetation. For the farmer it is a question of helping the soil to bring forth and to overcome its own death. He does not have a more immediate and efficient means than his own life. Therefore the rhythms of vegetation are accompanied, sustained, and exalted by the rhythms of man's life. The fusion of nature and man is here extremely facilitated. In Babylon at the New Year and at Memphis at the death of the Pharaoh one had to align nature with the complex life of a state, with its institutions, traditions, and social components. In the Baal rites of Canaan man and nature meet in their brutal expressions. One life passes through both of them. If only man manifests his instinctive life, the life of nature will give him a reply. Therefore do the Baal rites arouse life's instinctive forces to the extreme. In all ritual expressions we have first the appearance of the feminine element. The identification of the woman and the soil is felt immediately. Harlotry was not restricted to the temples but practiced in the open air, since the *power* of the act had to be communicated to the earth.[8] Erotic games, nakedness, and sexuality in all its forms are derived from this primitive tendency. Finally, orgies. For the orgy is the total ritual function of agrarian religion. It expresses not only the exuberant gift of life which is all but squandered. It marks man's penetration in a subterranean, nocturnal fusion beyond all forms and norms. The orgy breaks out when man becomes pathetically conscious of the death of the germ in the soil, of its decay which prepares for resurrection. Therefore the orgiastic rites are connected with the myth of the dying god of vegetation. In Phrygia and Phoenicia, and wherever that myth has been accepted, frenzy reaches its climax and turns into an orgy when the mythical ceremony calls to mind the death of the god. The orgy permits man then to cross over nothingness. By abolishing all frames and all restrictions, by re-establishing a kind of biological chaos, the orgy prevents man from disappearing. In the orgy death and life no longer have any meaning. They are transcended by an obscure dimension, which is unintelligible but victorious. Agrarian time does not go beyond the earth; it buries itself deeply in order to reappear on the surface. The orgy permits man to follow that road and to help in its construction without suffocating. It is the breath of men to whom life is not only a way up but also a way down; not only light but also darkness. Taking everything into account, ritual agrarian time finds its most authentic meaning in the time of orgy.

We do not have a detailed ritual of a Phoenician or Canaanite orgy and no systematic liturgy comparable to Babylonian and Egyptian texts. But the preponderance of agrarian elements in the mythology of Ras-Shamra, the sporadic and often organized survival of human sacrifices and of debauchery in Canaan in Biblical times are indications of an orgiastic orientation for what the Bible calls the religion of Baal. Most probably the Canaanites and Phoenicians tried in their own way to realize the harmony between man and nature through the ritualization of time. Like the Mesopotamians and the Egyptians they found in the rite only a partial appeasement, since the rite itself supported restlessness and also checked it. The festival of the New Year periodically reproduced the fights which prepared for creation. The coming of a Pharaoh underlined the meeting of life and death in human existence. The agrarian cult in Canaan and Phoenicia tried desperately to bring things to life in the subterranean regions where living man had no access. In spite of the efficiency of the rite, once it had been fully achieved there were many and irreparable times where man felt that he was alone in confrontation with nature, that he shared neither cosmic life above nor below, that he could really neither live nor die. Ritual time is a trying time, and its real sense lies in the fact that it must be stopped. "To live ritually in cosmic rhythms," writes Mircea Eliade, "means above all to live in multiple and contrary tensions."[9] One might apply this formula without any change to the magic, divinating, cultic, and orgiastic prophecies which rely on ritual time. When prophetic time is only a rite, it reveals man's contradictions, despairs, and shortcomings.

Cyclical Time

From the origins of human thinking up to man's most complicated and modern expressions, from the first attempts through full-fledged systems of religion, philosophy, and science, one can observe the outlines of an interpretation of time which, contrary to the ritualist concept of accepting and enriching time, weakens it instead. When time is wrapped up in a rite, it enhances its meaning. It is multiplied by a series of mythical resonances, in which human life finds an extension which is sometimes painful, but always rewarding. Ritual time is a time of imagination. But in the history of the human spirit there exists a basic tendency to do without time, to consider it negligible and alien to oneself—unworldly. This tendency is revealed in the *cyclical* concepts of time.

At the present state of our knowledge it seems that the cyclical interpretation of time, as far as it is essentially religious, appeared in Hindu thought. Otherwise its essence is rather cosmological in the ancient Orient. However, it is hard to define precisely the areas of ancient thought. There were no barriers between science and religion. Chaldean astrology, with its notion of identical, endlessly repeated cycles, was a religious as well as a scientific representation of the world. Perhaps it did not have the full metaphysical significance which we find in Hindu cosmology. At least we do not know anything about it. But it did have religious inspirations and translations, one of the most remarkable of which, as previously mentioned and as will be discussed further, is the symbolism of the ziggurat. In Egypt the important idea of survival is attached to the cycles of the stars. The dead do not have a dwelling place which is determined once and for all. They are neither in heaven nor in a nether world. They participate rather in the cyclical movement of nature, they travel with the stars, around the earth, and are sometimes above, sometimes below. This is again an eminently religious aspect of cyclical time, since survival was the main concern of Egyptian religion. Finally, nearly everywhere in the East, and more or less clearly, there was the idea of the Great Year, the cyclical renewal of the world. That idea had somehow been grasped by the first

Greek thinkers and adopted by the Pythagoreans. It has determined the development of a philosophy of time in the subsequent history of Greek thought.

What are the outlines of that tendency which was so common in antiquity, and which Greek philosophy has transmitted to modern thought? The direction seems clear—it is entirely negative concerning time, the essential aspects of which it is opposed to. It is against the mobility of time, since the cycle, which is self-enclosed, does not change. It is also against the irreversibility of time, for nothing begins, nothing ends, since everything starts all over again. Clearly, in the cyclical view, time does not have a quality which is inherent in the entire world. It is a particularly human accident, since nature is outside time and spatial. The man-nature antithesis is here not expressed in homogeneous terms. It is not a meeting of two different times but of man-time and nature-space. The disparity of the terms explains the modalities of the conflict.

The time-space dialectic entraps human destiny wherever it turns. Every religion, philosophy, and ethic gives it a particular meaning. From the primary sensation of an opposition between motion and stability one rises gradually to the great abstractions of event and being, dispersion and identity, provisional and eternal. Among the primitive, probably those who had an intensive history, the migrants and conquerors, became aware of the divergent distribution of time and space. One, the element of passage and usage, was man's own domain. The other, the element of stability and permanence, characterized nature. For the most distant migrations and the stormiest movements of human masses were finally brought to a halt by space. The world was always vaster than man, and even the mightiest and most stable empires eventually succumbed. The world was always more stable than man. Man could only consider himself to be inserted in nature, outflanked and enveloped in it. Time was merely an accessory of space.

We cannot follow up the steps which ancient Oriental thought took in working out a cyclical time. We do not know it well enough, and we have only indications rather than a doctrine. Greek philosophy, on the other hand, presents here a coherent development. Since it was probably influenced by the Orient, we may suppose that it organized tendencies which must have been known to the East too. To the Greeks, the world is a cosmos, an orderly and immovable universe, space. In such a cosmos time in its proper meaning has no reality. To the Pythagoreans it is repetition and identity, and to Plato, "image" of eternity. To Aristotle, it is a number in the cycle of the stars, a circular and uniform movement. Therefore, man's life and existence, his *time*, his uniqueness and his history, are not sources of knowledge. Man can discover himself only through the expedient of science or philosophy, both of which were at first spatial and geometrical. Only by leaving space can man know himself. This space is only partly outside him, since man shares in it through the cyclical movement of time, be it real or imagined. But nothing could be more illusory for man than to rely on time by isolating it from space and grasping it in his human solitude. This would mean disappearance and collapse.

One attitude that is common to all thought systems which rely on the idea of cyclical time, is that they ignore history, for history cannot rise in the immovable, in a system without beginning and end, without a change in its circle. Man's real *time*, his uniqueness and history, does not concern people whose life is stable. Even when events oblige men to become aware of movability and changes, even when a moving history develops effectively before a new cycle starts, even then does that history not achieve a precise meaning in man's consciousness. History is then merely a series of anecdotes which people can tell each

other for the purpose of distraction, but they have nothing
to do with human destiny. Typically, the Greek related
history to philosophical investigation and to rhetoric. To
them, historiography was an interest in the past but not
a "creation."[10] True, the Greeks had a history, but they
did not base anything on it. To have a history meant to
them to know the past and how it could happen again. It
did not mean to influence the structure of the world. The
knowledge of historical time cannot be reconciled with the
idea of an eternal recurrence.

But side by side with this outstanding feature the notion of a cyclical time presupposes others which have
grave consequences for man's behavior.

One of these is restricted to Hindu thought. There the
cycle is felt as *pain*. The whirlpool of transmigration, the
samsara, is a path of suffering and misery, a path which
has been traced by human deeds, be they good or evil.
The only salvation lies in deliverance. One must cross the
fatal river and reach the other side, and this is only possible through the end of all deeds.

Another consequence is less dramatic. It no longer sees
a painful but neutral fatalism in the cycle. A general *indifference* characterizes the movement of the cycle. Since
people meet each other again after some time in the same
situations, their behavior has no metaphysical resonance.
The doctrine of the endless return has no religious fruitfulness. Only fateful relations, not ethical ones, can be
established between man and the gods. Where the myths
were expressed in rituals, the gods were considered the
guarantors of justice and retribution. To the degree that
the myths were sublimated into philosophy, or, as with
Plato, lost their ritual correspondence in spite of their
remaining sub-real, the gods became removed. Their vigilance was replaced by their eminence. Ethics did not have
a religious foundation but became an aspect of politics.

But the ethical indifference, which was a consequence of

the idea of the cycle, blunted the belief in the political efficiency of human deeds. The Greeks did not believe that their conduct could correct, amend, or direct the future. By neglecting to work for it, they made it entirely rigid. The Greek world was rotting because the Greeks allowed it to die. Greek prophecy has remained unfruitful because cyclical time prevented it from being active and made it apathetic.

Mystical Time

By abolishing all barriers between man and God, *mystical time* brings about the total fusion of the divine and the human. Although it is implied in certain rituals and philosophies, it cannot be really identified beyond a moment in ritual or cyclical time. This fact is of a fundamental importance—mystical time is the most complete reduction of time, which is not only weakened but rejected. It is the time of the ecstasis, of a man who transcends himself, who leaves his human condition and thus also time. We are no longer dealing with time but with an experience of a *point* in time, not an extension of time.

Ancient ecstases must have known of that mystical moment of the fusion with the divine. Enthusiasm must have seized man in that supreme instant when, in the recital of a liturgy or during the discipline of contemplation, he became one with the divinity. But we have no systematic description of that culminating moment. Trance and contemplation are only the secondary signs of an experience which is made difficult to describe because it is directly opposed to human categories.

Nevertheless, Hindu thought provides a complete description of transcending oneself. As we have seen, here the cycle is the source of suffering. One must cross the fatal river and reach its other side, and this can only be achieved by annihilating all activity. Asceticism corresponds to a progressive diminution of active life, to the elimination of the influence of former deeds. Two aspects strike us because of their contradiction with the ritualization of time: instead of grasping time in the liturgy, one tries to escape it; instead of introducing one's own person in the act of the rite, one abolishes all action. The rites of asceticism are not active but disciplinary. They do not create a relation between man and time, but they make him realize the nakedness of his nothingness.

If, in the Orient, every mystery includes a particular meaning and wants to lead its disciples to precise goals, it is nevertheless tied up with all the other mysteries by purely exterior manifestations which are even more significant. The mysteries have this in common, that they identify themselves with a cult and impose a certain discipline on their followers. This applies to the orgiastic cults of Cybele, Adonis, Ishtar, Tammuz, and Dionysus in Thracia, Phoenicia and Mesopotamia, and later in Greece. It also applies to the sacrificial and powerfully symbolic cults of Osiris in Egypt and Mitra in Persia, and the cultic, fervent, and occult communions at Eleusis in Pythagorian Greece wherever the Gnosis made its influence felt. Finally, we have the cult of the Christian sacrament. In mysticism, the cultic rite is defined as the lever of the mystery, the key to the secret passage. In ancient cults it had the gross form of material and even biological demands. Man gives himself up entirely to the rite, he fills himself with sacred beverages, with blood, and he offers his manhood and his person to the divine. The Gnosis transforms the rite into an occult alchemy and arithmetic. Christianity transfigures it by grace and faith. But these are as indispensable to the mystery as is the sacrament itself. Discipline, which is also variable, joins the rite. In the ancient cult is is a discipline of enrichment, of excess, of an explosion of the personality, and delirium and frenzy are the vehicles of enthusiasm. The more real the ecstasis is, and the more it carries man beyond himself through intoxication and the dance, the more efficient it seems to be. In Greece, in the Gnosis and in Persia, where Mazdaism was associated with the cult of Mitra, we observe a tendency towards an inner effort, a diminution of the biological vitality in favor of an exaltation of intellectual forces. Christian asceticism, which cannot be separated from Christian mysticism, develops in the Middle Ages in a direction which is quite loyal to the Mystery of the Cross to which it was tied, if not ritually, at least in its discipline. The mystical union, which is the goal of all ascetic efforts, can be achieved only by pulling oneself together before reaching one's full personality. Only the passage through death allows man to participate in the Mystery of the Cross.

It is important to point out that, contrary to Hindu mysticism, Christianity does not make annihilation the end of the mystical experience. It is only part of it, and Christian mystical experience presents itself here as the experience of a real time. In Christian mysticism we have the feeling of an extension, a hierarchy, and a progress, which are characteristic for an evolution. The mystical union with God, which remains the final goal of the experience, can only be attained by a long pilgrimage from awakening to purification, from illumination to the fusion. At a certain moment this time is rudely interrupted by a stagnation, a decline, a pain, a crucifixion—the dark night, death. This, then, is a period of nothingness, which seems to be indispensable to the meeting with Total Love.[11] In Christian mysticism this interruption by nothingness evidently corresponds to the acceptance of the Mystery of the Cross. It is, however, characteristic for any mystical experience of time. Mystical prophecy seems to be dominated by this idea of a rupture. Besides the important fact that the vision is limited in time, it yet shows, even when it is extended over a longer time, the experience of an interruption and suspension. The mystical prophet tends to be the man of whom Tauler[12] speaks, and who stands before the Highest Being without knowledge, love, works, or spirit.

Notes

1. See Frankfort, *op. cit.*, p. 292ff.
2. Mircea Eliade, *Traité d'histoire des religions,* Paris 1949, p. 337. See Hubert and Mauss, *La représentation du temps dans la religion et dans la magie,* Mélanges Hist. Rel. 1909. G. Dumézil, Temps et mythes, Recherches philosophiques, V, 1935–36.
3. Frankfort, *op. cit.,* p. 401.
4. *Ibid.,* pp. 152ff.
5. *Ibid.,* pp. 403ff.
6. Jeremiah 7:31; 19:5; 32:35.
7. II Kings 3:27; Micah 6:7.
8. Without a doubt there is a connection between the rites of harlotry and the fact the Canaanite temple had a sacred space in the open air.
9. Eliade, *op. cit.,* p. 340.
10. See Jean Guitton, *Le temps de l'éternité chez Plotin et saint Augustin,* Paris, 1933, pp. 356f.
11. St. John of the Cross has written an entire book on this subject *(The Dark Night).*
12. Ferd. Vetter, *Die Predigten Taulers,* Berlin, 1910, III, 70.

PART II
The Hebrew Setting of Prophecy

1

The Biblical Dialogue between
God and Man:
The Spirit and the Word

The Spirit

In every prophetic revelation there is an encounter between the human and the superhuman, the natural and the supernatural. The Hebrews, too, were conscious of standing before the Divine, of facing an Other One. But that feeling was explained in a singular way; they saw in it not an accidentally repeated meeting that took place at certain intervals, but rather an essential human disposition that had to do with man's place in the world. In the encounter with the Divine, the Hebrews saw not a rupture but an accomplishment of their condition. As far as revelation meant the spontaneous manifestation of God within the world of man, it seemed to them as conceivable, and almost necessary, since it corresponded to certain directions of their thinking and to certain implications of their experience. Nevertheless, they remained surprised by God. For them, too, the dialectic of the Divine and the human harbored a mystery.

In the Bible, that mystery is described by a certain term, namely, *ruach*, which the Greeks translated as *pneuma;* we call it *spirit*. The superior Biblical personalities, those who dominate either by virtue of intelligence or strength, are *inspired*. Their energy derives from the spirit which God places or raises in them. The remarkable military or political investitures are due to the spirit. Thus, Joshua, the Judges, Saul and David are "full with the spirit."[1] Those who excel in wisdom or art, like Joseph or Bezaleel, receive their abilities from the spirit.[2] Prophetic revelation is revelation of the spirit, and therefore the prophet is a "man of the spirit."[3] Sometimes the spirit is the sign of permanent grace, and the prophet makes use of it regularly and almost unconsciously[4]; at other times it bursts out suddenly, and remains restricted to the experience of a dazzling moment.[5] It can be transmitted to others, so that Joshua and the Elders receive it from Moses, and Elisha receives from Elijah twice as much as his master had possessed.[6] Certain instances are noteworthy for the variety and the intensity which they lend to the prophetic spirit. The fantastic revelation which God gives to Ezekiel is from beginning to end an effect of the spirit. A *ruach* comes from the north and like a mighty stream it animates the heavenly chariot and its cosmic servants.[7] Then the *ruach* penetrates the prophet and takes him to the exiles.[8] Later on, it is again the *ruach* which creates in the prophet the astonishing feeling that he is again in Jerusalem, in the precincts of the Temple.[9] The *ruach* places the prophet in the Valley of the Dry Bones, and, coming, by the prophet's bidding, from the four directions, it revives those bones.[10] Furthermore, the "shoot" from the stock of Jesse, as foreseen by Isaiah, is the receptacle of a sixfold *ruach:* wisdom, intelligence, intuition, power, knowledge, and the fear of God dwell in him as emanations of the divine spirit.[11] Finally one day, according to Joel,[12] God will pour out His spirit on boys and girls, on old and young, on slaves and servants. Then the human community will become a prophetic society because it will be a spiritual one.

We know the exceptional outcome of that theory concerning the *ruach.* By and by the system of the "Holy

Spirit" is worked out, and rabbinic Judaism as well as Christianity were to introduce it into their respective sacred systems. But the basically Jewish notion of an inspiration from the *ruach* is of Hebrew origin. A reading of the pre-Exilic parts of the Bible shows that that idea is based on an original and ancient conception of the relations between God and man.

I.

In its inner structure the spirit is many-faceted and even contradictory. In its highest point, the *ruach* is the Spirit, in all its grandeur, majesty, solemnity, and even uniqueness. Though rarely, in the Bible it is already the *spirit of holiness*,[13] but more frequently the *Spirit of God*. This term becomes especially solemn when it is placed in the mouth of God: *My Spirit*. In that small word, *ruchi*, the Bible concentrates the entire sovereign and still condescending meaning of God in His relation to the world and to man. The spirit of God is a superior principle of activity and creation in the world. God sends forth His spirit, causes it to hover, gives it to some and takes it away from others. In this sense the spirit is not an attribute of God but an absolute principle of revelation. In several Biblical texts the spirit of God is the plenitude of the universe and the intimate presence of God in His creation.

This is particularly the case with Ezekiel's visions mentioned above. The spirit is the element of supernatural life. It impregnates the world as does a liquid substance. The heavenly chariot is carried by it, and it advances majestically on its flow. Then the parts of the chariot are affected by it, since the spirit of living beings enters the wheels and makes them turn. The prophet basks in that atmosphere of the *ruach,* and it is not surprising that the motion of the *ruach* seizes him too, and like a chariot, he

is taken away by the *ruach*. By virtue of its flowing movement, one and the same *ruach* generates the mysterious
movement of the world and the prophetic vision of man.

We have the same description in Genesis 37. The
ruach is everywhere, nestling in the four corners of the
world. Called upon by the prophet, it develops, fills the
universe, and in passing takes hold of the dry bones and
revives them. Here the *ruach* is a life-giving fluid; without
it the world is motionless and dead.

In the first verses of Genesis[14] we find an important
nuance. Whereas the divine *ruach* is still described as fluid
—the verb is even very expressive, the spirit "hovers"
over the waters and spreads out its wings like a bird—
it is detached from the chaos and watches over it as the
very source of life. This is God's first revelation to the
world, the first reflection which it has of God. It is, so to
speak, the pronouncement, the germ, of future revelations.
The world which, at its creation, was caressed by the
wings of the divine spirit, preserves something of that
contact. After having wakened the world, the *ruach* will
remain in its life.

But in the Bible the *ruach* is not always all-embracing
and objective. Sometimes it is a subjective quality of God,
an attribute of His character, and the spirit of God is
referred to, just as His soul and His heart. The spirit is
then only a fragment of the divine Person, His intention,
the direction of His will, if not His will itself.[15] In that
case the spirit of God is no different from that of man.
The perspective is an anthropomorphic one, since man,
too, has a *ruach,* the seat of his emotions and passions.
Man's *ruach* is exalted, joyous, sad, afflicted, panting,
heavy,[16] and the spirit of God, too, knows these ups and
downs, these outbursts and remorses.[17] We have here a
psychic aspect of the *ruach,* as different from its metaphysical and cosmic one.

But we must go deeper. The spirit of man is not only

the seat of his passions but also of contradictions. It is the place for the abnormal and the morbid. Biblical man sometimes has an *evil spirit,* which is no longer a simple quality of a human being but an objective principle which is placed in him for a certain time and with a greater or lesser intensity. As is always implied, that "evil spirit" is derived from God. It is the spirit of God which dwells temporarily in an individual or a group.[18] But whereas the common "spirit of God" cheers a man up, the evil spirit destroys him, as happened in the case of Saul. In the case of the people of Shechem, it led to disorder. We meet different nuances of the evil spirit. While, generally speaking, it is "evil," it becomes a *lie* in the mouth of the prophets,[19] *lethargy* and *impurity* in the heart of the people.[20] This term is of great importance, for its opposite, purity, is a manifestation of the *ruach* of God.[21] This is no longer the anthropomorphism mentioned above. When man is seized by such a *ruach,* which attacks him in order to corrupt him, there is a shade of demonism. The paradox is thus complete. On the plane of revelation the spirit of God concentrates the spiritual power on all its levels, from an abstract and supreme spirituality to a magic emanation, from purity to impurity, and from God to Satan.

The Hebrews were well aware of these different levels of meaning, and it is in this very concentration of everything unexplainable and inaccessible in one notion, namely, that of the spirit of God, wherein lies the importance of the Hebrew *ruach.* Since the whole world belonged to one God, it was His with all its contradictions. In the perspective of the *ruach* therefore, the dialogue between God and Satan is only a monologue within God Himself.

The phenomenology of Biblical prophetism must take this into account. The spirit of the prophets is nothing else but the spirit of the world and the spirit of plain people, or rather it had no other basis than in these spirits. What was later called the "holy" spirit was in the Bible *the* spirit. Inspiration did not drive man out of the situation in which he had been. It was just the reverse: only through his situation could man attain inspiration. This was made possible because man had a spirit, which means: he was alive.

II.

The *ruach* is an image of life, and the very etymology of the word explains why it has been selected—in order to understand life in all its complexity and density. For *ruach* means wind, air, the prolonged absence of which leads to asphyxiation and to the loss of life. While man can do without food or drink for a long time, lack of air soon leads to death. In the desert, where the world is without concrete substance, where man has only the unreachable sky above him and the barren sand at his feet, something lengthens his life—between the sky and the sand there is air, the wind, the *ruach*.

The same air is in the human body as breath. As long as that physiological *ruach* functions, as long as man exhales and inhales, he is alive. Once it stops, death is imminent or has been reached. Inside and outside of man, the *ruach* is the sign of life.

But Biblical thought has derived an exceptional conclusion from that etymological evidence. Out of the symbol of life, it made a symbol of the imperishable. Instead of an animistic perspective, we now deal with one of participation. Human breath, as far as it stands for biological existence, is called *neshama* or *nefesh,* whereas man's *ruach* stands for that part of his being which is open to another *ruach,* through which he stops being himself, in order to participate in something else. The *nefesh* or the *neshama* can only be tied or joined to another *nefesh* or *neshama.*[22] But between one ruach and another one there

THE BIBLICAL DIALOGUE BETWEEN GOD AND MAN 95

exists an intimate communication, an interpenetration. The dimension of the *ruach* goes beyond that of physical bodies, so that it does not seize them in their localization or individualization but in their communion. In possessing the *ruach,* man has not acquired *one* life, but life itself. The *ruach* is the very spirit of life.[23] As soon as that spirit encounters another life, it communicates with it. Herein lies the secret of the encounter between God and man. Since in the Bible God is *alive,* man's spirit of life shares in the spirit of God.

The texts of Ezekiel and Genesis quoted earlier show that there is a relationship between the spirit of the world and the spirit of man. Since the world is full of the *ruach,* men share in it. The *ruach* of the world extends the divine *ruach* which "hovered" over it while the earth was still chaos. Since man is part of the world, he participates in the divine *ruach.* Certain Biblical texts declare that man's life depends on the divine spirit, that man lives only when touched by the *ruach,* and that he dies when it leaves him. God sends forth His spirit, which spreads out like waves and seduces the beings. When God recalls the *ruach,* He deprives man and sends him to his death:

> "If he set his heart upon man, if he gather unto himself his spirit and his breath, all flesh shall perish together, and man shall turn again unto dust."
>
> Job 34: 14, 15
>
> "Thou hidest thy face, they are troubled; thou takest away thy breath, they die and return to their dust; Thou sendest forth thy spirit, they are created . . ."
>
> Psalms 104:29f.
>
> "As long as the spirit of God is in my nostrils . . . as long as I am not dead" . . .
>
> Job 27: 3, 5

Psalm 104 is interesting, because it makes no distinction between the *ruach* of God and that of man. The *ruach* is a participation, a dimension of the encounter between God and man.

As Claude Tresmontant has shown, there is a system in this concept.[24] Biblical anthropology joins with cosmology in order to complete the theory of the *ruach*. "Man's *ruach* is that part in him which enables him to meet God's *ruach*, and due to which the indwelling of the spirit of God is not an intrusion from the outside but is expected . . . The contrast which Biblical tradition introduces between the flesh and the spirit is a contrast of two orders. The flesh is man in his frailty, which comes from the dust from which he was created. The spirit is his supernatural part. . . . In Hebrew, the flesh is synonymous with the soul. "All flesh," or "every soul" means man, humanity. The contrast between the flesh and the spirit is not a duality inside a nature like the substantial dualism between soul and body, but rather the opposition between the order of nature and the supernatural order."[25] Certain verses reduce clearly the opposition of the divine and the human to a contrast between the spirit and the flesh:

"My spirit shall not abide in man forever, for he is flesh."

Genesis 6 : 3

"The Egyptians are men and not God, and their horses flesh and not spirit."

Isaiah 31 : 3

Tresmontant goes on as follows: "Biblical anthropology opens up a new and characteristic dimension, the supernatural dimension, which is peculiar to Biblical revelation."[26] The theory of the *ruach* enables all men to become prophets. Moses did not express a naïve wish when he prayed: "Would that all the Lord's people were prophets, that the Lord would put His spirit upon them."[27] This is quite in accord with the system of the

THE BIBLICAL DIALOGUE BETWEEN GOD AND MAN 97

divine and the human in the Bible. Hebrew thought could consider man only as having a share in God, and this gives the whole Bible its dialogical structure. But this general and sometimes vague participation presents itself in the Bible also in a very exact form, which we call prophecy, in the restricted and narrow sense of that term. What is the cause for the singularity of that prophetic participation? With what surplus is Biblical man, who is already gifted with the *ruach,* and thus a prophet, with what surplus is he invested when he receives the additional *ruach* of a *navi?* It seems to us that Biblical man becomes a prophet, and that the potentiality of Biblical man becomes a reality, when instead of encountering the Spirit, he meets God. He no longer meets a principle but a Person; not an essence but a *living* and *feeling* Being.

III.

We must give the idea of a living God an authentic and full-fledged meaning. God's life in the Bible must neither be moralized nor rationalized. It admits of God's holiness, His consuming character, His wrath and His zeal as well as His love. God's life is essentially irreducible to the rational but it reveals itself in the category of mystery. The spirit of the living God is *numinous.* An analysis like the one given by Rudolf Otto succeeds quite well in showing His fearsome and majestic character.[28] God's life is the mystery. It is felt as being outside of man, dominating, "wholly other." It inspires a sacred terror as well as an appalling and fascinating one. This is also true of the *ruach.* It comes from the outside, it *in*spires in the literal meaning of the preposition. The verbs which stand for inspiration indicate that something from the outside chooses a dwelling place for itself. Thus the spirit "clothes" Gideon, Amasai, Zechariah[29]; it "overwhelms" Samson, Saul, and David[30]; it "falls" upon Ezekiel.[31] The *ruach* is outside of man, and also above him. The sovereignty of the *ruach* is shown by the preposition "on," as in falling *upon* a man. In Hebrew we do not really have an inspiration. The spirit emerges from a certain place which dominates man in order to settle down in him. The *ruach* is terrifying by its very arbitrariness, since it appears and vanishes at the pleasure of God. It is something extraneous, and the man thus surprised is above all conscious of one thing: that he has become *someone else*. But this change does not set the inspired man aside in his relation to other people nor in his relation to existence. It only means that he is no longer alone. Biblical man does not become a prophet by secluding himself but by getting in touch with others. He was a navi through the knowledge that he participated in another reality besides that of his own life—the life of God.

The *ruach* of God is also feeling, *pathetic*. This is a truth which no idealism or spiritualism can weaken, still less eliminate. Only through a pathetic conception of the Spirit is it possible that one and the same term, *ruach,* refers in the Bible to the purest and most spiritual dimension and also to psychic life in all its contradictions. The Greeks had not been able to work out such an idea. Their philosophers thought that motion, and therefore also emotions, could not be reconciled with the divinity. The Greek people knew only egoistic divinities, whose passions centered around themselves, and who were concerned with man only when he bothered them. The Hebrews, on the other hand, saw in history and its movements a manifestation of their God, whose emotions were the levers of a history in which men were the inevitable actors. God's emotion was like a roof over the human condition. The Biblical description of God may well be called anthropopathic, meaning that God appeared to Biblical man in the polarity of His *pathos,* in His love and anger, in His harshness and His forgiveness. God's *ruach* judges itself and—repents. God's repentance alone would be enough to show that the Biblical God is not tied to an abstract and general principle. He is not the God of universal principles but rather the God of the Unique, of the historical moment. The *ruach* is not spiritual stability but living emotion.

The critical school believes in a purifying evolution of the Hebrew idea of God, so that a demoniac *ruach* had by and by been replaced by a spiritual one, and the rule of terror and justice had progressively yielded to one of ethics and love. If this were true, we would have not one Biblical prophetism but two. The first of them would correspond to the primitive representations of the *ruach*, being a magic and animistic approach to the divinity. The second one, radically different from the first, would coincide with the elaboration of ethical monotheism. But in reality Biblical prophetism presents one impressive continuity. It has always faced a God who was terrible and kind at the same time, and whose *ruach* vibrated between punishment and pardon. Biblical prophetism did not aim at emptying out the idea of God but rather at knowing His pathos. The Prophets, who were the only ones to have that precious knowledge, had neither the right nor the power to modify it in any way whatever. They only took part in it. This was fundamental.

All this has been vividly portrayed by A. J. Heschel.[32] His explanation of Biblical prophecy is based on an analysis of God's pathos, which he considers to be the basic category of prophetic theology. In the prophetic experience God is not the object but the subject. To grasp God means to be grasped by Him, and to see God means to be seen by Him. God's pathos means the attention He gives to the world and the interest which He has in it. God's pathos is directed towards man, which Heschel calls anthropotropism. Taking part in this, the prophet knows God's actual pathos and is in *sympathy* with God.

Prophetic religion is a religion of sympathy, as Heschel has shown in referring to the politics, the ethics, the theology, but above all the psychology of the Biblical prophets.

The first incidence, and one with which we shall deal further in this chapter, shows how autonomous Biblical prophets were in relation with other ancient and modern prophets, who depend on magic or ecstasis. The Biblical prophet finds his inspiration somewhere else. When the *ruach* approaches him from the dark regions of demonism or the bright ones of mysticism it is so only in order to remove him from there. Affinities of the *ruach* with animism and ecstasis are negative. They mark the boundaries between those areas in which the prophet's experience resembles that of other prophets and those in which the *navi* has an experience which is entirely his own.

God's living and pathetic revelation in the *ruach* does not establish a *relation* between God and man but it creates a *knowledge* between them.

All magic implies a relation, an automatic contact between the divine and the human. Ecstasis, too, calls for a relation between God and man, a psychological ripening, a progressing in the soul. The soothsayer and the mystic seek God and apply certain means to discover Him. In the Biblical world, on the other hand, God is in search of man. Heschel has taught us that the Bible is less a theology for man than an anthropology for God.[33] In Biblical revelation it is God who starts, it is He who takes the first step, and man is enveloped by Him. The divine call precedes the human expectation. If one wishes to explain prophetic revelation, one must get rid of all magic and psychic theories. There is no "conductor" in the spiritual current which leads from man to God, there are no guiding lines or psychological, intellectual or instinctive forces capable of sharpening the prophet's conscience towards a revelation and of getting him there with greater speed and assurance.

One can hardly find a proper term for the prophet's situation at the moment when God calls him. He is neither void nor passive, for we shall see presently that the prophet meets God out of a fullness. There is a call, God invites man and seizes him. God is there, suddenly, even before man expects Him or calls on Him.

The analysis of this lack of an approach from the side of the prophet allows us to point out certain important differences between the Biblical prophet and other ancient prophets or mystical ones of modern times.

First of all, there is no *magical* relationship between God and the prophet. God does not owe the *navi* anything, and the technique of material magic does not affect Him. Unlike ancient soothsayers, the Biblical prophet cannot unravel the message of God by looking at the flesh of sacrifices, the flight of the birds, or "signs" in nature. Still less can he arouse the presence of God by acting on occult elements which supposedly chain God to nature. The Bible knows so well that the almighty God *can* let Himself be provoked by magical practices that it tells us that God agreed to yield to the divinations of Balaam.[34] But Balaam is not a Biblical prophet. He is a false prophet for many reasons, and his successes in the field of magic are one of these, as if to underline that one of the authentications of a true Biblical prophet is that he does not rely on magical practices.

Nor is there a spiritual magic between God and the prophet. Nothing—neither a prayer nor a solicitation—can force God to reveal Himself. Often, when there is great need, the prophet calls on God, just as he would call on someone else. But just like "someone else," God can refuse to listen to him and remain silent.[35] Neither a long introductory intimacy nor an exceptional devotion

assures a dialogue between God and the prophet. Prophetic tradition indeed abounds with such voids. God's
word is then "rare," and the prophet cannot force it into
existence. God's silence—not His mystery but His silence,
which, like all other divine attributes, can be analyzed by
dogmatic theology—is all-important for the prophet
who experiences it.

God's sudden appearance in the prophet's spiritual life
constitutes an essential difference between the *navi* and the
mystic.

The prophet meets God in a void. Between him and
the moment of the meeting there is nothing at all, at
least no decision, no preparation, no cause, not even that
very pure meditation which the Bible knows of, and which
it reveals with acclaim in connection with pious souls.
This is called *the search for God*. Between the mystic and
the meeting, on the other hand, there is the entire long
and detailed preparation, the *way*, the *pilgrimage*, where
grace can be attained step by step, from awakening to
purification, from asceticism to illumination, and passing
through the *dark night* before reaching the union in the
meeting. Through a thousand different forms the mystical
experience always remains the same—it is an ascent,
and the true encounter with God, where everything becomes exchange and reciprocity, is reached only at the
top of the ladder.[36] And, again in a thousand different
forms, the prophetic experience, on the other hand, reveals itself as an unexpected shock. It is a thunderstorm
out of a blue summer sky, and it takes an unprepared man
by surprise.

It is true that this phenomenon is not without exception
in the Bible. Magical techniques, trances and elements of
ecstasis appear sometimes in Biblical prophecy. But this
reestablishment of the *relationship* between the divine
and the human coincides with epochs of Biblical history
where the consciousness of being wrapped up in God

yielded to the feeling of being tied to Him. The ecstatic forms of Biblical prophecy are contemporary with its cultic forms. Now the cult by itself does not imply any knowledge but is a *religion*. The more prophetism became identified with religion, the more it developed within itself elements of a connection and a relation with God. In the autonomous visions of prophecy the *relation* was secondary and therefore unnecessary. *Knowledge* took its place.

IV.

But what kind of *knowledge* is it which is deprived of any magical or psychic relation? According to Heschel, it is the supreme postulate of sympathy.[37] We might better say, it is sympathy itself. If we were to look, in the language of the Bible, for a Hebrew equivalent for sympathy, we would find *the knowledge of God*.[38] In the Messianic prophecies of Isaiah, it is majestically associated with the *ruach*. When the time arrives that the *ruach* of all men participates intimately in the *ruach* of God, when "inspiration" will no longer be a prophetic accident of the human condition but its very essence, when all men will be "prophets," the whole earth will be full of the *knowledge of God*.[39] Then all men will have that experience of sympathy which so far had been the privilege of the prophets.

I have shown elsewhere[40] that there is something *immediate* and *penetrating* in the Biblical notion of *knowledge*. One's whole being is involved, due to the identification of that term with the act of union of man and woman. Contrary to Plato's "longest road," prophecy experiences a sudden and instantaneous revelation which is complete from the first moment—a blossoming forth of love. We shall soon see what deep meaning the prophets ascribed to the reality of love, how they conceived of their universe as one great marriage adventure between God and Israel. They were aware of living through something similar in their private sphere. To them revelation was neither a technique nor a gift. It was rather the discovery of love. The encounter with a living and feeling God revealed to the prophets neither a spirit nor an idea, but a Partner.

One of the essential aspects of Biblical prophecy is therefore that it is an experience, and an experience for two. Prophetic experience is the foundation for the certainty of a call. There is something painful in the fact that the difference between *true* and *false* prophecy lies only in the intuition of the true prophet. There is no other sign of distinction. Nothing shows the observer that the *ruach* is one of lies. Only the prophet knows, in the intimacy of his experience, that the *ruach* is true. As will be discussed later, at different times in Biblical history people have indeed tried to codify prophecy and to establish a theory of false prophecy. But they could never establish a code for true prophecy, since it was confined to the experience of the prophet. However, that experience was so strong and real that deception was out of the question. Without the strength of their experience Michayu and Jeremiah would not have had the courage to contradict so brutally the reality in which they lived. They had to experience within themselves a stronger and more absolute reality in order to be able to stand up against the things they witnessed. In order to be called a defeatist or a traitor in the midst of a fanatically chauvinistic people, it was not enough to harbor a vague wish or a generous but illusory idea. They needed a well-founded conviction. The prophets found that certainty in their *knowledge*, in the absolute reality which dwelled in them.

This allowed them to *share* the experience. As mentioned before, it was an experience for two, an encounter with a Partner. Amos has described that feeling in a famous passage. Without a doubt, the accumulation of images shows that the prophet was in search of an authentic symbol, and that none of those used by him corresponded entirely to the experience through which he had lived.

"Will two men walk together unless they have agreed? Will a lion roar in the woods when he has no prey? Will a young lion cry out of his den if he has taken nothing? Does a bird fall into a snare on the ground unless there was a trap? Does a snare spring up from the ground when it has taken nothing? Is a trumpet blown in the city, and the people are not afraid? Shall there be evil in a city, and the Lord has not done it? Surely God will do nothing unless He has revealed His secret to His servants, the prophets. The lion has roared—who will not fear? God has spoken—who can but prophesy?" Amos 3: 3-8.

God and the prophet depend on each other as the lion and his prey, as the bird and the snare, the roaring and the terror. They walk together. Hosea has tried a more exact description—two wrestlers. Even if those verses should refer to God and Israel, the picture can apply equally to a prophetic encounter.[41] Again Hosea takes up the theme of the encounter between Jacob and the angel where, according to Genesis[42] they met face to face, just as was the case with the prophetic revelations accorded to Moses, and on Mount Sinai, to the entire people. For those theophanies, too, occurred face to face.[43] The *knowledge* of God by the prophet is a bodily struggle, as is shown in detail in the text of Genesis in connection with Jacob's meeting the divine Being.[44] Finally, Jeremiah uses for his own experience an image which Hosea had applied to Israel.[45] He compares the prophetic encounter with that of two lovers:

"Oh Lord, Thou has seduced me, and I was seduced,
Thou hast overcome me, and hast prevailed."
Jeremiah 20: 7

The wrestling and the embracing of love, the pathetic violence, those are symbols which the prophet considered adequate for a description of his *knowledge,* and it has here the very same meaning which it has so often in the Bible: knowledge through the love of the partners. Jeremiah uses this symbol in order to express what he lived through in his own prophetic revelation. Elsewhere he uses it, as do other prophets, to describe the history of Israel.

But knowledge goes one step further, namely from personal revelation to collective revelation. Inspiration through the *ruach* concerns only the prophet's private and inner drama. But prophetic experience presents itself also on another plane, not any longer in intimacy but in public life. The prophet is not only called upon but also sent forth. Revelation is succeeded by confrontation. This does not take place any longer in the realm of the *ruach* but in that of the davar—the *spirit* finds its fulfilment in the *word.*

The Word

Is the word—*davar*—in Greek *logos,* an autonomous category of prophetic revelation, or is it linked with the manifestations of the *ruach?* Certain historians believe that the *ruach,* in its emotional and irrational complex, has been sublimated by the great prophets into a more "spiritualized" revelation, namely, that of the *davar.* According to them the spirit and the word are like the degrees of a revelation which becomes purer and purer. This is a theory which deserves to be investigated. To Volz and Mowinckel,[46] for example, the spirit and the word are two different forms of revelation which correspond to two unequal periods of religious experience. The ancient prophets, those who lived before the eighth century, express the feeling of being possessed by the *spirit* of God. This spirit works in them like a demon, with a magic and blind force that is sometimes harmful. Such "possessed" prophets are hardly distinguishable from fools. Popular opinion of that period mentions prophets side by side with fools.[47] We are told that the great prophets, from the eighth century on, react against such a sentiment. They say that they are not seized by the spirit but by the *word* of God. Far from being possessed, they are possessors of the divine word. They distrust the possessed, pneumatic prophets and even consider their inspiration by the *ruach* as a criterion for deception. Only at the time of the Exile does the *ruach* reappear in Biblical prophecy. By that time Babylonian influences make themselves felt. These were to be strengthened by Persian elements, and the idea of the *ruach* was to predominate in the formation of post-Biblical thought. But between Amos and Jeremiah, during two hundred years of "great" prophetism, the prophets escape the influence of the *ruach*, and the irrational aspects of revelation become sublimated. They do not have the feeling of being seized by God but of hearing His word. Even if the mechanism of the phenomenon remains a mystery, the contents of the word assures revelation something eminently rational. The spirit does not have any content; it can only be judged by the man who is seized by it. But by virtue of its verbal expression, the word is subject to the scrutiny of intelligence and moral sense. The use of the *word*, which serves the *spirit*, proves, side by side with other elements, that the "great" prophets stand on the level of an *ethical* monotheism.

Let us point out first that in order to be right that thesis must do away with a great number of verses which explicitly mention the value of the *ruach* in the experience of the great prophets of the eighth and seventh centuries. It was Hosea who created the typical expression "man of the spirit,"[48] in order to compare him with the prophet, and to contrast him with the fool. Micah declared that he was full of strength, of the *ruach* of God, of justice and power.[49] Furthermore, in that instance the synonym used gives the *ruach* a positive and exalting value, not a debasing one. Isaiah mentions that the *ruach* inspires the good, creates life, crowns the offspring of Jesse, and is opposed to *mortal* flesh.[50] One cannot very well erase those verses which are in perfect accord with Isaiah's entire message. Indeed, the argument of the exegetes impresses us only in regard to the two prophets who limit the period of the *davar*, Amos and Jeremiah. Whereas the former knows the *ruach* only in the meaning of *wind*,[51] the latter identifies it, in his prophetic inspiration, with lies.[52] But neither the absence of the spirit in one of these nor its debasing use with the other one appears to us to be decisive, since it is not the word that counts but the idea. Now, as we have seen, Amos described revelation as a force, a seizure, one might say a rapture. He is *given over* to the *word* of God, just as his predecessors had been given over to His *spirit*.

Faced with the priest of Beth El, who treats him as a visionary, Amos does not develop a "rational" theory of prophecy. God has taken him "from behind the flocks," frightening him, and forcing him into prophecy. He is surprised by the *word* of God, just as the prey is surprised by a lion. All this does not constitute a sublimated description of prophecy. Election through the word means to Amos as much of an irrationality as revelation through the spirit means to other prophets. Also, as we have stated, Jeremiah pathetically experiences prophetic knowledge as a violent seduction. Not many prophets have equaled Jeremiah in the poignant and tormenting sensation of being *possessed* by God. That possession comes from God's *word*, not from His *spirit*. But in either case it is irrational and disruptive, and if Jeremiah allows himself to be treated as a fool, this is doubtless because he had the appearance of one possessed to a greater degree than those prophets whom he accuses of uttering a deceitful *ruach*. In him the *word* is psychologically identical with the *spirit*.

This profound resemblance between the spirit and the word seems to us to be essential. They are neither separated by two different religious epochs nor by two different concepts of the divinity. One and the same God inspires and speaks, and His word is as pathetic as His spirit. The theophanies through the *word* are no more rational than the revelations through the *spirit*, as is shown precisely by the "great" prophets. God's word is sent forth just as the spirit, and exactly like the latter it "falls" upon man (Isaiah 9: 7). It is likened to fire and to a hammer:

"Is not My word like fire, says the Lord, and like the hammer which shatters the rock?" (Jeremiah 23: 29)

Jeremiah 20 shows that these feelings apply not only to the effect which the divine word has on its listeners. They concern rather the prophet's personal experience, and it is he who senses the *davar* as a devouring and blazing fire. Moreover, Jeremiah 23 is a diatribe against the false prophets, who depend on a vision and the *ruach*. Jeremiah denounces the lack of feeling in their experience as well as their psychological insensibility. These prophets do not feel, as he does, the upsetting effect of the *davar*, which makes Jeremiah's soul fly into pieces. On which side of this antithesis of two types of prophecy can the irrational experience be found? On the side of the *word*, and not that of the *spirit*, which Jeremiah mistrusts only because it does not possess, for his contemporaries, the gripping force it had heretofore, and which Jeremiah himself experienced in the *davar*.

There is another meeting place of the *davar* and the *ruach* in the realm of the irrational. In spite of its awesome character, the *ruach* is, like the *davar,* a source of exaltation and joy. The typical ambivalence of the numinous is as valid for the word as for the spirit. Two prophets expressed this in a remarkable context—Jeremiah, who ignored the *ruach* in its literalness, and Ezekiel, who is deeply moved by it. Both experience the joy of the divine word at the very moment that they *consume* it:

> "Thy words were found, and I did eat them;
> And thy words were unto me a joy and the rejoicing
> of my heart . . . " (Jeremiah 15 : 16)

> "And he said unto me: 'Son of man, eat that which thou findest; eat this roll, and go, speak unto the house of Israel.' So I opened my mouth, and He caused me to eat that roll. And He said unto me: 'Son of man, cause thy belly to eat, and fill thy bowels with this roll that I give thee.' Then I did eat; and it was in my mouth as honey for sweetness." (Ezekiel 3 : 3).

This mechanism of the logophagy which is felt simultaneously by two prophets who radically differ in their concept of revelation shows that both of them experienced the *davar* no differently from the *ruach.* Just like the spirit, the word penetrated and invaded them, united with their personality and gave them a vivid joy. It is doubtful whether to them logophagy was but a symbol. It had sometimes to be expressed in physiological sensations. The *davar* certainly led to psychic changes which were as real as those of the *ruach,* and one could become a fool through the *davar* as well as through the *rauch.* Just as the spirit, the word lent to the prophetic experience certain aspects which a rational intelligence might well call pathological. When approaching the limits of their manifestations, both the word and the spirit are pathetic.

II.

The spirit and the word are therefore in the Bible two forms of revelation which run constantly side by side. Both of them must be considered irrational, but each of them has a function of its own. Although a prophecy through the spirit is *like* one through the word, they are not the same, and it is important to point out the differences.

The *ruach* is *ambiguous*. Its etymological vagueness influences its content, too. Is it a spirit? Is it a wind? The *davar*, on the other hand, does not have such ambivalence. It is *the* objective word, and it has hemmed in the revelation, allowing nothing to escape. The objectivity of the *word* is clear in opposition to the *vision*. In the system of Biblical revelation, a vision cannot contradict the word. Only rarely is it used to support the word. It is only its frame or accompaniment. Often the vision even comes under suspicion when it contradicts the word. A real criticism of the vision could even develop in Biblical times, and the line which separates the false prophets from the true is often the same which distinguishes visionaries from the prophets of the word. Where we find a conflict between authentic prophets, it can only come from the contradiction between two words. This is the result of the fundamental ambiguity of the *ruach*. The vision is the domain of the *ruach*. It is obscure and must be deciphered, whereupon the result must be verified by God. The *ruach* is enigmatic. Amos, Jeremiah and Zechariah are questioned about the meaning of their visions, and they are told that they have "seen well." It could have been different.[53] Only when God, instead of letting them see or feel, *speaks,* is the truth of the revelation definitely acquired. In order that *knowledge* be joined with *absolute certainty,* the spirit must crystallize itself in the word.[54] The word is the maturity of the spirit. When the spirit is sown, it can give life to a plant or to a parasite, and only the word can prove that the spirit has reached its end. The entire domain of the *ruach* remains subjective. We have here a relation of the first person. The "I" of the prophet has an experience which he can describe, understand, and know, without, however, being able to detach himself from it and judge it. There are dreams, visions, ecstasies, and they are referred to in the first person: I had a dream, I saw, behold. . . . The domain of the *davar* is objective. The "I" of the prophet is replaced by "He": "the word of God, the speech of God. . . . " The words no longer need a reiteration or an interpretation. They are. They have an existence of their own. In the experience of the *davar* there is already the hint of a feeling of separation. The *ruach* of God and the *ruach* of man are in danger of becoming one. But when God speaks, God and man are two. The word is a dialogue. We shall discuss this further. For the moment let us remember that the *ruach* is only a prologue to the *davar,* the *logos.*

We have seen that this prologue is intensive enough to interrupt the magic or ecstatic relation with God. The *ruach* arises out of its own. Neither the techniques of magic nor the disciplines of an ecstasis lead to the *ruach.* The *davar* is even more transcendent in relation to these. The word is the very antithesis of silence. Both magic and mystical ecstasis need silence. The *word* cannot be reconciled with either of them.

Magic power is silent. It reveals itself in a contact, in an obscure discharge. It does not say anything to man, except that is there, facing him in its terrifying mystery.[55] Man busies himself in *divining,* in interrogating the signs, those accessories of the revelation. He cannot touch the essence. And even in the divination of appearances he receives no certainty and remains unsure. Magic power is eternally wrapped up in silence, whereas the prophetic word unravels something. A transcendent clarity breaks into the natural world. If the *ruach* is already the movement of God in the direction of the world, the *davar* is the goal of that movement. The mantic must approach a god who refuses obstinately to reveal himself. The prophetic *ruach* shows the will of a revelation, and in the *davar* that wish is materialized. In the face of the word, man has nothing to divine or to guess but—to obey. It is doubtless still a mystery but no longer a secret.

Ecstasis, too, is silence, at least at its apex. This is found true in cultic ecstasis, the influences of which are felt at certain periods of Biblical prophecy. Phrygian frenzy, which reached Phoenicia and Canaan at the very same time that Hebrew prophetism was born, brought along an orgy of noise. But neither the music nor the wild dances carried significant words. Cries, but no songs, and a breathless frenzy of dance. The homophagic enthusiasm was a giddy and vibrant silence. Sacred flesh was torn and eaten, and no sound was permitted. On the other hand, the word, no matter how loudly it was uttered, has always an intellectual meaning. It is a song or a phrase, never just a voice.

Through the *word* prophecy becomes a dialogue. As we have tried to show, the *ruach* creates a dialogical dimension because it allows man to have a share in God. The *davar* invigorates that dimension through a strict distribution of the roles. "As one man talks to another"[56] —in the word, God and man are essentially two. In the *ruach* they are so only formally.

A man who faces a god who reveals himself has quite another calling than one who is invaded by a divine revelation. Knowledge through the spirit is inviting. It orientates man towards God. The *ruach* has mystical roots and directs man towards a fusion with God, towards enthusiasm. Knowledge through the word sends man back to himself, so that he must be ready for an answer and a discussion. Dialogue is not, as in the *ruach*, the form of the revelation but its goal. God's *davar* expects a *reply*.

III.

The reply which God's *davar* expects is sometimes an objection formulated by the prophet, or a prayer. There are numerous examples for this, from the harsh reproaches of Abraham to the violent exhortations of Moses, Amos, and Jeremiah. But that reply is turned towards God. It reduces the exchange to a monologue in the soul of the prophet, a monologue which can be pathetic and seem like a struggle but it is not different from the pathetic struggle within a prophet seized by the *ruach*. The true reply to God's *davar* is to repeat that *davar,* to become God's mouthpiece, to extend the inner dialogue to an exterior one, to put the meaning of the *davar* to a test by introducing it to the world. By addressing *certain* people, a prophecy by the *davar* wants to reach *all* of them. This is not an easy task for the chosen mouthpieces. There is nothing mechanical in their transmission. The prophets are not simply relays. Their experience with the *davar* acquires a new dramatic note when it is to be transmitted to others. Then it becomes a "burden," too heavy for them, but they must perform their task. Or else it is a fire burning in their chest, a fire which they cannot long withhold.

The *davar* as pronounced by the prophet, and no longer received only by him, has certain original characteristics. The *ruach* is only transmitted in the form of another *ruach*, it is essentially indivisible. But the transmitted word is not identical with the word as it was received. After the prophet has been granted the word, it takes on a new meaning when he expresses it.

What meaning? This depends, in each case, on the interpretation we give the word *davar*. It does not only mean "word," but also "order," and "action." God's words on Mount Sinai were commandments.[57] The words of King Solomon imply his conduct.[58] There are many examples of the use of these various meanings of the word *davar*. The prophetic *davar,* too, means order and action. To *listen* to God's word means to obey Him. When the word leaves the prophet's mouth, it is not directed towards the listener's ear but towards his will. The *davar* itself creates action. Isaiah knows that God's word does not return empty to Him; once it has been sent forth it is like a seed—it creates.[59] Similarly, in the description of the Book of Genesis, the *ruach* can only hover above the chaos, but the *word* organizes it. *God said: "Let there be light."*[60] God's word is creative. The same creative function is inherent in the prophetic word. Some people wanted to detect a magic power in the prophetic word. They said[61] that the prophet uttered his words because they knew that they would magically influence reality. But this is not so. The influence of the *davar* has nothing to do with magic. Through the prophetic word God continues His work of creation. Sometimes he asks for man's obedience—*davar* is then an order—sometimes he modifies the word through the *davar,* in its meaning as creation. Thus the *davar* is God's intervention in the moral and physical evolution of the world. It is noteworthy that in Biblical language the word *davar* is one of the primitive words for "history." "The words of Solomon"—that means his actions, his history.[62] The words of the days—that means the chronicles. Here we come to the ultimate differences between the *ruach* and the *davar.* The prophetic universe has a dialogical structure. By admitting revelation, the prophets believed a contact between the divine and the human to be possible. But that universe remained static when it was only "inspired." The *ruach* introduced into the world a living God who did not, however, modify it. God is present in the world through the *ruach*. But through the *davar* God cooperates with man. God and man meet in the *Covenant*.

Notes

1. Joshua: Deuteronomy 34:9. Judges: Judges 3:10; 6:34; 11:29; 13:25, and *passim*. Saul: I Samuel 10:6, 10; 16:14. David *ibid.*, 16:13; II Samuel 23:2.
2. Joseph: Genesis 41:38. Bezaleel: Exodus 28:3 and *passim*.
3. Hosea 9:7.
4. I Samuel 16:13.
5. Typical cases: Samson: Judges 13:25. Amasai: I Chronicles 12:19.
6. Numbers 11:25; II Kings 2:9.
7. Ezekiel 1.
8. *Ibid.*, 3:14.
9. *Ibid.*, 11:1.
10. *Ibid.*, 37.
11. Isaiah 11:1f.
12. Joel 3:1f.
13. Isaiah 63:11; Psalms 51:13.
14. Genesis 1:1f.
15. For examples of this meaning of the *ruach* see Maimonides' *Guide for the Perplexed* I:40.
16. Genesis 45:27. Joshua 5:1; 2:11. I Kings 10:5. Isaiah 54:6. Psalms 51:19. I Samuel 1:15.
17. Genesis 6:3.
18. Saul: I Samuel 16:14 and *passim*. The people of Shechem: Judges 9:23.
19. I Kings 22:21, 23.
20. Lethargy: Isaiah 29:10. Impurity: Zechariah 13:2.
21. And not saintliness.
22. Shechem and Dinah: Genesis 34:3. Jacob and Joseph: *ibid.*, 44:30. Jonathan: I Samuel 18:1.
23. See O. Procksch: *Theologie des Alten Testaments.* Guetersloh 1950, p. 460.
24. Claude Tresmontant: *Essai sur la pensée hébraique,* Paris 1953. Concerning the whole problem of the *ruach* see also Paul Volz: *Der Geist Gottes und die verwandten Erscheinungen im Alten Testament und im anschliessenden Judentum,* Tuebingen 1910.
25. Tresmontant, *op. cit.*, p. 108.

26. *Ibid.,* p. 109.
27. Numbers 11:29.
28. See Rudolf Otto: *The Idea of the Holy.* Also his *Aufsaetze, das Numinose betreffend,* Munich 1932.
29. Judges 6:34. I Chronicles 12:19. II Chronicles 24:20.
30. Judges 14:6, 19. 15:14. I Samuel 10:6, 10; 16:14; 18:10.
31. Ezekiel 11:5.
32. Abraham Heschel: *Die Prophetie.* Krakow 1936 (The essential part of Heschel's theory can be found, rendered into English by the present translator, in: *Judaism,* vol. II no. 1 (January 1953); (see also his *The Prophets,* 1962, esp. chapters 12, 14, 15, 18. Tr.) Compare also Heschel: *Man Is Not Alone.* 1950.
33. Heschel: *Man Is Not Alone,* pp. 125ff.
34. Numbers 23:4, 16.
35. Jeremiah 42:6f. See also I Samuel 28:6.
36. Compare J. M. Leuba: *Psychologie du mysticisme religieux,* Paris 1925.
37. See Heschel: *Die Prophetie,* p. 169.
38. See E. Jacob: *Le prophetisme israélite d'après les recherches récentes,* Revue d'Histoire et de Philosophie Religieuses, 1952, I, p. 69.
39. Isaiah 11:1ff.
40. André Néher: *Amos, contribution à l'étude du prophétisme,* Paris 1950, pp. 34ff. and 258ff.
41. Hosea 12:5.
42. Genesis 32:28, 31.
43. Deuteronomy 5:4; 34:10.
44. Genesis 32:25.
45. Hosea 2:16.
46. Paul Volz, *op. cit.,* S. Mowinckel: *The Spirit and the Word in the Pre-Exilic Reforming Prophets,* Journal of Biblical Literature 53, 1934, pp. 199ff. See also H. H. Rowley: "Nature of Prophecy in Recent Study," *Harvard Theological Review,* 38, 1945. pp. 16ff.
47. II Kings 9:11. See later Hosea 9:7 and Jeremiah 29:26.
48. Hosea, *ibid.*
49. Micah 3:8.
50. Isaiah 28:6; 11:2; 29:10; 31:3; 32:15.
51. Amos 4:13.
52. Jeremiah 5:13. See also Micah 2:11.
53. Amos 7:8 and 8:2. Jeremiah 1:11. 13. Zechariah 4:2.
54. See O. Grether: *Name und Wort Gottes im Alten Testament,* Giessen 1934. pp. 97ff.
55. See Heschel: *Die Prophetie,* p. 107.

118 THE PROPHETIC EXISTENCE

56. Exodus 33:11.
57. Exodus 20:1. Deuteronomy 5:19.
58. I Kings 11:41.
59. Isaiah 55:10f.
60. Genesis 1:2f.
61. See A. Lods: *Les prophètes d'Israel*, pp. 58f.
62. I Kings 11:41.

2

The Dialogue in Time:
the Covenant

The Time of the Covenant

The intimate dimension of Biblical time is the *covenant*. Everything leads to it, everything derives from it. The concept of a covenant between God and man, and not only that of a simple relationship, is the most original contribution which Hebrew thinking has made to the religious history of mankind. It confuses man's feeling about God. It arouses in man a choice which no other divine revelation has been able to suggest: neither religion nor veneration nor the cult but—love. That man's vocation should be to love God, this is the secret which the covenant grants to all those who adhere to it. Biblical time is the rhythm of that vocation.

No religious thought of antiquity could rise to that notion of a covenant. Although the gods were not always man's adversaries, and some of them even established friendly relations with human beings, there were, in the ancient world, nearly everywhere *partial* divinities, who jealously and exclusively protected a certain group or certain individuals. Especially in the Semitic world, there were *related* divinities to whom the tribes owed their lives and their progress. There is the Adon, the *Master,* or the *Melech,* the *King,* who *chooses* his tribe or his city, to live and disappear with them, and who *chooses* his human vicar to represent him on earth.[1] As if to insist on

119

the difference between its own idea of the covenant and all other forms, Hebrew thought accepts them all, but only in order to raise them to a higher level and thus give them a transfigured form. Like other nations, the Hebrews saw in God the jealous guardian of their tribe and the champion of their wars; like all other Semites, they saw in Him the Father of His children, the Master of His servants, and the King of His subjects.[2] Thus they speak the language of all their contemporaries. But they give a particular name to the covenant which is the root of those relations, a name which has no parallel in other Semitic idioms, and which stands for a specific temporality. That is the *brith*.

The Biblical brith has often been analyzed in the singularity of its meaning. As we have shown elsewhere,[3] it includes basically a division of responsibilities. The Biblical covenant is not a protection and not even a simple election. The divine choice gives man a precise task. The brith is a joint endeavor.[4] The attempts at an alliance as they were conceived in non-Biblical thought led only to the techniques of a religious feeling, at a kind of systematization of the respect due to a protecting divinity. The revelation of the presence of a god had taught man only gestures of imploration or recognition. Only the Biblical revelation of a covenant calls upon man for an action which does not remain a technique, an action which does not restrict itself to arousing God to act in accordance with man's prayers and devotions, but which runs parallel to the divine act. The brith is less a covenant of man with a god whose help is indispensable to them than a covenant of God with man whom He needs in order to create His work. Herein lies the singularity of the Hebrew brith. It places men in the time of God who calls them.

This call is characteristic for the brith. Whereas when other Semitic nations state that they are the allies of a

god they can tell us nothing about how they have become
so, the Hebrews introduce each of their stories about the
covenant with the description of a divine invocation. In
the Bible God addresses man in order to offer him a
clearly defined covenant. This clarification of the divine
intentions transforms the alliance into a brith. Men know
what God wants of them when He allies Himself to them.
The brith is an alliance which implies a *law*.

The concurrence of the *covenant* and the *law* is given
a great deal of emphasis in the Bible. It seems that the
Hebrews could not think of a covenant without its being
accompanied by the revelation of a divine will. The first
brith is concluded between God and Noah, and it is completed by the so-called Noachidic legislation. God gives
laws to post-diluvian humanity by associating with them.[5]
With Abraham God makes two alliances, both of which
formulate demands whose spiritual and material character corresponds, as we shall see later, to the Biblical
definition of the rite. Abraham must *believe,* then he must
practice *circumcision.*[6] Finally the Hebrews as a people
are called upon to ally themselves with God at Mount
Sinai. In the short account of the ritual act of the covenant at the foot of Sinai the divine demand is put into
the words of a book.[7] It does not matter whether this
means the Decalogue or supplementary legislation. The
divine will was announced at the moment when the covenant was concluded. That covenant, too, concerned practice and faith, since when the Hebrews were asked for a
reply, they answered: " . . . we will do and obey."[8] The
more grandiose and less ritual theophany of Exodus 19
and 20 summarizes what the Hebrews meant by brith.
Everything centers around the divine call, around the
clarification of the divine will:

"Thus shalt thou say to the house of Jacob, and tell
the children of Israel: Ye have seen what I did unto

the Egyptians, and how I bore you on eagles' wings and brought you unto Myself. Now therefore, if ye will hearken unto My voice and keep My covenant, ye shall be Mine own treasure from among all peoples; for all the earth is Mine; and ye shall be unto Me a kingdom of priests, and a holy nation. These are the words which thou shalt speak unto the children of Israel." (Exodus 19: 3ff.)

Thus the covenant includes a social organization, a kingdom of priests, the foundation of sacred nation. The Decologue lays the groundwork of that organization.[9] But even more is involved. God creates a vast and durable plan of action, and He asks the Hebrews to take part in it. The brith is a divine *project,* in the psychological and geometrical sense of that word. In suggesting it, God follows a precise intention (this is the imperative of the *law*) and plans to realize it in the future with the help of men (this is where the *covenant* comes in). The close and indissoluble association between the two changes the whole idea of a covenant. What elsewhere was an obscure and temporary consciousness became with the Hebrews a clear and permanent act. Through the brith the existence of the Hebrews changed to *history.*

Although the Semites were unable to express time in anything but mythical formulas, they, too, had the idea of a future, of history. But that history was not only different from the historic consciousness of the Hebrews because their myths made it burdensome and sometimes restrained and annihilated it, but because, even in its animated periods, it was apart from the wish of the gods. To say that man is conscious of progressing in history is something very vague, because no details are given concerning man's assurance of treading the path of history. But here precisely lies the difference between Semitic and Hebrew history. It is true that the Semites had the impression of living in a sacred history. The godheads were mixed up in their existence, but the connection was not made clear. In general, history developed by rules of accident. The good and the evil that came from the gods were equally surprising, and their will was obscure. An entire system of soothsaying had as its goal to rob the gods of the secrets of their intentions, and this was done in an atmosphere of piety overlaid with fear. The Hebrews, on the other hand, could not imagine that they could be in history except *with* God. The covenant and the law gave historic progress its clarity and its direction. Since God's and man's intentions were identical, the covenant supported the optimistic appearance of the march. By revealing God's will, the law implied that the road was a good one. What elsewhere was trial and error was, with the Hebrews, a reassuring and serene progress, due to the covenant and the law.

This progress lends the Bible its typical structure. There is constant cooperation between God and man. God watches over the realization of His plan, and man aids Him in His task. History consists in that cooperation between God and man. But it is a *dialogical* history. Man replies to an uninterrupted call by God or, if you prefer, to a continuous series of calls. Nothing hinders the immediate encounter of God and man. Neither nature nor heroes place themselves between the divine and the human. There is neither a ritualized nature nor a deified sovereign to serve as mediator between the transcendent and the immanent in the universe of the brith. On the contrary—between God and man there is a face-to-face confrontation. Creation, the Deluge, the Tower, the New Year, the agrarian ritual—whatever supports or spans ritual and mythical time is being reshaped in a different time. In the Biblical world ritual time is expressed in terms of the covenant. We shall show how new and unique these terms are.

The Covenant and the Myth

The Hebrews, too, have used the ritual myth in order to solve the grave problems of their religious existence, and we find in the Bible substantial elements of a ritual interpretation of time, which are, however, mixed with a different and quite particular conception.

We have seen that the fundamental disagreement between the time of man and that of nature was expressed in Babylonia through the rites of the New Year, the aim of which was to re-establish a thoroughly interrupted harmony. Those rites had their parallel in Egypt at the time that a new king was enthroned. Now a New Year's festival existed also in Israel. More and more historians interpret it in the sense we have indicated. They ascribe to that day an all-important place in the religious history of the Hebrews. Such a festival had to acquire an extraordinary meaning if it was practiced in the manner described by the exegetes. According to them, all that happened was that basic themes of ancient ritual thought were being adapted to the Hebrew religion.[10] Since it occurred in the fall, it counterbalanced with its rites the abrupt passage of the seasons, and at the same time it evoked the cosmic dramas of the creation, where chaos and order, life and death met. The festival allowed for ceremonies of the enthronement of the God of Israel who, like Marduk in Babylonia and Horus in Egypt, could regain His power only after temporary eclipses and battles. Processions, parades, and the sounding of the horn mixed accents of anxiety with triumphant acclamations in honor of the lost and found God. In the great national sanctuaries—in Beth El for Samaria and in Jerusalem for Judea—the sovereigns were associated with the festival by appropriate rites, just as in Babylonia the important phases of the enthroning of Marduk were accompanied by ceremonies of which the King of Babylonia was the center.

All the constituting elements of that festival have to do with myths, whose salutary influence they wish to restore, or whose harmful reach they wish to limit. The choice of time is not arbitrary. In Jewish tradition the beginning of the fall is linked with the birth of the world, and the exegetes find in the first stories of the Book of Genesis Hebrew myths of *creation,* as they underlie the rites of the festival of the New Year. Those myths are supposed to reveal in a superficial monotheistic version, perfect analogies with the Mesopotamian myths. The *waters* and the *abysses* represent the primitive chaotic duality, in the Genesis of the Bible, just as do their parallels Apsu and Tiamat in the Babylonian cosmogony. The beings erupt only at the price of violent conflicts with these elements which are themselves antagonistic. These mythical fights and contradictions haunt the rites of the Hebrew New Year, and are therefore comparable to the Babylonian New Year. According to certain historians, the fact that in Israel the fall season was chosen rather than that of the spring, is because in Hebrew tradition the fall is the season of rain. Thus the festival would indicate the expectation of the rain, which was indispensable to agricultural life, and its arrival was made easier by such rites. Foremost in the meaning of the Hebrew New Year would no longer be a myth of *creation* but one of the *deluge,* a myth which Genesis tells us about in terms which allow easy recognition of the Babylonian parallel. When Jeroboam, the first sovereign of the kingdom of the North, established the festival in the eighth month, this was perhaps simply a political act by which he wished to break the tradition of Jerusalem, which observed it in the seventh month.[11] According to the Bible story, the eighth month is the month of the deluge. Thus Jeroboam gave the festival a character which was more in accord with its primitive inspirations and he tied it up with the myth of the deluge, which the tradition of Jerusalem had toned down in favor of the myth of creation.

Other scholars think that we must go even further. If the festival was celebrated in Jerusalem in the seventh month, it is because in a mythical way that month reminded people of the exodus from Egypt and the passage of the Hebrews through the desert. That event, which is so important for the history of Israel, is connected with two ritual observances at two different times of the year. The first one reminds us of the Passover sacrifice and the festival of the unleavened bread, which comes in the first month, hence in the spring. Such a reminder may be called historical. The Passover week commemorates the date of the exodus. The second reminder comes in the fall, on the occasion of the ritual week of the Tabernacles. Thus we no longer have the observance of a date but the concentration, within a sacred and limited time, of the *reminder* of the exodus and the sojourn in the desert. This would be a mythical procedure par excellence, for the rites restore, within just a few days, the presence of a prolonged event in the past. Now the festival of Tabernacles is sometimes confounded with that of the renewal of the year.[12] Would the liturgy of the New Year, celebrated in the seventh month, not be the mythical development which the Passover liturgy applies in the first month to a historical diagram? Alfred Haldar[13] has tried to reconstruct that *myth of the exodus and of the desert,* which Hebrew Biblical tradition could only preserve in the diluted form of an historical account, but which the rites and liturgies of the Hebrew New Year evoked, according to Haldar, in its plastic reality. In the language of myth, the desert stands for the subterranean regions and hell. The enthronement of the divinity, celebrated at the New Year, corresponds to the ascent of the divinity after a prolonged stay in hell. The god of Israel would then be a chthonic divinity with the features characteristic of the various Phoenician godheads. The singularity of Hebrew religion would thus have been that it gave that myth the historical appearance of going down to Egypt, staying in the wilderness and entering Canaan. The real significance of the festival of the New Year would lie in the persistence of the original power of the myth. The Hebrew New Year would then have that particularity that although it may be compared to the Babylonian New Year because of the common utilization of the myth of creation, it is based on a supplementary myth of its own, namely the myth of the exodus and the desert.

In addition to the New Year, agrarian rites have impressed the historians of Hebrew religion[14] which is supposed to be replete with them in various forms, from the consecration of ritual periods to great acts of vegetation, leading to sacrificial and erotic excesses as shown in the agrarian rites of Canaan. In the Israelite epochs of Canaan, just as in those of the pre-Israelite, there were many instances of human sacrifice. They may be found as late as the seventh century in the valley of Hinnom near Jerusalem, and the contemporaries of Jeremiah probably did not see in the Melech, to whom they offered their firstborn, a foreign divinity but the divine King of Israel.[15] At the beginning of that same century, at the time of Micah,[16] pious Israelites asked themselves with a naïve self-assurance whether the sacrifice of the firstborn was not a normal ritual demand of their god. Temple prostitution was common in the sanctuaries of the Northern kingdom. It had even reached the Temple of Jerusalem, but in the seventh century King Josiah expelled the male and female prostitutes.[17] Israelite religion would thus have been familiar with the cruel excesses of the Canaanite agrarian rites. How much more so did they include the rites of agrarian time in their cult, like the consecration of the time of the first sheaves, the first fruit, of harvest time, and the first rain. According to most historians, the ritual complexity of agricultural life among the Israelites was but a replica of the Canaanite cultic organization, and was by and by adopted by the Hebrews after they had settled in Canaan.[18]

Beneath those rites sociologists try to discover myths to explain them. They find them above all in the general repertoire of the agrarian myths, which are valid for all primitive peasant societies. But it seems that in this realm of the agrarian cult, as in that of the ritual of the New Year, a myth which was typical for Hebrew-Canaanite civilization acquired a predominating significance. The universal theme of the death of the seasons has in Canaan a local variation which is revealed by the texts of Ras-Shamra. Whereas elsewhere one and the same divine force produces the vital forces for vegetation, and perishes when vegetation dies, there are two different spirits in the pantheon of Ras-Shamra. One of these, Mot, lets the grain ripen, and the other, Baal-Aleyin, fertilizes the ground with rain. In Egypt and Mesopotamia, the power of the waters is concentrated in the swelling of the rivers. Dummuzi and Osiris penetrate vegetation through these swellings, with which they identify themselves. In Canaan Mot and Baal-Aleyin are opposite gods. The death of the one is necessary for the ascent of the other. This can be explained by the climate of Canaan with its well-defined seasons. The reign of Mot is the summer drought, and the winter rains are the reign of Baal-Aleyin.

The mythical value of the waters therefore presents a very typical aspect in Canaan, since it is connected with the fertilizing function of the rains. From this derives probably the importance which is acquired by the beginning of the rainy season in the fall, which, as we have seen, would have been felt in Israel and Canaan as a real renewal of the year, at least as well as would have been

the case with the spring season. From this derives also
the emphasis which is put on an erotic interpretation of
agrarian life. To the fundamental identification of the
fertile soil with the womb—an identification which in
itself suggests erotic rites—a mythology which centers
around the rain adds the similarity between the sexual act
and the penetration of the rain water in the ground. Baal-
Aleyin, the god of rain, "fertilizes" the soil, and in ritual
translations that verb assumes an entirely brutal meaning.
The exegetes are struck with certain Hebrew texts which
apply a purely sexual terminology to the meteorological
phenomenon of rain. Isaiah 62: 4f. knows and uses the
general theme of the ground as a woman:

"Thou shalt no more be termed Azuvah (Forsaken),
neither shall thy land any more be termed Sh'mamah
(Desolate) ; but thou shalt be called Hefzi-bah (I delight
in her), and the land B'ulah (Married)."   ,

The earth is being compared to a woman awaiting her
husband, or better: her master, her Baal. The literal
translation of the verb which we render as "married"
would be "possessed by her husband." One cannot express more clearly the idea of a sexual relation between
the divinity and the earth. But at another place Isaiah
applies that same idea to the rain, or better, since he
wishes to show the fertilizing power of the divine word,
he compares it with the fructifying quality of the rain:

"For as rain and snow come down from heaven and do
not return there before having watered the ground, and
made it bring forth and bud, so as to give seed to the
sower and bread to the eater, so shall the word which
comes out of My mouth not return unto Me empty, but it
shall fulfill what I plan and prosper in the thing for which
I sent it.   (55:10f.)

The rain enters the soil as the semen enters a woman's
womb. Vegetation is the result of this meeting between
the rain and the earth. This unpolished mythological style

can be found in later Jewish tradition. In Talmudic terminology the *Field of the Baal* is the field which needs
irrigating, i.e., the field which waits for its Master, the
Baal. Rabbi Judah declares plainly: The rain is the Baal,
the husband, or the Master, of the earth, and he is supported in his exegesis by the verse in Isaiah.[19] Although
such traces are found much later, historians find them
meaningful, for they seem to indicate that the Israelites
preserved elements of a Canaanite myth for a long time,
and it strongly penetrated Israelite religious life at the
classical time of the Bible. Its presence would explain the
strong erotic shades of Hebrew agrarian rituals.

Do ritual mythologies which certain exegetes believe
to have discovered in the Bible really have a place in the
Hebrew world of thinking? A more thorough study of
the fundamental *myths* allows us to answer that question
in the negative.

Creation

The *myth of the origins* is presented in the Bible in an
inaugural chapter in which moderation and harmonious
arrangement are made even more impressive by a comparison with a similar Sumero-Babylonian myth. But this
is not merely an esthetic change or a logical refinement.
Hebrew thought was not content with putting in order a
complicated theme by giving it the simplest possible form.
The chapters mentioned are truly Hebrew by the very
plan of the account, and the narration does not reflect
the method of Hebrew thinking but rather its content.
In speaking of Hebrew religious thought one often uses
the term "demythologization." This word defines exactly
a certain process to which myths, rites and ideas have by
and by succumbed after having been introduced in Hebrew
society or having been adopted by it. When Hebraism
refined these during a breathing space, it changed them in
form and content and made them more logical and moral.

Nevertheless, the word "demythologization" has its limits, and it no longer has any meaning whatever where no progress exists, when the theme used by Hebrew thought is entirely its own property, worked out by the latter, and in no way borrowed from others. A demythologization can exist only due to antimythological forces. Such forces have created original ideas which had never had to cope with the myths, and which characterize Hebrew thinking. The account of Genesis is built on just such ideas. Compared with the Babylonian myth, it is not a moralized myth but no myth at all. The difference lies squarely in the fact that contrary to the Babylonian story it is not a *mythical time* on which the account in Genesis is based but *historical time* which alone among all similar attempts in ancient times Hebrew thought elaborated.

Various attempts have been made to point out what seemed to be essential in the reflections concerning the origins of the world, as described in Genesis. In the beginning there was the spirit, in the beginning there was the word. . . . But the very Hebrew word which introduces the account, breshit, shows that what mattered to the narrator was not what was in the beginning but rather that there was a beginning. For that word does not mean "in the beginning" but "as a beginning." The creative act occupies time. God starts creating, and He distributes creation over seven days. *Time* itself is of the uppermost importance. Creation manifests itself by the appearance of time.

That time is absolutely new. This is indicated by the Hebrew word *bara*—the second word in the chapter—which stands for the creative act and is used in the Bible only in reference to God. Only He can create, that means produce in a sudden and sovereign way. Such a creation is *ex nihilo,* since it breaks with whatever precedes it. What came before is nothing compared with the new thing which constitutes creation.

These first facts go a long way toward stating the problems of the origins of Being in a manner which is radically different from that of the myth. In the latter, one and the same time applies to Non-Being and Being alike. The existence of the creative God antedates creation, and that existence plays a major role in the creative act. Mythical creation implies a personal drama of the divinity, and therefore questions arise which have to do with the birth, the acquisition of a creative power, and the final victory of a divinity who triumphs over the Nothing by creating Being. Mythical time attains cosmogony only by passing through a theogony and theomachy. In the Babylonian myths we find such aspects clearly developed, and the account of the creation centers around the dramatic adventures of Marduk and his rivals. This is not necessarily an outcome of Babylonian polytheism, for the problem of the birth of the god must be stated even if one assumes the existence of one great primitive divinity. The mythical dimension demands that the question of the origin of the world takes in also the origin of God.

On the other side of the picture, it is not enough to point at Biblical monotheism in order to explain the absence of a theogony and a theomachy in Genesis. A supplementary account about the origin of God would throw no aspersion on the monotheistic character of the report in Genesis. Moreover, later Judaism has evolved legends concerning God's behavior before the creation.[20] Such meditations do not conform with Biblical perspectives which do not want to know God prior to His creative act. God's existence before creation is something entirely different from His appearance in the creative act. In the Bible the same account cannot cover what is before creation and what is after it, because what was before cannot be told at all, since that is not an event but a non-event. Mythical creation supposes a before and an after—creation and what came after it. Biblical creation implies timelessness and time. Creation is the very beginning of time.

Another variation in the problem of the Being is not concerned with His origins but with His relations to the created world. In the myth, the time afterwards is identical with the time before, and just as there is a mythology of the origin there is one of the coexistence of the divinity and the universe. The world is then not entirely created but still has vestiges of all kinds of forces which had been subdued by the creative god before he came to power. Therefore the creative divinity and the created world are in a state of latent hostility. The god must defend himself against his own creation whose incompletely tamed forces awake from time to time and rise against the creator. In every mythical concept there is a hidden but permanent dualism. Good and evil, light and darkness, cosmos and chaos are in a perpetual contradiction. Whereas polytheism sharpens and multiplies such opposites, they exist even in a monotheistic system although it is not based on the notion of mythical time. The originality of Hebrew thought is not only due to the fact that it connected creation with a unique God, but that it established a historical and no longer a mythical relation between that God and the world He created. That historical relation is the *covenant,* and it leads to two equally important consequences—God's transcendence and immanence. In the Biblical view there is no contradiction between God and the world but rather an antithetical situation within God Himself in relation to the world. God is equally close and distant, outside of the universe and penetrating it everywhere. He is Being and Becoming.

God's transcendence stems from the fact that nothing that has been created is contemporary with God. Since all of creation was realized in historical time, none of its elements existed in God's timelessness. God's exteriority in relation to His creation is truly absolute, and it will

recur at the end of time. Once history is ended, creation
disappears, and only God remains in His timelessness.
In the form of eschatology the plan of the *end* constitutes
the replica of the cosmology of the *beginning*.

But if the creation is not contemporary with God, God
is contemporary with His creation, penetrating it, impreg-
nating it, without, however, identifying with it. We must
see in Biblical *panentheism* the original Hebrew attitude,
as opposed to the transcendentalism or pantheism of the
philosophers.[21] In the account in Genesis, pantheism vac-
illates between two expressions, each of them valuable
and meaningful. The first of these has to do with God's
spirit, the second with His *word.* The *spirit* of God "hovers" above the waters, which cover the chaos and the
darkness of the abyss. This gives access to a confrontation
of God and matter, since the water is outside the spirit.
Created matter is unorganized, dark, massive, and im-
mobile. Opposite it is the spirit, in motion, and that motion is soft, like a caress which protects one's sleep or
arouses from it. The image suggests that God's spirit
embraces the world without, however, penetrating it.
This penetration is rather the task of the *word.* From
verse three on God speaks, and His *word* takes root in
the world and becomes incarnated in created matter.
Each new word of God's brings forth a new phase in
creation. God's *word* accompanies creation as its rhythm.

We have shown which role the *spirit* and the *word*
play in the Biblical system of revelation, and how the
relationship between the divine and the human works in
this instance, namely: the *spirit* reveals God to man, and
the *word* establishes an active participation between God
and man. We see now how this system of revelation is
achieved, and how Biblical man has thought it out in depth
and range. The *spirit* and the *word* do not only apply to
the relation between God and man but they are also the
categories of the relation between God and the world as

a whole. Just as the Spirit offers man a number of ways through which to know God, it offers them to the universe. The world created by God has not become detached from Him like an arrow in random flight, but God and the world see and face each other, even in their contradiction, since a unified and moving spirit is faced with multiplicity and apathy. The silent and peaceful coexistence suggested by the second verse of Genesis is the more remarkable as the partners are absolute opposites: matter and spirit, darkness and light, immobility and motion, disorder and unity. That verse places the encounter between God and the world on the level of the encounter between God and man, where the imperishable and the perishable come to face each other in the *spirit*. When the *word* emerges, the heretofore silent confrontation becomes dialogical. The world responds to God's *word* by creating itself, by *becoming,* just as man responds to God's word in a *becoming*. The creation does not remain *outside* God but follows obediently the movement of His *word,* it advances, and in the process of self-creation it adds one layer upon another in the domain of becoming, and one day to the other. Through the *word* a *history* of creation is being established, whose plot eventually absorbs the great contradictory forces of light and darkness, heaven and earth, the dry land and the waters, and then the cosmic and stellar rhythms, closing with all living beings, from plants to man.

Thus the relationship between God and the world is not a mythical but a historical one, since the categories of the *spirit* and the *word* lead to history. That conception radically changes man's position towards God. In a mythical conception of the origins man is a mere onlooker in a drama which is played between the divinity and its creation. Nature has a time of its own, which differs from the time of a god who has not attained a final triumph as well as from the time of man who does not occupy an organic place in creation. Nature is a reality outside of God, and man's efforts consist in adjusting himself to these two rhythms, neither of which chimes with his own, and which, in addition, oppose one another. This is the reason for the tense and torn existence of ancient man and for the elaboration of cyclical rites and concepts whose appeasing effect is attained at the price of passions and degradations which they call for. The historical concept of the origins as suggested in the Bible attributes to nature no more of a *supernature* than it does to man. This is so not only because both nature and man are *creatures* and therefore both subordinated to God and even like nothing in relation to Him. This *devaluation* of nature is certainly inscribed in the account of Genesis but only because it stipulates the transcendence of God. Beside a transcendent God nature has no superior value at all, and there is no reason for man to fear or to revere it. But we have already pointed out that in Genesis God's relationship to the world is an ambivalent one, being transcendent as well as immanent. On the level of immanence we have an *evaluation* of nature, since the world faces God in the *spirit* and the *word*. But this evaluation is exactly the same as is man's, since he, too, faces God in the *spirit* and the *word*. One and the same time surrounds man and nature, the time of God's *word*. In nature man does not detect a strange sound which interrupts his own and alienates him from God. God, nature, and man live in the same time. Man can *subdue* nature (Genesis 1:28) not because he is the last and supreme creature dominating all others, but rather because the domination of nature does not arouse him against himself nor against God. Nature neither destroys itself nor does it rebel against God. For if God is transcendent, nature is merely a collection of inoffensive objects. If, on the other hand, God is immanent, nature does not reveal itself but God; it does not give us idols but a divine history.

Thus we see that by ascribing an identical time to nature and to man, the account of Genesis has introduced the ideas of the *spirit* and the *word* in the creative act. But the Biblical narrator has given it an additional expression. Being concerned with harmonizing man and nature, he first describes God's revelation to nature in the same terms as His revelation to man. He further employs the identical terms in the description of the history of the creation as later *history*. The terminology of the creation again opposes history to the myth. The time called for by creation is already part and parcel of history, and the Biblical narrator underlines this idea formally by describing creation in terms of history.

How, then, does the Bible deal with history? First we have the word "day." What we usually render as "chronicles" is really expressed as "words of the days" or "acts of the days." In Deuteronomy (32:7), "the days of old" define history in the wider meaning of a becoming. That terminology is supplemented by another—"the generations," although that Hebrew word really means "children." History is thus thought of as an intimate and permanent connection which links the parents to the children and vice versa. "The years of many generations" of the same verse are synonymous with "the days of old" as a term for "history," as is indicated by that parallelism in Deuteronomy.

Now the very same double terminology is applied in Genesis. In the first chapter, creation is formulated in seven "days." What meaning must we give to that term? In that one chapter, it actually has three different meanings. In verse 4 it stands for "light." Thus it has a cosmic meaning, and is an element of that great contradictory chain of forces "light—darkness." In verse 14, the same word has an astronomic meaning and stands for the daily revolution from one sunrise to the other. Everywhere else that the word appears at the conclusion of a section of the creation story it has a different meaning again: a certain period, a succession of moments, and it is this way that the Hebrew word *yom* is used further on in the Bible in order to indicate the articulations of history. It does not matter that the seven days of creation are not equally distributed in their relation to the sun. This is so because they are not astronomical but, let us say, chronometrical, days. They suggest the mobility and the progress of time —history. These seven days are no more mythical than the creative act itself. They are the first in a succession of days which will from then on divide the life of the creation. In the Biblical view this is not prehistory but the beginning of history.

The second chapter relinquishes the scheme of periods and resumes the work of creation in one day, " . . . in the day that the Lord God made . . . "[22] But the very same verse spells out that the story of the creation is that of the "generations" of heaven and earth. Here we have the other word which means "history." The day that heaven and earth were created was a day in history. It was the beginning and the launching of later history, which was to be divided up by means of the rhythm of "generations."[23]

Thus, one and the same language is used for the epoch of creation and subsequent periods. The origins of the world are not removed from human intelligence, as if man had to discover them elsewhere, namely, in a dimension which could be reached only by surpassing the human condition. They can be perceived and understood within the very same history from which they stem. In order to remain connected with the origin, man does not have to transcend history and arrive at a mythical dimension but he finds the extension of the origins in his own history, accepting it and abandoning himself to it. This is the profound meaning of the creation in the Biblical system. Since creation is history and not a myth, it does not overburden Biblical religious thought. It does not force man to hide behind rites or in a doctrine of the eternal return. Man is not haunted in any way, but creation invites him to progress in his history of which it is the liberating source. Since Biblical creation began a flow of history, he was quite aware of a sense of direction. He knew of his origin behind him, and was conscious of marching towards a goal. Every moment of Biblical history looks back towards the creation and from there towards a future. The canonical structure of the Bible gives an account of that system. The double terminology of "days" and "generations" which is used by the Biblical narrator to characterize the creation and the further development of history serves also for the end of history. To the "beginning of the days" corresponds an "end of the days."[24] The "days" of history have a beginning and an end. Likewise, the "generations" of history proceed towards a goal. Parallel with the symbolic character of the word "generations," the end is here described in a metaphorical way. There may be faults and breaches in the chain of the generations, but final redemption consists in mending the tears and in fashioning a faultless product. This is clearly expressed in the final vision of the prophet Malachi (3:24), the last canonical prophet of the Bible: "And he shall turn the heart of the fathers to the children, and the heart of the children to their fathers." It is the task of the divine messenger to repair something; he must renew the missing stitches and enable a continuous and progressive reading of the succession of the generations. Continuity and progress—those are the characteristic features of historical time, made possible by the Biblical interpretation of the creation.

The Deluge

The Biblical story of the deluge differs from its Babylonian counterpart by its *ethical* character. This has often been stated before, but it might be interesting to go a little deeper. The ethical aspect of the Biblical story does indeed not only consist in the fact that it carries a moral lesson, that the deluge was not the outcome of the whim of the gods but a just punishment, and that only one righteous human family was saved. There is a moral in the structure of the story which goes beyond the moral of the narration. The Babylonian myth of the deluge has a nonhistorical structure. It is based on a conception of a deadlock in history. Things have become so confused in the world that there is no other way out than to destroy everything and start again from scratch. Postdiluvian humanity has nothing whatever in common with prediluvian mankind, since the saved individual is not a man but a half god. He could jump over the abyss only because he is a hero. Utna-Pishtim is not shaped by the standards of human history, and therefore he could survive the total disappearance of mankind. One history is swallowed up in the flood, and another one begins; what is in between is outside of these histories. We find the same structure in the Greek version of the myth, where neither Deucalion nor Pyrrha are human beings. A new human race is being created by their superhuman intermediary. The structure of the Biblical account is diametrically opposed to all this. Although in an obscure verse (Genesis 6:4) the existence of *heroes* is mentioned and they have somehow to play the role of agents at the time of the deluge, at the crucial time it is a man of purely human lineage who survives and whose existence forms the link between prediluvian and postdiluvian mankind. History does not come to a deadlock but clears a path. It, too, enters the Ark and is carried off by Noah's family. It leaves the Ark with the same human family and the connection is uninterrupted, since the deluge is not a break in history. The passage way is certainly narrow—one single man assures its opening, but after all that man is there, and through him the continuity of history is realized. David Koigen[25] has shown that the concept of a progressing, uninterrupted history, looking for constant realization, has found its logical fulfillment in the idea of the *ethos*. Strained existence asks for acts of righteousness and self-perfection. The account of the deluge illustrates that fact by connecting the survival of history with the justice of human conduct or, better still, the justice of one single man. This theme, which is so often found in the Bible—the prophets were to apply it to the destiny of Israel in the midst of other nations— and which contains the seed of the highest ethical values of Biblical religion: sufferings, sacrifice, redemption, is inseparable from the idea of a progressive history. Since history wants to go on at any price, ethical demands are made and strike human conscience in its deepest recesses.

In Genesis two important theological ideas are closely connected with the story of the deluge: the *covenant* and the *law*. God makes a covenant with Noah and the renewed world, the sign of which is the rainbow. God gives a law to Noah and to his sons. Should we consider that Noachidic covenant and law to be merely casual themes? We rather believe that they, too, are basic elements in the account of the deluge. In the account of the creation, Genesis presents history as a covenant. In the account of the deluge, it associates the idea of a law with that of the covenant, an association which, as we have seen, is inherent in the very principles of Hebrew thought.

If the covenant and the law of Genesis have a Noachidic character, it is so because the Hebrews could look at man in the same way as they looked at themselves— under the sign of the covenant and the law. In this respect Hebrew prophets did not differ from the priests. By accepting the Israelite covenant and law, they accept also the Noachidic ideas of the covenant and the law and they remind us often of it. It is possible that the men who lived before the deluge are hardly ever mentioned in prophetic literature[26] because we do not see clearly how these people stood in relation to the covenant and the law. True, there are certain hints. The *benedictions* which God places on man and other living beings on the seventh day are signs of a covenant, and the commandment He gives to Adam is a law.[27] But the formulations are not exact enough. It is quite remarkable that in Judaism thoughts about prediluvian mankind began only after the prophetic period. The prophets were only superficially interested in it. This is due to the fact that in a certain sense and in spite of the apparent harmony in the Biblical account, the history of prediluvian mankind is not of the same nature as that of Noachidic mankind, since the former were not connected to the covenant and the law. To the prophets, the human situation in history began with the covenant and the law.

The Tower of Babel

Just as Hebrew thought had a quite original approach to the creation of the world, it dealt also in a particular way with another important problem in the series of moral and religious questions with which humanity is beset, namely, the question of human autonomy and conquests. At first this is a physical problem of interest primarily to conquerors.

The increasing political power of the empires lusts for more and more territory, and there is no reason for coming to a halt. Once one country has been subdued, one becomes conscious of what lies beyond, and again the conquering appetite is stimulated, and will only be satisfied when the boundaries of the empire are identical with those of the earth. The impossibility of reaching such a goal keeps the greed of the would-be conquerors in constant tension, and also creates in their minds the tantalizing anxiety which derives from failure.

However, the problem has also a metaphysical aspect which can be appeased more easily. A total conquest is

not only concerned with the earth but also with heaven.
The universe is an entity, and horizontal expansion is
completed by a vertical one. Man wishes to become the
master of the heavens as well as the master of the earth.
The attempt to dominate man is joined by the ambition
to install oneself in the abode of the gods. Conquest leads
therefore to two risks: an unlimited power on earth and
the replacement of the gods by men in the heavens.

Whereas in the myth of Prometheus the Greeks tragically widened the basis of the problem and denied the
possibility of a solution, the Sumero-Babylonians tackled
the problem ritually and solved it through the symbolism
of the ziggurat.[28] These spiral towers, twenty of which go
back to Sumerian, Babylonian, and Chaldean epochs,
constitute the basic religious symbol of the Mesopotamian
conquerors. The tower of the building is of primary importance; the temple secondary. The sacred significance
rests in the upward direction of the structure; it leaves
the earth in order to lead to the heavens. When the Babylonian kings ordered the construction of a ziggurat they
specified that the top reach to heaven. In the uppermost
story is the abode of the divinity, almost always a celestial
one. One can reach the sun, the moon, and stars in their
cosmic residence, since the temple which shelters them at
the top of the ziggurat goes as far as the plane of heaven.
The steps and ramps which go from floor to floor remind
us with a clarity rarely found in similar religious buildings
of the idea of going up, of a journey towards the heights.
Frequent rites, collective processions or individual ascents,
probably gave the pilgrims the feeling of a victorious
march towards the heavens.

The ziggurat was thus a meeting place of earth and
heaven, and the different names which it bore, according
to the localities, corresponds to this foremost destination.
For it was called "house of service between the heaven
and the earth" (at Larsa); "house of the foundation of

the heaven and the earth," "link between the heaven and the earth" (in Babylonia) ; "temple of the masters of the heaven and the earth" (at Borsippa). Like all other sacred places it then became a center of the world, the place through which the axis of the universe passed, and in which the entire earth was concentrated in one spot. The square, massive basis of the building symbolized that earthly center, and from there one rose towards the apex, crossing on the way cosmic spaces which were represented in the galleries. But the basis of the ziggurat had another meaning, which was quite original. The earthly element which was concentrated in that basis had not only a cosmic value but also a human composition. All men, all peoples were found gathered there in a compact and crowded mass, and that total humanity got ready for the ascent and the conquest of heaven. The Biblical account which has to do with the myth of a ziggurat clearly illustrates that thought. The Babylonian tower rises at the exact place where all people are united, side by side. The togetherness of the first human group in Babylonia expresses that very important meaning of the ziggurat. It is not the earth which is supposed to be linked to the heaven but living humanity which occupies the earth. The problem is stated in terms of human history. In the hieratic work of its ziggurats Sumero-Babylonian religion proclaims the victory of the conquerors over the totality of cosmic space and its inhabitants. The earth has been conquered, and all nations are concentrated in a single place. From that place and base starts the conquest of the celestial sphere, and is realized whenever a ritual march takes people from floor to floor to the highest summit, where they settle in the abode of the gods. This is the symbol of a firm belief in the possibility of a physical and metaphysical conquest of the world by man.

The Hebrew concept denies this belief categorically. The Biblical account of the Babylonian ziggurat takes into consideration the essential elements of its symbolism.[29] It is a tower constructed by an undivided humanity, the incarnation of all the peoples concentrated at the foot of the tower. The top of the tower should reach to the heaven and thus link mankind in its totality with the God of that mankind. This is indeed the function of the ziggurat. But in the Biblical lesson the ziggurat remains unfinished. Before it can reach into the heaven, God *comes down* from heaven to meet man, and with a vigorous gesture He stops their enterprise. He scatters them to the four corners of the earth, everyone in his own language and in his own individuality.

There are two spiritual directions in this Hebrew interpretation of the myth of the ziggurat. The first is the descent of God, who intervenes in man's ambitious attempts. This is not the transcendent Power against which all human action must fail. It is rather the violence which steps forth to seek man out and to halt him in his path. There is nothing like it in Mesopotamian mythology. There the battles of the gods are always metaphysical or cosmic, whether they fight each other or whether they battle against the great cosmic forces of the universe, like the abyss, the waters, the monsters, etc. The gods do not come face to face with man. Or else, the transcendence of the gods is absolute, and then their relation to man is simply a game, as in the Sumerian myth of the deluge. Or again, as in the ziggurat, man joins God, without a fight, by virtue of a rite. It is in Greece that we must look for an analogy with the Hebrew concept of God's approaching man. Just like the mankind of the Biblical Tower of Babel, Prometheus is stopped and pursued by the gods. Just as in the Biblical story, the idea of violence characterizes the immediate relations between the gods and man in the myth of Prometheus. There is even a certain aspect of *revolt* in Greek thought. But the Sumero-Babylonian universe knows only relations of force or slyness between the gods and man. The Hebrews and the Greeks know that a real meeting is possible—a dangerous but exalting struggle between God and man.

But we find another spiritual implication in the Biblical story of the ziggurat. Aside from God's descent, there is the unraveling of the myth—the linguistic and spatial dislocation of the people. Here there is no longer a parallel between Hebrew thought and Promethean myth, where man is chained by the gods and taught his powerlessness and insignificance. The Hebrews overcome this tragic pessimism by an optimistic faith in history. An anonymous mankind which serves as a pedestal for metaphysical conquests in the symbolism of the ziggurat, the isolated and self-enclosed individuality of a Prometheus, are replaced in Biblical thinking by the community of peoples, each with its own language, working out their own destinies and playing a concrete and well-defined role in history. This is the Hebrew reply to the problem of the autonomy of human conquest. Earthly and cosmic space cannot be mastered by conquest but by *time* and by progress in history, where all nations have a chance. But that history is a constant meeting with God, and what seems to be an accident reveals itself by and by as the history of a *covenant,* a Noachidic and universal covenant, which is completed by the particular covenant between God and Israel. We shall show later what importance this has in the thinking of the prophets of the Bible.

The Covenant and the Rite

The mythical universe of creation, deluge, and human conquest is replaced in Hebrew thought by a universe without a myth, where creation is a constant eruption of history. Thus the deluge is the continuity of history through the covenant and the law; human conquest is a joint march in history. In such a universe, time is grasped at the source, as an element of progression and equilibrium, and there is no need for its being grasped in a rite. The absence of a mythical interpretation of the world corresponds in Israel to the lack of a ritual time in the sense in which we have defined it. Here we must reconsider one by one the great rites which have been discovered by historians in Biblical religion and investigate once again their true meaning.

Let us stress first the remarkable fact that in Israel there was no rite of the ziggurat. Some scholars wanted to see in Beth-El a miniature ziggurat, and believed that the anointing of Beth-El by Jacob (Genesis 28:18) was a myth regarding the joining of heaven and earth.[30] But aside from the fact that, as in connection with the account of the Tower of Babel, the Bible insists on man's inactivity or impotence (Jacob's sleep; the drawbacks of a polyglot humanity), and on God's descent to man (God's word addressed to Jacob; God's actual descent towards Babel), which contradicts the lesson of the Babylonian ziggurat, which hints at man's ascent and at his reception by God, no comparison can be made between Beth-El and the ziggurat. "Beth-El" means the abode of a god, a residence without a special mythical significance except that of pointing at a theophany. In the Northern Kingdom the sanctuary of Beth-El was considered a reminder of its patriarchal founder, and was thus considered a site of divine revelation, and as a sign of a covenant between God and Jacob. There is no indication that a special cult was connected with Beth-El, or a rite that reminds us of the meaning of the Babylonian ziggurat.

The Babylonian festival of the New Year was based on the Babylonian creation myth. We have already seen that in Israel creation did not figure in the category of a myth. Thus the Israelite New Year could not respond to the haunting of the great cosmic conflicts and the longing for an appeasement, since the account of the creation, as far as it could be conveyed in a liturgical text, neglected the basic discords of the universe. But this does not mean that the Israelite liturgy of the New Year corresponded to that other and more characteristically Israelite myth, namely, that of the exodus and the desert. For that myth, which identifies the God of Israel with a chthonic divinity, has never been expressed in Hebrew thinking. Any symbolic interpretation of the exodus from Egypt and the sojourn in the desert is contradicted by the constant affirmation found in the Bible that those events and ideas had a historical character. The exodus and the desert are the pillars of one of the best-founded traditions in Hebrew history, and, outside any rite, they are the basis for two permanent and concrete concerns in Hebrew society, from the earliest times on—*social legislation* and *nomadism*. Hebrew social legislation is not the fruit of a long moral meditation. It is rather inherent in a society which, from its very beginning, considered itself a society of the emancipated. This explains why the Levites held such an important place in that society, and the rights granted to the underprivileged, such as slaves, strangers, and the poor. All that legislation, which was handed down in such an obstinate way and became the authentic basis for Israelite society rests on the historic reality of the slavery in Egypt. The social interpretation of the exodus was on a higher level than any ritual uses, and it also included a historical definition: to the Hebrews, the exodus was not the migration of a god but the emancipation of a people. The ritual applications of the exodus, too, underline that social character, as Hebrew tradition has often accented it in connection with the rites of Passover and Tabernacles. We must not consider those "Deuteronomic" explanations to be of a recent date. They are as old as Hebrew society itself. From the first Passover on, God's allies knew that they were eating "the bread of affliction" (Deuteronomy 16:3). Likewise, from the first Tabernacles on, they knew that they were leaving their solid houses in order to live in a succah, a flimsy and temporary tent (Leviticus 23:43). The Feast of Tabernacles was not a mythical copy of the historical Passover, but like those of the Passover its rites gave life to the historic definition of the exodus and the passing through the desert, *the* moments "of affliction."

The rite of Tabernacles is but a rite of impoverishment. This is also a nomadic rite, and here we come to another permanent concern of Hebrew society—nomadism. This is not the place to write in detail about the reality of that tendency which, all through Biblical history, has found a shape in ideological systems, in institutions, and sects. For the moment let us remember that nomadism irrevocably gave the notion of the desert its concrete and historical value. For people who were haunted by nomadism in all its forms—as a regret or as an ideal—the desert could not become a mythological ideogram. It was rather the Arabian Desert at the borders of Canaan, through which the ancestors had wandered after having left Egypt, and even before they had become a sedentary people and Israel was but a nomadic tribe. The return to the desert, which the prophets of the eighth century foretold, was the spiritual replica of the return to the desert as practiced by the Rechabite nomad sects of the ninth century, who themselves continued customs which had been transmitted without interruption. We do not see by what detour the idea of a desert could have been transformed, since an unfailing nomadic tradition preserved its clearly historic meaning.

But if the Israelite festival of the New Year does not correspond to any precise myth, does that mean that we must deny its ancient character and follow those historians who think that it was only instituted during the exile? This we cannot believe, although we are persuaded that its importance was immeasurably exaggerated by certain scholars. The Israelite festival of the New Year celebrated the royal attributes of the God of Israel, and hymns from the Book of Psalms have preserved the elements of a liturgy which underlined those attributes.[31] But nothing in that liturgy or festival has anything to do with an "enthroning" of God. It is not a representation, not even in outline form, of a drama, or of the advent of a god who had temporarily lost his power, but an old and important idea was affirmed, namely, that God is King. This is one of the fundamental expressions of the covenant, and we shall have to investigate its meaning, which, from the historical point of view, gave the Israelite New Year a meaning that was strictly opposed to that of the Babylonian or Egyptian New Year. For in the latter rituals the earthly king indeed occupied a central place. He was the incarnation and the vicar of the heavenly king, and through his mediating function in the ritual of the New Year people became conscious of the divine drama.

But such a concept was out of place in the Israelite ritual. The proposition of the alliance, *"God is King,"* had two aspects: *"Ye are My servants"* and *"There is no other King."* These propositions, which were kept alive in the nomadic institutions of the Hebrew state, gave the New Year a character of transcendence, and were also pointed out in certain psalms that, even at a later, dynastic epoch, contain no allusion to an earthly king in Israel.[32] However, the change in the political regime in the tenth century (the beginning of a kingdom) brought with itself a danger for the transcendence of the New Year. The relations between the heavenly King and the earthly king had to be defined, and this was done in the frame of the covenant. But certain kings broke this frame by assuming religious functions similar to those of other ancient sovereigns, and they changed the rites of the New Year by introducing their own person. This was notably the case with the kings of Samaria, and it is possible that in the ninth and eighth centuries the festival of the New Year underwent profound changes in the Northern sanctuary of Beth El. Through the agency of King Joas or Jeroboam they evoked perhaps the anxieties of a divine drama, the myth of a dispossessed god who was restored to his royal power. This phenomenon necessarily found its parallel in Jerusalem, at the time of Uzziah. If, as is probable, his spectacular attempt to enter the Holy of Holies[33] coincided with the period of the New Year, it also modified profoundly the range of the ritual of the New Year at the Temple of Jerusalem.

Here we have typical examples of a crisis in Biblical times. By assuming roles of meditating sovereigns, two fascinating kings, Jeroboam and Uzziah, left the covenant. But this rupture did not only constitute a personal sin. By echoing in a certain number of rites, it gave the faithful the impression of participating in a time different from that of the covenant, namely, a ritual time with all its tensions and contradictions. The religion of Biblical man no longer moved in Biblical time but in the ritual time of a religion.

The existence or reabsorption in Israel of agrarian rites shows a similar crisis. The catalogue of "Canaan" rites mentioned earlier is certainly contradicted to a large degree by a list of Biblical protestations against those very rites. Although human sacrifices are offered near Jerusalem, they are strictly forbidden by all Israelite sacred legislations, and the patriarchal story of the substitution of an animal sacrifice for Isaac demonstrates in pathetic phrases the revulsion which the Hebrews felt concerning human sacrifices (Genesis 22). Harlots were present in the sanctuaries, but the law rejected them unanimously and severely, and in the north as well as in the south a bitter struggle ensued against the practices of those who called themselves "saints," but who, by popular opinion, were rather referred to as "dogs" or "prostitutes" (Deuteronomy 23:18-19). The prophets were the most outspoken enemies of orgies, and in this respect they followed a long tradition, as is shown by sacred legislation. The harmony of these testimonies allows us to assume that from the very beginning the Hebrews had an austere and stubborn mentality which could never adjust itself entirely to the complex Canaan civilization.

But we should investigate further the sources of that mentality. The agrarian rites rest on certain myths, and on the level of those myths we may find the essence of the Hebrew opposition. Once the Hebrews were installed in Canaan, they became sensitive to the importance of rain in the climate of that country. But they rejected the myth which systematized the sequence of rain and drought. Instead, they retained its irregular and unnatural character and developed an entire theory of catastrophes (long droughts, torrential floods), which rested on very simple ethics connecting the regularity of the rain to the obedience to the covenant (Deuteronomy 11:10-21). This concept was not only an outcome of Hebrew monotheism but also of the fundamental nomadism of Hebrew society. When the Hebrews faced their divinity, they did not feel themselves to be chained to a certain soil, as did the Canaanites. Their god was not the Baal, the *proprietor* of the field, but a God with whom they were always strangers (Leviticus 25:23). Therefore they did not have to *exorcise* the Baal through rites and appropriate sacrifices, but they had to find a religious formulation for the relations between God the Master, who was the Baal of the soil, and the strangers who, grouped together in His covenant, did not wander around with Him but were tied to the soil whose Baal He was.

That formulation is one of the most characteristic and also pathetic of Hebrew thought. The Hebrews realized it by changing, through a simple but important nuance, the basic identity of agrarian religions. They identified the soil with woman. This identity had already appeared in the verses of Isaiah quoted earlier (62:4-5; 55:10-11), but the Hebrews varied it by giving the word "woman" the meaning "wife," and the excerpts from Isaiah should be read in this sense. They are arranged around the subject of God's being the husband of the earth. This theme corresponds to the larger but similarly inspired one of God's being the husband of Israel and Israel his wife. We shall soon investigate the incidence of this theme in the definition of the covenant. Let us for the moment remember that in the realm of agrarian religion the identification of the soil with the wife replaces the idea of *property* with that of *loyalty*. What in the Canaanite Baal religion is a relation of possession is, in Israelite religion, a relation of faith. From this derive the two great currents which endlessly contradict each other in the Bible. There is a Canaanite current which passes through the existence of the Hebrews for whom the earth is "possessed" by God the Master. A different current upholds the existence of the Hebrews for whom the earth is beloved by God the Husband. The two currents meet in the ambivalence of the word "Baal," which means master as well as husband and which designates the Canaanite divinities, while at the same time they may also be applied to the God of Israel. The Hebrews, who were conscious of this double meaning, had to choose between two times: a Canaanite time, where Baal was the master, and a Biblical time, which broke radically with the views of an agrarian religion, because Baal was no longer the master but the husband. Even in the agrarian domain the concept of a covenant triumphs over ritual or mythical concepts. Here the covenant between God and the land is expressed with the same term that defines the covenant between God and man, namely, the faithfulness of husband and wife.

Notes

1. See J. M. Powis Smith: "The Chosen People." *American Journal of Semitic Languages,* vol. 45, 1928–29, p. 73.
2. Deuteronomy 14:1; Hosea 11:1; Isaiah 63:16. (Other examples for the father-son relationship below, pp. 289–291). God the Master: Leviticus 25:41 and the constant use of the word Adon for God. God the King: examples below.
3. See our book Amos, pp. 36ff. To that bibliography should now be added H. H. Rowley: *The Biblical Doctrine of Election,* London. 1950. J. Pedersen: *Israel, Its Life and Culture,* London 1926–47, III. pp. 263ff.
4. *Amos,* pp. 45f.
5. Genesis 9.
6. *Ibid.,* 15:6ff., and chapter 17.
7. Exodus 14:1ff.
8. *Ibid.,* 24:7.
9. The present trend among exegetes is to accept the Mosiac authorship of the decalogue. See the excellent resume of the debate by H. H. Rowley: "Moise et la décalogue," RHPR 1952. I, pp. 7ff.
10. The two most remarkable contributions which the Scandinavian School (Pedersen, Engell, Mowinckel, Haldar) has made to Biblical studies are the discovery of a connection between the cult and the most spiritual phenomena of the Biblical universe; and, in the cultic domain, the importance of the rites of the New Year. We found it interesting to deal at length with these facts, not so much because we accept them in part as that we must indicate their limitation.
11. I Kings 12:32f.
12. Exodus 23:16; 34:22.
13. A. Haldar: The Notion of the Desert in Sumerian-Accadian and West Semitic Religions. Upsala, 1950.
14. See above all, René Dussaud: *Les origines cananéennes du sacrifice israélite,* Paris, 2nd ed. 1941.
15. Jeremiah 7:31f; 32:35.
16. Micah 6:7.
17. II Kings 23:7.
18. Dussaud, *op. cit.*

19. Babylonian Talmud Taanit 6b.

20. Cosmogonical speculations in Rabbinic times allow investigation as to "what happened before the creation." The Mishna (Hagiga 2:1) deplores this and tries to limit it. Nevertheless, even outside any Greek influence, one finds this problem dealt with again and again in Talmudic literature.

21. Leon Roth: "Le pensée juive dans le monde moderne," in *Le legs d'Israel,* Paris, 1931, p. 443, applies the term panentheism to the theological concept of the Bible.

22. Genesis 2:4.

23. *Ibid.,* 5:1; 6:9; 11:10, 27; 25:12, 19; 36:1; 37:2.

24. *Ibid..* 49:1. Numbers 24:14. Deuteronomy 4:30; 31:29. Isaiah 2:2. Jeremiah 23:20. Hosea 3:5. Micah 4:1.

25. David Koigen: *Das Haus Israel.* Berlin 1933, p. 24.

26. Prophetic historiography seems to consider the Noachidic epoch to be original, as quoted by Isaiah 54:9 and Ezekiel 14:14, 20. To the prophets, as to later Judaism, humanity is less Adamite than Noachidic.

27. The Talmud connects the Noachidic law with Adam. The verse in Genesis 2:16 would imply the entire legislation developed in 9:1ff. (Babylonian Talmud Sanhedrin 56b.)

28. See A. Parrot: *The Tower of Babel* (Studies in Bibl. Archaeology, no. 2, New York, 1954.

29. Genesis 11:1ff.

30. M. J. Lagrange: *Etudes sur les religions sémitiques.* Paris 1905, p. 192.

31. Psalms 29:95ff.

32. With these psalms we have already arrived at the stage of a kingship liturgy of God, which can be found in the Rabbinic ritual of the Festival of the New Year. The association of that idea (Malchuyoth) with that of remembering (Zichronoth) shows the *historical* and not the *mythical* sense given in that liturgy to the evocation of the divine royalty.

33. II Chronicles 26:16ff.

3

The Dialogue in Society—
the Law (Torah)

The Covenant Community

The *idea of the covenant* is connected with that of the *community of the covenant*. The covenant is not only the underlying idea of the Biblical universe, but it works out doctrines and institutions which give Biblical society its particular physiognomy. That society is the place of a history. The Hebrews experience their own existence as a part of history which is divine as well as human. Their community associates divine intention with human enterprise. Therefore two elements predominate in the structure of Hebrew society—the acceptance of time and the presence of God.

The value of time in Hebrew society derives negatively from the *nomadism* which has always animated it. There is something remarkable and almost unique in the persistence of the nomad tendency within Hebrew society. In spite of their long stay in Egypt and long after their definite settling in Canaan, the Hebrew people continue to harbor nomad aspirations. Legal institutions like Levitism keep a wandering group alive among the sedentary tribes.[1] When they became inefficient, sects like the Rechabites revived the institution and lived their nomad ideal with a touching obstinacy.[2] At the outset priesthood was purely Levitic and centered around the sanctuary of Shiloh, where the sacred objects preserved

their temporary character, and only after the establishment of the kingdom brought about the idea of a fixed
sanctuary, which, however, could only be established on
the ruins of Shiloh and its nomad clergy.[3] The prophets
supported a latent nomadism and gave it, from the eighth
century on, an acute expression. It is possible that this
obstinate persistence favored the development of a rigor-
ous monotheism and an austere system of ethics. But
this would still leave unanswered the question why no
other ancient nomad tribe has risen to that ethical monotheism, and we would have to find the supplementary
causes which gave Israelite nomadism such great strength.
As a matter of fact, even if the consequences of Hebrew
nomadism have been only imperfectly brought out, the
problem of the causes of such obstinacy has been still less
clearly investigated. Why has the nomad spirit not van-
ished in Israel, as it has disappeared everywhere else,
where it has been absorbed by strong tendencies towards
a more sedentary life? If the Hebrews did preserve a
nomad instinct, romantic feelings can only have played
a minor role. The truth is that they have always carried
within themselves that nomadism, because this was really
an instinctive tendency of their spirit. Hebrew nomadism
is essentially a refusal to overestimate space. Just as in
the spiritual world of the Hebrews the refusal to overestimate space led to a historical dimension of time, so
did, in the social life of the Hebrews, nomadism, which
rejected the temptations of space, breathe a new spirit
into collectivity. Nomadism changed the social life of the
Hebrews from a collection of facts placed side by side
into a working tool.

Besides nomadism, the awareness of a divine presence
gives Hebrew society its specific character. This feeling
is allied to that of the covenant: God is *with* Israel.
No other ancient society has given this "with" such a
concrete meaning. Many different expressions have been

used to determine the ancient Hebrew community.[4] Whether these are fitting or not, they must make use of the divine element. Hebrew society cannot be imagined without God. It is characterized by a divine absolutism which not only places God above the people but associates the people inseparably with God through a *covenant* and through a *law*.

The Torah

The ideal of the Hebrews was to become a *nation of priests* or a *nation of prophets*.[5] Although these desires remained unfulfilled, they indicate that the Hebrews had the feeling of being linked to God in a priestly or charismatic way. In any case, numerous institutions confirm this pretension in Israel, the most important of which being the Torah. Etymologically that word means "to point out," to make a path or a line of conduct.[6] But the fact that, as was shown above, the Torah always appears in the center of a Brith, a covenant, links its ethics with God. The ethics of the Torah is the will of God. In the ancient world this was a scandalous assumption, since it was believed unthinkable that the godhead should be concerned with morals, let alone social morals.[7] But this is the very center of Hebrew ethics. The basic commandments of the Torah, like "Be ye holy," "Do justice," "Love God and thy neighbor" tell us not only what is *good* but how man can share in God's intention. The Torah is not the conduct of *an* existence but that of an existence *with* God. Just as Biblical time, Biblical *holiness, justice,* and *love* are defined in terms of a *covenant*.

Holiness

In the Torah, *holiness* is the imperative of personal ethics. "Be ye holy," "sanctify yourselves"—this is how the Torah addresses man when it speaks to him in the second person, in the dialogue of the imperative. It does not say to him, "Be just," "be good," "be honest," "be pious," since justice, goodness, honesty, and piety— and we might well add more ethical qualities to that list— derive from *holiness,* as if it were enough for man to concentrate his efforts on holiness in order to achieve all other virtues.[8] In the ethics of the Torah, where man receives his directives from an immediate divine revelation, the obligation to become holy excels all others, because it is their principle and seed. Moreover, the Torah itself explains the reason for this pre-eminence of holiness: *"Ye shall be holy, for I the Lord your God am holy"* (Leviticus 19:2). On the moral plane, this is the equivalent of the covenant. For if the covenant brings man close to God by unifying their intentions, *holiness* does the same by unifying the meaning of their acts. The covenant means that man meets God, and holiness means that man tries to be like God. By making holiness the first commandment, the Torah inserts ethics into the covenant. There is no holiness without a partner, and trying to be holy means, for man, trying to imitate God.

This definition, which suggests itself by a plain interpretation of the Torah, shows that *holiness* is not considered synonymous with *purity.* Holiness calls for an imitation of God which purity strictly denies, for the simple reason that in the Torah God is not defined through purity.[9] Whereas the Torah does say that God is holy, it never declares Him to be pure. Therefore man does not imitate God by purifying himself. He remains with himself and acts according to his own lines of conduct. By becoming pure, he does not really enter into the covenant. To do that, he must rather strive after holiness. Thus purity and holiness are two different states, and this is important for the understanding of the ethical value of the Torah. In all other religious legislations purity is identical with holiness, so that by entering holy

places and coming close to God, man makes a choice between what is pure and what is impure. The great inno-
vation of the Torah is the distinction between the domain of purity and that of holiness. The polarity of
purity and impurity is presented in the Torah as simply
a technique, or better, as a preparation. It leaves man in
a discussion with himself. Man can reach God only by
striving for holiness.

This observation allows us to assign an exact place to
the ritual discipline of cleanliness and uncleanliness which
the Torah introduced in its code, and which plays such
an important role in Levitic legislation. The critical
school has called that part of the Torah together with
its cognate elements "The Code of Holiness." They could
not have chosen a more inappropriate term. It is rather
a code of ritual purity, as it is found in most ancient religious societies. But whereas elsewhere that code was
all there is to religious wisdom and it sufficed to accept
it in order to be in touch with the divinity, to attain the
good, which was "pure," and to avoid the evil, which
was "impure," the Torah denies that ritual purity has
any metaphysical or moral value. It is not essential to
holiness. If the sanctuary were to disappear there would
no longer be any purity or impurity but the call to holiness would remain as before.

But how is this demand translated into acts? What
attitude does the Torah demand of man when it invites
him to holiness? Is it moral purity? In that case the ad-
vantage of Biblical ethics over contemporary religions
would mainly consist in a turning inward of the idea of
purity which, instead of being of ritual concern as is the
case elsewhere and on primitive levels even in the Torah,
would by and by be filled with a moral sense. But in fact
moral purity, too, was only a by-product of holiness, with
which it is never identified. This demand was not due to
an evolution, but is, as we shall soon see, organically

linked to the idea of *tsedek,* as the Torah implies in its primitive and basic formulations. A psychological discipline of purity corresponded to a ritual technique of purity. But neither of these led to holiness.

In order to understand the striving for holiness we must not forget that it is a striving for the imitation of God. Man's relation to the world had to be the same as God's relation to it. Apparently this was a logical contradiction, which could be solved only in a supreme effort in deeds. "Ye shall be holy, for I am holy." God is transcendent as well as immanent, separated from the world and entering it. This should also be man's position—rejecting the world and accepting it. In the face of a *transcendent* God everything is profane, and man must always be aware of it. He must secularize all great components of the universe, cosmic nature, time, space, life, and man himself. In opposition to all those who declare all or some of these forces to be holy and worship them, the man of the Torah must consider all this to be profane. But in relation to an *immanent* God everything is sacred, and the man of the Torah must be aware of this, too. The entire profane universe is made holy by God, nature, time, space, life, man—but being created by God and penetrated by Him they acquire a *value* in the dimension of the sacred, and the demand for holiness is the same as the effort to discover and to reveal that value. This effort is served by the *rite* in the Torah. It does not tame the physical forces but sanctifies them. Its aim is not to reconcile two contradictory domains, that of nature and that of man, but to make metaphysical what is profane in nature and in man.

But that man is not asked by the Torah to imitate *one* God but *the* God, the Only One, and here we have another basic aspect of the call for holiness and of the rites which correspond to it in the Torah. A polytheistic theology admits the postulate of a multiplicity of the Being.

The holy and the profane appear there to be unavoidably and radically different. Whereas monotheism recognizes such an apparent multiplicity, it does not accept it as the last word. Just as in the Divine Being everything is essentially One, so there exists in the human being the possibility of unifying the diversity of his aspects. The *rite* of the Torah—santification of a profane creation by the obedience of the creature to the Creator—is also a santification of the creature by his becoming aware of his unity. The sacred and the profane divide man only when he allows himself to be mutilated by them. But when man restores their essential unity by the rites, he experiences them as truly unified reality, achieved by the accord of the partners, who, conscious of belonging together and far from contradicting each other, recognize each other in the dialogue.

Justice

If holiness is the imperative of personal ethics in the Torah, justice represents the demand of social ethics. Perhaps the insistence on nomadism has had a share in stirring up an acute sense of justice during the entire range of history in Hebrew society. In a nomad society power is not subjected to the great variations and perturbations known in a sedentary society. It is fairly distributed, and the imbalance ends sooner or later by being taken up in time. The mobility of a nomad history prevents the definitive fixing of the power of an individual or a given group. By remaining loyal, if not to the nomad reality then at least to its ideal, Hebrew society constantly maintained the demand for justice. As we shall presently see, institutions like Levitism must, in principle as well as in accordance with practice, prevent a rupture between the possessing class and the poor. Likewise, certain demands of the Torah, like the Jubilee and its consequences concerning the land and lending of money (Le-

viticus 25), transformed social life in a provisionary experience, which could be reconsidered from time to time.
Thus in the long run time corrected possible abuses and
excesses of power. We do not know whether the Jubilee
was ever put into practice; but even if its demands were
purely ideal, they furthered ethical thinking in which the
terms *right, equity,* and *justice* occupied an important
place; and even if they were not always applied, they provided at least a constant source of reflection. One could
refer to them in a natural way.

Such reflection was centered around God. The principles of righteousness and justice were God's own *justice*
at the time of the conclusion of the *covenant,* a unique
movement in history, shortly after the exodus from Egypt,
when the Israelite community as a whole formed a society of emancipated slaves. It was to a society without
a hierarchy, without influential members, without tradition, without legal authorities that the Torah had been
revealed by the only Being who assumed the role of the
leader of that society—God. God was the unique and
absolute legislator of a community where not only all
were alike, from the oldest to the carrier of water, but
where all were made equal by a God who loves justice.
"I am the Lord your God, which took you out of Egypt,
out of the house of bondage." This is the first "word"
of the decalogue (Exodus 20:2), and the first affirmation
through which the *covenant* became *Torah.* The Torah is
not revealed to a people that was brought forth by nature
but to a people that had left another people in revolt.[10]
Only a people like Israel that had been subjected in Egypt
to the experience of misery and revolt, slavery and liberty,
suffering and redemption, only such a people could understand and accept the Torah. God placed the Torah into
the heart of slaves whose chains He had just broken.

This is God's *justice.* It preserves within the life of the
covenant something of what it had been at the moment

when the *covenant* was being concluded. *Justice* is here *justification,* since the Hebrew word has often the meaning of *victory* or *innocence.* At Sinai God's revelation was justified by His previous intervention in Egypt. The Torah was not placed like a yoke on the necks of slaves. It was the outcome of a struggle in which God had been right. God could not be blamed for anything, since His victory over the Egyptians freed Him of all suspicion. He appealed to the religious servitude of people whom He had socially liberated, as if to stress the fact that new servitude could not wipe out the freedom which had been so recently acquired. The Torah was from the beginning part of a plan of *redemption.* The exodus had been a redemption, and so was the Torah.

Human *justice* as demanded by the Torah is also part of that plan. It was not enough to practice justice, which, though important, had already been vouchsafed by the semi-nomad constitution of Israel. It seems that through justice the Hebrews were called upon to cooperate with God's plan in history. To practice justice did not only mean to act morally within society but to take upon oneself an eminently religious vocation; it meant to do one's share in bringing out God's *innocence* and to assure His *victory.* Such a vocation plays its role on a practical as well as on a theoretical level. Practically it means to eliminate injustice and sin, which prevent God from being victorious. Evidently one had to begin with himself, but one must also try to win others over to that moral perfection without which God's game is lost. Theoretically it means to work out a doctrine that is capable of explaining suffering and evil without holding God responsible for them. It is a doctrine that declares God to be innocent, and man guilty. In Hebrew society it is the *just* who undertake that double task, since their piety comes under the term of *justice.* Through their actions and thoughts they share in God's justice. They are the all-important

THE DIALOGUE IN SOCIETY

artisans of social justice, of moral purity, and of the technique of repentance.

The difference between the design of *holiness* and that of *justice* seems clear. Holiness risks imperfection and sin, as long as the act of sanctification is all-comprising. Justice evades such a risk, and its very purpose is to abolish imperfections and to reduce sins. Therefore the Biblical *saint* is not identical with the Biblical *just* or righteous man. If they are to meet, there is the need for another agent. This is *love,* and it is so strong that its demands force holiness and justice to undergo a change.

Love

Love is more than *justice.* For whereas the latter admits imperfection and acknowledges the existence of sin, which it tries to correct, love is unconditional. It is not concerned with darkness but immediately accepts light. "Thou shalt love the Lord" (Deuteronomy 6:5). "Thou shalt love thy neighbor" (Leviticus 19:18) no matter who they might be, or in what condition they might be. You must love God, even if you consider Him to be "guilty." You must love man in spite of his sins and unworthiness. Love knows no method or techniques. Love is an absolute demand.

Love is also more than *Holiness.* Holiness calls for an imitation. We must imitate God in His way of acting towards the world and man. God and man work at the same task, but in their own particular dimension. Love unites God and man in their common dimension. "Thou shalt love God . . . . Thou shalt love thy neighbor." The same love is demanded for both. The transcendent and the immanent, timelessness and time, the absolute and the relative—all are entrusted to one and the same feeling in man's heart—love. Through the demand for love, man's heart becomes the meeting place for God and man. Love is the dialogue between God and the world within man.

The prophets were well aware of the pre-eminence of love in the Torah, doubtless because of their prophetic vocation they themselves were constant meeting places between God and the world. They experienced that meeting as love and described it as such in the broadest terms, as we shall soon see.

But although we must leave a deeper analysis of love to a later chapter, we should underline at once that in the Torah the demand of love, too, is an expression of the *covenant*. Just like holiness and justice, love is an answer to a call which comes from God. Of the utmost importance in love is not that God loves man, although this is evidently a very significant idea and one to which the Bible attaches great importance. But that idea is also found in other religious doctrines, more or less clearly outlined. Certain chosen creatures had the impression of being loved by God.[11] But it is typical of Biblical love that man is called upon to love God,[12] and this is not found anywhere else. In the Bible the idea of a loving God is enriched by that of loving man. Thus we return to the dialogical structure of the *covenant*. It looks as if God revealed in the Torah the demand for love because He Himself wants to be loved. God longs for the love of His creatures, and therefore He concludes a covenant. Israel has not only been chosen because of God's love but because God expects love in return.

Levitism

Levitism is a domain entirely typical of Hebrew religious society. Whereas in Israel the "priest" is called a *cohen*—a word that is found in many other Semitic languages—the word "Levi" has no parallel outside of Israel. Therefore the problems connected with Levitism begin with an interpretation of the very word "Levi."[13] The first series of hypotheses has a mythical-historical character. It sees in the historical Levitism of the Bible merely a later reconstruction of what had originally been only a myth. Accordingly, the tribe of Levi had no real existence before the last years of Judean kingship and was built around a mythical theme whose hero was a person out of ancient nomadism. Wellhausen,[14] whose views on the matter have become classic, derives the word "Levi" from "Leah"—Levi's mother in the Genesis "myth"—and connects both terms with "Leviathan," the cosmic serpent whose figure reappears in the cult of Moses, the "legendary Levi." Another hypothesis of a similar character holds that the Levites of Israel were a group of priests with parallels among the institutions of ancient Arab tribes. Minean inscriptions which possibly go back to the fifteenth century B.C. do indicate that the servants of the god Wadd are called lv or lv't, and we may have here a linguistic relationship with "Levi." This information would be the more interesting, as that tribe lived in northern Arabia, the same region in which the Bible places the Midianites, with whom the Hebrew Levite Moses was connected. Thus the hypothesis of Midianite origins of the Mosiac religion could include Moses' adoption of the Midianite term "Levi" for Hebrew priesthood.[15] Jastrow, however,[16] prefers to establish a relation between "Levi" and the priestly term "laba" found in the texts of El-Amarna. The common root would be "lb," a lion, an animal whose name, in the form of "ari," is also used in the texts of Ras-Shama for persons who have religious functions, a kind of priest-prophets.[17] But aside from the fact that the Midianite or Egyptian origin of Moses' religion is of a very hypothetical character, the linguistic interpretations are extremely frail and debatable in any case. We are led back to the purely Hebrew meaning of the term "Levi,"[18] which is also confirmed by the Hebrew text itself. The meaning is an *associate*.[19]

But linguistics cannot tell us with whom that person

is "associated," and historians are divided on the point. In the Bible we meet two communities of Levites, who differ greatly from one another. One, a lay community, is one of the "tribes" of Israel. Were they called "Levi" because of their close "association" with the tribe of Simeon, which they seem to have joined in military exploits which were not underwritten by the other tribes?[20] But the Levites are also individuals scattered within the rest of Hebrew society, where they did not constitute a political group but rather an association with a religious character.

The name "Levi" would then be a religious term rather than an ethnic one.[21] It would be used for "clients" of sanctuaries, men attached to the service of a temple or cult. In order to solve the problem of lay vs. religious tribe of Levi we must go back to the historic plan suggested by the Bible. The lay sense preceded the religious, and only later were the Levites transformed into a religious brotherhood, which replaced the ethnic group constituted at the beginning. That change was made suddenly, and on the occasion of events in which Moses, a Levite himself, was the hero. The Levites connected their investiture to the tradition of the desert. There, on the occasion of events whose range was to be decisive for their later vocation, the Levites experienced the true meaning of the name they bore. From then on they were associates of God.

For this association with God is the true meaning of Levitism. I do not know why the object to which the Levites were attached must be reduced to a sanctuary or a cult.[22] They were not the clients of a temple nor those of a religion in a narrow sense. They were rather the vassals of the sacred. But with all their vassalage they preserved something of their secular independence. Unlike the priests, they were not anointed in a ritual which identified them with the sacred. A remarkable legislation treats the Levites as functionaries,[23] for they serve in the Temple only from their twentieth to their fiftieth year. Their life has then two obligatory nonpriestly time limits. Another rule[24] gives them the choice of accepting or rejecting their ritual functions in the Temple. Thus they are not "consecrated" but available. They may enter the holy places at a time convenient to them and still hold on to the freedom of their secular lives. This situation, which makes of the Levites perpetual intermediaries between the sacred and the profane is a concrete illustration of the covenant, for that doctrine, too, relates in a constant way men to God, and secular existences to sacred intentions. Exactly where Hebrew thinking believed in the possibility of a development of history based on a belief in God and in men—a joining of heaven and earth, of the transcendent and the immanent—there also arose the development of Levitism as the social incarnation of the covenant.

Biblical tradition discovered the true meaning of Levitism by connecting its birth to the very moment when the covenant arose. If one were not to admit that the spiritual and political history of the Hebrews is based on the conviction of a covenant concluded with the God who had delivered the Israelites from Egypt, Levitism does not contain more than Hebrew history itself. But if we give due recognition to the idea of the covenant, Levitism must be understood in its situation as a twin brother of the covenant. Levitism is a spiritual and social movement which has saved the covenant in one of its very first crises. By upholding the purest elements of the covenant against hostile currents, sometimes with a certain extremism, it has obstinately preserved its character as an avant-garde. When we analyze Levitism throughout Hebrew history, we discover the covenant in its first eruption and in its basic and irreducible affirmations.

If we were to search Hebrew society for a group most

like the Levites, we would arrive at the "gerim," the strangers, who are really "sojourners." Their main characteristic is their nomadism, and indeed the Bible uses that term to describe the nomadism of the Hebrew patriarchs. They refer to themselves as *gerim,* their life is a pilgrimage *(magur),* and the land on which they pitch their tents is also one of pilgrimages.[25] In Egypt the Hebrews are *gerim,* not because they are strangers, but because as a nomad tribe they have come to "sojourn" on Egyptian soil. They did not forget that their presence in Egypt was a provisional one, and although there were attempts to implant themselves in Egypt, to become sedentary there and to assimilate with the natives,[26] it was certainly the preservation of the mentality of *sojourners* which did its share later in rallying the Hebrews to the notion of an exodus. After having invaded Canaan, the Hebrews did stop being *gerim,* but their society held numerous *gerim,* in whom we must see not only strangers, native Canaanites in particular but also Hebrews who rebelled against a final settling down in the land and who led a nomad existence. Among these are the Kenites, who are tied to the Hebrew community by family relationship but prefer to live in tents rather than in houses.[27] It is true that they live on the margin of society, on the frontiers of the territory. Nevertheless, it is from them that in the ninth century the first Rechabite sectaries get their recruits, at a time when nomadism is no longer felt to be a simple style of life but as a proper means of saving the very principles of the covenant. The Levites, too, must be counted among the *gerim* of sedentary Hebrew society. We can well understand their loyalty to nomadism if, as the Bible indicates, they were the avant-garde in Egypt of those who refused to settle permanently. The outstanding role that certain Levite families played at the moment of the exodus must be explained as an outcome of their determination to remain *gerim*. They were willing to leave, to become nomads again, because they had never given up their status as nomads. In any event, after Hebrew society settled in Canaan, the Levites were a tribe without any land.[28] This implies a number of things.

First of all, the rejection of the land means a rejection of space. Space offers many temptations, and we have noted that ancient religions, and even Hebrew religion at critical times, were in this manner led into taking refuge in ritual or cyclical mythologies. Levitic nomadism remains true to a basic aspect of nomadism, the attachment to time. The existence of the Levites recognized a proper concept of time.

The religious consequences of this metaphysical aspect are inestimable since they have kept alive the concept of historic time. This also has sociological connotations. In rejecting the land, the Levites rejected at the same time the Canaanite civilization, which was essentially sedentary. Economic life in Canaan rested on agriculture and trade, the latter being furthered through natural exchanges between Canaan, a land of agriculture, and Phoenicia, the land of industrial resources. The cultural ties between Phoenicia and Canaan were established on the economic community of the two countries. But the Levites were never assimilated. They were the only ones among the Hebrews who never embraced farming, as the Hebrews did from the moment that they entered Canaan, nor commerce, as the Hebrews were to do later when they had taken over the richest parts of the land.

Since the Levites thus refused a rural or commercial existence, we must ask ourselves how they subsisted. By raising cattle, which is the most natural means of existence among nomads and which also supported the Hebrews of old before they became settled? No. The Levites lived on—nothing. Their existence depended on the charity of others. They were poor. Their rejection of the land was also a rejection of wealth.

This comparison shows that the attitude of the Levites was neither romantic nor sentimental. The poverty of the Levites is an uneasy condition, and they must have had important considerations in order to maintain it. These considerations had to do with the time that the covenant was established, a time with which the Levites were so intimately associated. After the exodus and during their sojourn in the desert the Hebrew community was a society of the emancipated. There were no hierarchies and prerogatives. People who had been made equal by virtue of their recent slavery stood before God, ready to become His partners. Every one of them, as well as the group as a whole, could always be reminded by God of their slavery which they had escaped with great difficulty. The covenant was concluded with just such a society of pariahs, and in order that the covenant somehow preserve that character it was necessary that the poor should always be in relation with God. The poverty of the Levites expressed this social meaning of the covenant. Through the poor Levites, who are associated with God, God associates Himself with the lowest classes, the strangers, the widows and orphans, the poor and disinherited. In this way the society of the covenant cannot suppress the problems posed by a suffering existence. Social evil is a concern of God's. Hebrew society works out a religious doctrine of suffering and social ethics. Parallel with the movement which leads from Levitic nomadism to Rechabism we have another movement which leads from Levitic poverty to the doctrine of the *anavim,* the poor.[29] The Rechabites as well as the anavim are in search of salvation. The first find it in an integral nomadism, the others in a moral exaltation over their own condition:

God loves them *because* they are poor. Both groups are inspired by the example of the condition of the Levites.

The poverty of the Levites is strongly underlined by legislation which holds public charity responsible for their subsistence.[30] But it is also evident, in a more direct and even harsher way, from certain suggestions found in the Biblical text. In a brief outline of the Levitic charter,[31] Deuteronomy affirms that the Levite knows not father, mother, brothers nor children, if circumstances demand it. The Levitic community is not a caste, and it does not give its members the solace of a dynastic or hereditary feeling. The Levite is one of those men who, although having inherited his position, must be ready to live all by himself. Opposite the hereditary transmission of his condition, there is a *charisma of existence,* which imposes itself upon him with an absolute power, and in order to lighten its weight, he cannot rely on the help of family, property, or title. We must see in him the *orphan* of society, and it is not by a mere coincidence that we find in the Bible an orphan mentioned side by side with the Levite. They have a common destiny. For the same reason, the Levite is related to the stranger. Just like the Gibeonites,[32] he performs menial work in the sanctuaries, where he is a hewer of wood and a carrier of water. Just like the Netinim[33] he is *lent* to the priesthood. Now in Hebrew society the Gibeonites and the Netinim are true strangers, since they are of Canaanite origin. Thus we find the Levites associated with the foreigners, and the quality of "ger" has the meaning of stranger rather than that of nomad. The poverty of the Levite is not a monastic one. It allows him to join the lowest classes of society, lay as well as priestly. This double presence gives Levitism its true religious efficiency. Levitism *links* the profane and the sacred, but through the lowly ones. Through this constant role as an agent between misery and the sacred,

Levitism invaded another spiritual domain to which it had already been predisposed by its nomadism—that of teaching.

It was not only from the exile on that education had been entrusted to the Levites. Max Weber has shown[34] that steady contact with the people authorized the Levites to serve as chaplains, as guides of conscience, and to be consulted as such, and this from the very outset in Hebrew history in Canaan. The moral preaching of the great prophets of the eighth century could not have been understood if it had not been preceded by a vast current of education which had popularized the principles of a *law*. That law, the Torah, in part written down, in part oral, was commented upon by the Levites, who had held that monopoly ever since the Hebrew community had become one of the covenant, in the wilderness. Deuteronomy presents the transmission of the Torah to the Levites as an institutional act (31:9). The account in Exodus is more dramatic. There the Levites acquired their titles by their own strength, when they repudiated the Golden Calf (32:26ff.) Their choice provided the Levites at once with a fierce anti-Canaanism. They would neither submit to the sedentary existence incarnated in the Baal nor to the orgies to which the fertilization cult led. The Levites made that double rejection the rule of their later life. By becoming the *gerim* of the community of the covenant, they remained loyal to nomadism, and by becoming the apostles of the charter—the Torah—they remained loyal to the ethics of the covenant. On the plane of those ideal demands the community of the covenant could count on the Levite. But within the community there appeared also another figure, one who helped and took the place of the Levite, not only by undertaking to *teach* the demands of the covenant and the law but to *live* them. This was the *prophet*.

Notes

1. See below.
2. Jeremiah 35.
3. I Samuel 4.
4. See the discussions concerning the terms theocracy, confederation, no-mocracy, theopole, in our *Amos*, pp. 237ff.
5. Exodus 19:6; Numbers 11:29.
6. See A. Néher: *Moses and the Vocation of the Jewish People*, London, 1959.
7. The definition of virtue which Cicero gives *(De natura deorum* III, 36) is typical for the spirit of pagan antiquity: "But this is the way with all mortals: their external goods, their vineyards, cornfields and olive-yards, with their abundant harvests and fruits, and in short all the comfort and prosperity of their lives, they think of as coming to them from the gods; but virtue no one ever imputed to a god's bounty. And doubtless with good reason; for our virtue is a just reason for others' praise and a right reason for our own pride, and this would not be so if the gift of virtue came to us from a god and not from our-selves. On the other hand when we achieve some honor or some ac-cession to our estate, or obtain any other of the goods or avoid any of the evils of fortune, it is then that we render thanks to the gods, and do not think that our own credit has been enhanced. Did anyone ever render thanks to the gods because he was a good man? No, but be-cause he was rich, honored, secure. The reason why men give Jupiter the titles of Best and Greatest is not that they think that he makes us just, temperate or wise, but safe, secure, wealthy and opulent."
(The above translation of Cicero's text is taken from A. Rackham's version, done for the Loeb Classical Library. Permission to use this translation, granted by the Harvard University Press, is herewith gratefully acknowledged. Tr.)
8. This statement is further developed in Jewish theological tradition by excluding the Law of Holiness (Leviticus 19:1) from the classical number of the 613 commandments of the Torah.
9. Whereas the expression "The Holy God" is current in the Bible, the term "Pure God" appears only in post-Biblical Jewish literature, never in the Bible itself.
10. See Franz Rosenzweig: "The Builders" in: *On Jewish Learning*, tr. by William Wolf, New York, 1955, pp. 72ff.
11. Evidently we are dealing here with partiality, not with real love. The expression "beloved of the gods" corresponds to "favored of the gods," found in non-Biblical religious literature. It does not carry the senti-

mental note which, in the Bible, led to the conjugal symbolism, where the one beloved by God is loved like a woman by her husband.

12. Deuteronomy 6:15; 10:12; 11:1, 13, and *passim*.

13. For a methodology of studies related to Levitism see K. Moehlenbrink: "Die levitischen Ueberlieferungen des Alten Testaments," in: *Zeitschrift fuer die alttestamentliche Wissenschaft*, vol. 52, 1934, pp. 184ff.

14. Wellhausen: *Prolegomena zur Geschichte Israels*, 1896, p. 141.

15. See G. Hoelscher: article "Levi," in: Pauly-Wissowa: *Real Encyclopaedie der klassischen Altertumswissenschaft*.

16. Jastrow: *Dictionary of the Targumim*, vol. II.

17. See Haldar: *Associations of Cultic Prophets*, p. 82.

18. *Ibid.*, p. 91f.

19. Genesis 29:34 (association between husband and wife); Numbers 18:2, 4 (association with a sanctuary).

20. Genesis 34; 49:5ff.

21. Dhorme: *L'évolution religieuse d'Israel*, I, *La religion des Hebreux nomades*, Brussels, 1937, p. 226.

22. This is the hypothesis of Maybaum: *Die Entwicklung des altisraelitischen Priestertums*, Berlin 1880, p. IV.

23. Numbers 8:23, 26.

24. Deuteronomy 18:6ff.

25. Genesis 17:8; 28:4; 36:7; 47:9. Exodus 6:4.

26. Genesis 47:27.

27. Judges 4:7, and *passim*.

28. Numbers 18:20 and *passim*.

29. See A. Causse: Les "pauvres" d'Israel, Strasbourg, 1922. (See also Hermann Cohen: *Die Religion der Vernunft aus den Quellen des Judentums*, passim. Tr.)

30. Deuteronomy 14:27, 29.

31. *Ibid.*, 33:8ff.

32. Joshua 9:27.

33. Numbers 8:16, and Ezra 8:20.

34. Max Weber: *Das antike Judentum*, p. 181f. See N. W. Porteous: "The Basis of the Ethical Teachings of the Prophets," in: *Studies in Old Testament Prophecy*, Edinburgh, 1950, p. 143.

PART III
Prophecy as a Way of Life

1

Prophecy in History

Abraham and Moses

Abraham and Moses dominate the entire sequence of Hebrew tradition. Whereas the former is its herald, it is born with the latter. With them we come to the basic types of the prophetism of the Biblical canon. All the prophets of that canon are either prophets of the type of Abraham or of that of Moses. Although Biblical criticism denies their antiquity in the prophetic series, it must refer to them as to a beginning. At whatever time in history their characteristic features were definitely outlined, they represented Biblical prophecy in its most frequent and authentic forms. We shall try to define these forms and thus present, in connection with Abraham and Moses, a short survey of Biblical prophecy.

I.

Abraham is called *navi* once in Genesis (20:7). We may suppose that his prophetic function is alluded to a second time in the ancient prayer that was recited in connection with the offering of the first fruit (Deuteronomy 26:5).There we read: "My father was a wandering Aramean." The words "wandering Aramean" most probably refer to Abraham. But the expression "my father" implies not only a patriarchal meaning. "My father" is a technical term used at certain times for the prophets, who were addressed with the words "my father," and this was not only done by their disciples but by all those who talked respectfully of the prophets. Similarly, the prophets used the words "my son" when addressing others.

Those passages, however, are not as important as the way in which the Bible presents Abraham's personality. Even if the term *navi* were not found in the text, it would still be evident that Abraham's conduct is in many respects that of a *navi*. There are many proofs for this fact, since the text confers on Abraham many traits which appear only rarely with many another prophet. Somehow, his entire personality symbolizes prophetism.

Abraham is a prophet in the double sense of the word. He is *called* as well as *sent*. There are numerous stylistic expressions for the *call*. But two of these characterize Abraham and constitute the leitmotif for his prophetic vocation. One is "Go forth," which is used at the beginning and at the end of Abraham's career (Genesis 12:1 and 22:2), and which is also the theme of the investiture. It seems that this is how God addresses Abraham when He calls on him for a hard and important task. The other one is the very use of his name (Genesis 22:1 and 11). This is an intimate formula which we find with many other prophets.[1] Abraham's call is related to a mission; he is sent to other people in order to convey the divine message. The text limits the human community to Abraham's own family: "For I have known him, so that he may command his children and his household after him, to keep the way of the Lord, to do righteousness and justice; to the end that the Lord may bring upon Abraham that which He hath spoken of him." (18, 19). This important verse reveals the relation which exists between the election (designated by the term *yadoa*[2]) and the mission. The promise made to Abraham will not materialize because Abraham has been chosen but rather because he will have to convey to others—here, his family—the message he has received from God. This is the very prophetic

plan: the realization of the prophecy depends not only
on the revelation received by the prophet but also on his
communication with others and the use they will make
of it.

Although, according to the letter of that verse, the
message given to Abraham was only meant for his family,
the revelation and the encounter have widely different
forms. God reveals Himself to him in a word, in a vision,
and even in an ecstasis, since there is a great difference
between the nearly rational visions that we are told about
in Genesis 12:7; 17:1; and 18:1 on the one hand, and the
theophany of the fifteenth chapter on the other side. In
the former the vision is fast dissolved in a dialogue,
whereas in chapter 15 it is accompanied by a deep slumber,
a terror, cosmic incidents, and finally God's mysterious
passing between the "pieces" of the sacrifice. There is a
strange atmosphere, since the slumber and the anxiety
are possibly the phenomena of an ecstasis. In any case, in
this revelation Abraham is a prophet as well as a seer.[2a]

We meet with the same variety in the encounter. In
Genesis 20:7, where Abraham is called a *navi*, he is an
intercessor with God. In order to be cured, Abimelech
needs Abraham's mediation and prayer. This is a function he shares with all prophets. Jeremiah did not forget
that Moses and Samuel descended from those famous
intercessors (Jeremiah 15:1), and he as well as Ezekiel[3]
had on several occasions been solicited by the people.
We must, however, keep in mind that Abraham was not
solicited by the people but by an individual, as had been
the case with the very earliest prophets.[4] In Genesis 14
Abraham has the features of an *inspired warrior*. He resembles the "judges," whom the spirit of God sends into
battle. Elsewhere he is a *cultic prophet*. God's revelation
and call are often accompanied by the building of an altar
and a sacrificial offering. These are ritual acts through
which are manifested God's word to Abraham as well

as the latter's word to others. This connection with priesthood is vividly illustrated in the encounter with Malkizedek, where, facing the priest of Salem, Abraham is God's prophet-priest (Genesis 14:20).

And yet, these variations of Abraham's prophetic experience could be considered conventional, without touching the real nature of his prophetism, which, however, shows itself in other forms that are more substantial although they are not so clearly apparent.

The predominating aspect in Abraham's religious experience is the permanent dialogue with God. With a simplicity and a spontaneity which, even from a purely literary viewpoint, do not have their equal in the religious annals of other peoples, the Bible tells us that God spoke to Abraham, that Abraham spoke to God, and that there went on between the two a constant and simple exchange. This is also valid for those patriarchs who succeeded Abraham and for the entire subsequent history of the people who were chosen in Abraham. Here we find the most remarkable and typical feature of the Bible stories: the dialogue between the divine and the human is taken for granted, a natural consequence of the structure of the world. The *Word* is not offered to all, but it is always offered to some, and it is precisely the prophets who are invited to a divine intimacy. They reach a degree of revelation which the Bible calls "face to face," and which we see realized in a more or less perfect way in each of the prophetic revelations mentioned in the Bible. We see immediately a prophet in Abraham, because he is one of those who share in that dialogue.

But with Abraham that intimacy with God has a particular shading that we find only with the most prominent Biblical prophets. The admirable second part of Genesis 18 is not merely a pathetic dialogue between man and God but rather an account of a collaboration between the divine and the human within the progress of the world. God

needs man for the realization of His plans. He is not
entirely free to let His creation take care of itself but
He needs the assistance of His creatures. Justice is the
result of the cooperation between God and humanity.
"Shall I hide from Abraham what I am doing?" (Genesis 18:17). The prophets are the chosen ones on whom
God can and must count, and without whom God's work
is in danger of miscarrying. ". . . the Lord God will do
nothing without revealing His counsel to His servants
the prophets." (Amos 3:7). This thought is the basis
for that chapter in Genesis. The prophets were deeply
convinced that their intimacy with God and with His
plans and secrets was not simply part of the revelation
which God granted them but rather a necessary condition
for the fulfillment of the divine word. Thus the prophets'
interceding function takes on an entirely new meaning.
The prophets' main purpose is not to inform God of people's desires but the opposite: to serve as an intermediary
between the divine intention and the reality of the world.
The transmission of the divine Word into history is done
at the very moment when the prophet receives a revelation. This transmission is indeed necessary, for without
it the divine intention would remain suspended and would
never reach the world. Although this may appear con-
ceited, this conception seemed to the prophets to be as
unavoidable and naïve as that of a dialogue between God
and man. Since revelation was always possible, it could
be translated into terms of action only when it was con-
fided to the prophets. Abraham is one of those men to
whom God not only confides a message but His concern.
He is not only God's mouthpiece but His confidant. He
has a part in the divine mystery. He is a prophet in the
Biblical sense of that term.

Finally, Abraham is the prophet who is *on the march*.
The very first word which God addresses to Abraham demands an uprooting. The theme of change which appears

under different forms with all prophets[5] is presented in this case with the rigor of an absolute. Abraham becomes a prophet by leaving his kindred and birthplace shortly, by becoming someone else. On the way to Haran, Abraham walks alone towards the unknown, toward the "land which God will show him" (Genesis 12:1). God can find him anywhere. God makes a covenant with a nomad. Prophecy is a joint march, and Amos was to choose that very expression as a definition of prophecy. It comes to life in the existence of Abraham.

II.

Like Abraham, Moses combines in his own person aspects of prophetism which in other instances are found only separately. He has something of the martial exaltation of the Judges when he slays the Egyptian (Exodus 2:12) and later when he proclaims a holy war against Amalek (Exodus 17) and the Midianites (Numbers 31). More than Abraham, he is like a cultic prophet when he assumes the office of a priest at the nomadic sanctuary in the desert (Exodus 20). The theophany of Sinai, too, is preceded by a ritual act (Exodus 24), and cult and revelation seem to be inseparable there. Moses is an intercessor with God, and also His confidant, and God asks for his cooperation in order to carry out his intentions. He communicates with God through vision and the word. He, too, is a seer and a prophet; he is called upon and sent forth. Finally, and again like Abraham, Moses is torn away from his milieu in order to fulfill his mission, which is the beginning of a journey, an endless wandering.

But there is another experience which characterizes Moses, and which was unknown to Abraham. It introduces an important factor into Biblical prophetism. Moses experiences the *suffering* of the prophetic vocation. Whatever God told Abraham was accepted by him with equanimity—the call, the departure, faith, the struggle, and even the trial. He *believes* in God (Genesis 15 :6). Even when the divine command tells him to sacrifice his son, he does not hesitate, for there are only two possibilities: either God's demand is justified, so that it must be obeyed; or it is only a trial, for then God will show His justice. Abraham does not suspect God of a mistake or of injustice. His faith is absolute. He is the prophet of certainty.

Moses is the prophet of doubt, refusal, revolt. One must always come back to him when we look for an example of the prophecy of *suffering*.

The abundance and the firmness of the psychological features of Moses prove that we are not only dealing with a more intense experience than that of Abraham, but we get the impression of a different nature. Moses' prophecy is of a very different sort from that of Abraham. The prophetic type incarnated in Abraham is less complicated than that represented by Moses. It is above all less mysterious. Abraham is a *sheltered* prophet, whereas Moses is the prophet of surrender. The two correspond to different conceptions of the relations between God and man. For Abraham they are relations of confidence; for Moses they are relations of terror. With Moses revelation assumes a more tragic character, and the literary prophets were to hold on to this aspect of prophecy. This has to do with the fact that an Abrahamitic prophet is an individual, whereas the Mosiac prophet is implanted into the history of a people.

Abraham's only mission was to live, to believe, and to progress. His message was valuable only for a generation yet unborn. Moses' mission puts him in the very midst of a human community. This is the beginning of an encounter, of a struggle, of a dialogue between people. This is so much more difficult, so extremely different from a simple dialogue with God, and sometimes comes so close to failure that God offers Moses the option of becoming a new Abraham, a prophet-patriarch: "I will make of thee a great nation" (Exodus 32:10). What characterizes Biblical prophecy since the time of Moses is that the election of Moses is accompanied by the election of a people, and this is not for the distant future but in an immediate fulfillment, and that without the existence of that chosen people Moses' prophecy would have been radically different and would have had to start in an entirely new form. The materialization of the revelation made to Abraham depends on Abraham's faith, and then on the maturing of the work accomplished by God. On the other hand, the materialization of the revelation made to Moses depends jointly on the faith of Moses and of the people. A dialectic of the prophet and the people is added to that of the prophet and God. Just as, on the level of revelation, the divine and the human are tied to each other, on the stage of the encounter the individual and the community are linked to each other in their human expressions.

The Earliest Prophets

I.

"I raised up of your sons for prophets, and of your young men for Nazarites." In these words Amos (2:11) expresses the good things God had done for the benefit of Israel as the fulfillment of the clauses of the covenant made at the exodus from Egypt (2:10; 3:1). At the same time he mentions the spiritual models whom he uses in his capacity as a prophet. Although elsewhere he denies being a prophet (7:14), he is quite aware of the fact that he is in the line of the prophets. But he rejects the confusion with those prophets around him who are not truly inspired. Nevertheless he claims to be connected with the earlier prophets who, together with the Nazarites, were the living witnesses of God's concern.

The association between prophets and Nazarites is not only logical from a moral point of view, since both groups promoted the ideal of religious and ethical virtue, but it also corresponds to a historical reality implied by Amos in a formula which must not be limited to the ninth century, when the prophets around Elijah and Elisha and the Rechabite Nazarites fought for the same principles. Amos refers rather to a more remote period, the one immediately following the exodus and the conquest, both of which are mentioned in chapter 2, verse 10. Similarly, the period of the Judges, which was the beginning of political life in Israel, is characterized by the existence and the encounter of prophets and Nazarites.

The time between Joshua and Samuel is typical for a *charisma*. The political power is mainly a temporary one, and it belongs to the one whom God has chosen and invested with His Spirit. That investiture is done suddenly, by an exaltation of physical and spiritual powers. It confers to the chosen one a reign which ceases only when the divine spirit is withdrawn. The divine choice is arbitrary and surprising. Although sometimes it affects individuals who through their proper conduct had been predisposed to the reception of the power, it often also comes to people who apparently had not been predestined for such important functions, such as women (Deborah) and outlaws (Jephta). All this properly belongs to the domain of prophetic election, since both the investiture through the spirit and the arbitrariness of the choice are of the very essence of the prophetic experience. In that sense the Judge is a prophet, and we are not surprised to find that term applied to Deborah (Judges 4:4).

But at least one of the Judges is also called a Nazarite. Samson has the exterior signs of the Nazarite vocation —he drinks no wine nor cuts his hair. However, Samson is exceptional, for it was not he who sought his condition but his mother, who imposed it after being given divine orders (chapter 13). The child is "sanctified" from birth. Before birth he is prepared for an exceptional fate. This is one of the facets of prophetic election, and it reappears with Samuel (I Samuel 1). Jeremiah had experienced it quite clearly (Jeremiah 1:5). Thus Deborah is a judge and a prophetess at the same time, just as Samson is a prophet and a Nazarite. The charisma of his designation as a leader, which in itself would assure him the role of prophet, is being stressed by the mysterious notion of a predestination, whose importance for their own election had been experienced by other prophets.

Since thus prophetism and the state of Nazarite are associated at the time of the Judges, knowing the one ought to be helpful for the understanding of the other. While Nazarites existed all through Hebrew history, they did not always appear in the same form. In the Code of the Nazarite (Numbers 6) the moral form predominates, whereas elsewhere we have ascetic features. In addition, the Nazarite is equipped for battle, as if the acceptance of the vows released physical forces in him. Therefore he is a fighter.

Early in Hebrew society it is clear that the "struggles" engaged in by the Nazarites are real wars. It is noteworthy that the Judges, too, are elected for war. They appear and disappear, because of battles. When the spirit seizes them, it is to turn them into military leaders. Apparently the makeup of Hebrew society admitted at first of two radically different classes of warriors. Some were "heroes," professional soldiers, "hidalgos," according to the excellent notion of Max Weber.[6] These were recruited from among city dwellers who were able to arm themselves, which assured their political independence and power. This knighthood, which originally had been of Canaanite origin, admitted Hebrews after a while. The

more Hebrews settled in cities, the more of them entered
that soldierly nobility. At the time of the Judges certain
"heroes" were still Canaanites, whereas some were Hebrews. They represented a permanent knighthood, but
they followed the call by a leader only when they deemed
the fight necessary and profitable. The Song of Deborah
contains a complaint about the city of Meroz whose
"heroes" did not come forth to help the troops of Barak
and Deborah at a time when they were counted upon
(Judges 5:23).

Along with those professional soldiers there were oc-
casional Israelites. They did not enter the fight for political considerations but because of their enthusiastic
faith. They were conscious of defending an ideal and a
religious community, and they were driven on by the
spirit. We have in mind the Nazarites. During military
campaigns they felt perhaps bound by certain ascetic rules
which were meant to excite them.[7] In the Song of Deborah
they are called "those who offer themselves willingly"
(Judges 5:2 and 9), which implies the spontaneous character of their mission. Those soldiers of the faith must
have looked shabby in comparison with the "heroes."
They were usually fewer in number and had fewer resources and weapons (see Judges 5:8: "Was there a
shield or a spear seen among forty thousand in Israel?"),
but they had an exalted idea of their mission and unshakable courage.

Being prepared for a sacred battle was to remain a
predominating trait of Biblical prophetism. It arose and
grew during the first centuries of the conquest and the
subsequent installation of Israel in Canaan. At first we
see it animate the Nazarites and the Judges. But then
this quality appears also with the prophets. All prophets
are fighters for their faith. By and by their fights gain a
more spiritual character. But Samuel still fights on the
battlefield, just as Deborah and Samson had done.[8] Elijah

meets the prophets of Baal face to face.[9] As indicated, Deborah and Samson show additional features of the Nazarite. The investiture of Jeremiah, one of the last of the great literary prophets, is that of a fighter, and we know that he fought with the citizens of Jerusalem. In common with Samson and Samuel, he is predestined for his mission even from before his birth:

"Before I formed thee in the belly I knew thee, and before thou camest forth out of the womb I sanctified thee; I have appointed thee a prophet unto the nations." (Jeremiah 1:5.)

In the celibacy imposed on him (16:2) we have perhaps a Nazarite rule, at least in a symbolic way. In any case, and like all Judges of Hebrew antiquity, he knows that he has been called upon for combat and for war. The verses which describe his investiture could as well be applied to Deborah or Gideon. Although the climate is different and there is more at stake, the basic tendency remains the same. Just like the political charisma of the Judges, the political charisma of Jeremiah is still a call to war:

"See, I have this day set thee over the nations and over the kingdoms, to root out and to pull down, and to destroy and to overthrow; to build, and to plant." (Jeremiah 1:10.)

"For behold, I have made thee this day a fortified city, and an iron pillar and brazen walls, against the whole land, against the kings of Judah, against their princes thereof, their priests thereof, and against the people of the land. And they shall fight against thee; but they shall not prevail against thee; For I am with thee, saith the Lord, to deliver thee." (1:18-19.)

We may suppose that if the charisma of the judges constitutes the source of the concept of a prophetic fight, it can also instruct us concerning the scope of that idea.

The wars in which the Judges engaged have perhaps certain characteristics which the prophets did not take exception to either when they were ready to fight within their prophetic vocation.

The feeling of national unity expressed in the Song of Deborah[10] has often been emphasized. The Israelite tribes, who differ so much from one another, are united by the spiritual link of the national religion, best expressed in the covenant, which makes Israel the *people of God,* and God the *God of Israel.* The antiquity of these two terms is proven by their frequent use in the Song of Deborah (Judges 5:3, 5, and 11). They do not merely have a symbolic meaning as do other doubles in the terminology of the covenant (God the Father, Israel the child; God the Husband, Israel the wife; God the Master, Israel the servant), but they stand for the concrete link which ties a God to a people. These expressions do not owe their existence to a reflection on the situation of Israel, but they define that situation in a spontaneous way. They were to become familiar with the prophets, since all of them are carried away by a national fervor which measures up well with that of Deborah's epoch. Herein lies one of the prophetic aspects of the Song of Deborah. Just as the author of that Song, the prophets see in national unity a unity within a religious community. They always consider Israel to be an entity, and beyond all political dissensions and intertribal struggles they go on believing in an internal and spiritual unity of those associated with God. Elijah builds an altar of twelve stones on Mount Carmel which symbolizes the religious unity of Jacob-Israel.[11] All the great literary prophets are active in both the Kingdom of Samaria and that of Jerusalem. Their message is valid *for Judah and for Israel.* Finally, after the catastrophes, the surviving prophets of Judah cannot conceive of the return without taking in the tribes of the North. On every occasion the feeling of national unity has remained alive with the prophets.

But although the prophets were not the only ones who experienced that feeling and kept it alive, they expressed it in a very original manner. To them, loyalty and treason had nothing to do with politics. The unity of the nation did not depend on the patriotism of the Israelites but on their attachment to the covenant. A fight for God, or better *with* God was, according to the prophets, a just fight from the national point of view. A fight without God was impious and politically absurd. This opinion explains to some degree the attitude of a Jeremiah, whose evident political treason was indeed, in the consciousness of the prophet, the authentic loyalty to the covenant. Now a similar intuition can be found in the Song of Deborah. It seems to me very important to point out that from the very beginning there existed a feeling which was not given to the prophets by the great historical events from the eighth century on, but which was originally contained in Hebrew thinking.

The Song of Deborah tells of a battle in which not all Hebrew tribes seem to have been interested. What was at stake was probably the establishment or re-establishment, in the valley of Kishon, of routes of communication which had been interrupted between the north and the south. The frontier tribes of the valley—Issachar, Zebulun, and Naphtali—accepted the battle, whereas the more remote tribes did not respond to the call. From a merely political point of view, that refusal can be well understood. The faraway tribes had other concerns which seemed to them as urgent as the reconquest of the Kishon. But the Song protests against such a concept. The battle merited the unanimity of the members of the people of God, since it was led by God. The importance of the battle did not depend on political circumstances, like the re-

doubtable strength of the enemy or the value of the land
to be held or conquered. It depended solely on the fact
that God had entered the fight. God had the right to
count on His soldiers, on all of His soldiers. God had
indeed started the fight. He comes from Seir and from
Edom.[12] The earth, the heavens and the clouds have understood this and prepared a path for Him. The moun-
tains, like Sinai, make room for the God of Israel. Could
He therefore not count on His cohorts, on His own people? The stars of the heavens, the River Kishon on earth
have come to the aid of God and fought side by side with
Him[13]—and His own soldiers, in the midst of His people,
have deserted Him! This is the meaning of the reproaches
which the author addresses to the Hebrew defectors. God
led the battle, and they ought to have joined Him. This
is precisely one of the basic meanings which the prophets
were to give to the political fights which they were to
witness. They also adopted the opposite idea, one which
the Song of Deborah did not have an occasion to spell
out—that if God does not join the fight, one must keep
out of it.

II.

Gideon is the type of the Judge-Prophet. He was invested under miraculous circumstances in order to fight
the Midianite invasion, but he remained in constant dialogue with God. The martial charisma does not forsake
him for one moment. His battle cry "For the Lord and
for Gideon" (Judges 7:18) is a short résumé of the certainty which the Song of Deborah had expressed all along.
God is with Gideon in war, and the war is just, because
the revelation of the presence of God is ever at the side
of Gideon.

Interestingly enough, an incident occurs at the beginning of Gideon's career which is not directly connected

with the war against the Midianites. The text tells us
that on the very same night that God had invested Gideon as a military leader, He also charged him with an additional and more urgent mission, namely, to destroy the
altar of the Baal which belonged to his father, Joash, to
demolish the Ashera, and to build in their stead an altar
to God and to offer a sacrifice with the wood of that
Ashera. The undertaking was not without danger. Gideon acted in secret, then he fled, and the Israelites of
Ophra demanded that he should be delivered into their
hands for punishment (Judges 6:25-32.)

This episode is under suspicion by the critical school
which sees in it nothing but a later and even inexact mo-
tivation for the epithet of Jerubaal which Gideon had.
They also find it strange that Gideon should have been
the only Judge whose fight was not merely political but
religious. However, when we consider what the Baal and
the Ashera meant to the ancient Hebrews, we realize
that hostility toward the Baal could not appear more logically than at the very time of Gideon.

The literature of Ras-Shamra has brought to light the
fact that the Canaanite territory was the place par excellence for the cult of the Baal. Although the Baal was
worshipped virtually throughout the Middle East, the
cult was nowhere as systematized as in Canaan. In Canaan
every locality, every hill, every source had its master, its
Baal, and every place consecrated to the Baal had its
Ashera. Whether that Ashera was a pale, a piece of wood,
or the trunk of a tree, it probably represents the feminine
counterpart to the Baal, who in the cultic places is symbolized as a Matzevah, an erect piece of rock in a phallic
form. The Baal and the Ashera are a divine couple. Their
promiscuity in the elevated places of Canaan has promoted everywhere ritual excesses. When, at the end of the
tenth century, the Baal of Tyre, who himself was of
Phrygian origin, was introduced in Canaan, he was to

find a soil long since prepared for the orgiastic forms of the cult.

The influence of the Baal cult on the Hebrew conquerors is one of the fundamental themes of Biblical history. The gross enticements of the ritual excesses, and the simple fact that the religion of the Baals extended equally over the entire country, supported what prophets were later to call the *prostitution* of Israel to the Baal. This is a factor of assimilation, occurring frequently when an already civilized country is conquered by a new people. In Canaan, however, the problem presented itself by still another aspect. For here it was not two homogeneous nations meeting; the social structures of Canaan and Israel were diametrically opposed. The civilization of Canaan was sedentary and rustic. Even the big cities were nothing but market places for the produce of the countryside, which constituted the vital center of the land. The religion of the Baal was agrarian in essence and in its rites. We have alrady remarked that the presence of the Baal at a certain place guaranteed a proprietor's claim to his piece of land. The cult of the couple Baal-Ashera made the ground fertile, and the sexual rites contributed to the fecundity of the soil. The frequent presentation of the Baal in the form of a bull corresponded also to the farmer's need to have his god assure the seasonal productivity of his plot of ground.

Israel's civilization was just the opposite. When they entered Canaan they were a nomad people like all other nomad tribes bordering Canaan at the north, east, and south. Following the conquest by the Hebrews, two civilizations were at grips within Canaan, the one sedentary and rural, the other one nomad and pastoral. The latter weakened more and more, and the colonization of Israel in Canaan was accompanied by a slow but obstinate tendency toward a sedentary way of life. The Israelite nomads changed into peasants.

This movement was irresistible. Hebrew nomad society underwent a progressive reform, which also affected its religion. Hebrew religion became *Baalic,* not only because the cult of the Baals existed in Canaan, but because it was the cult of the sedentary peasants and also because in its brutality it answered the instinctive religious needs of the "man of the land," the *am haaretz.*[14] The prostitution to the Baal was thus the corollary of the progressive sedentary transformation of Israel. The more the latter developed, the more apparent became the former. The more the latter progressed, the greater did the threat of the former become for the very foundations of the ancient Hebrew religion.

Now at the time of Gideon sedentary life reached its culminating point. The Midianite invasion, which the Bible places at that moment, is an attempt by a new nomad people to invade Canaan. After the Hyksos, the Arameans, the Hebrews, and the Philistines, it was then the turn of the Midianites to try their luck. Coming from the south, the Arabian desert, they passed through Transjordania.[15] They then threatened to cross the Jordan, just as Israel had done several centuries before. A new confrontation is in the offing between a sedentary people and a nomad one, the Midianites, but this time the rural nation is no longer Canaan but Israel, that had succeeded in integrating itself more and more deeply in Canaan, eventually to supplant the Canaanite masses who had just achieved a sedentary structure. The hero of the Israelite resistance toward the Midianite invasion was the peasant Gideon, and this not by accident. For the Hebrew peasants were the first to feel the threat, and they felt that they were strong enough to organize a military defense. The war between Israel and Midian was a struggle between *barley bread* and the *tent,* between the symbol of the peasant and that of the nomad, as they are spelled out in a dream mentioned in the Bible, thus suggesting the true meaning of the conflict (Judges 7:13-14.)

It is therefore not surprising that in the same story we hear at the very same time the Israelite peasants had become familiar with cult of the Baal. It was quite a natural development that the adoption of the Baal followed the coming of a rural system. The change to sedentary ways corresponded to the change initiated by the temptation of the Baal.

Nor is it surprising to hear that at that very same hour the shameful cult of Baal had taken on an aggressive and violent form. The problem thus became unavoidable. In order to safeguard Hebrew religion from any Baalic contacts, one had either to regress to a nomad way of life or to demand of the peasant, who had become settled, to reject once and for all the cult of the Baal. Whether Gideon intervened personally in this dilemma, depends on the interpretation of the text. But we cannot reject the idea that the problem had to come to the fore in Gideon's time. According to the Biblical text, Gideon's intervention was preceded by that of an *ish-navi,* a man-prophet, one of those anonymous nomad emissaries who were inspired for one day, the primitive representatives of Hebrew prophetism. His brief message sounds authentic and ancient:

"The Lord sent a prophet unto the children of Israel; and He said unto them: Thus saith the Lord, the God of Israel: I brought you up from Egypt, and brought you forth out of the house of bondage; and I delivered you out of the hand of the Egyptians, and out of the hand of all that oppressed you, and drove them out from before you, and gave you their land. And I said unto you: I am the Lord your God; ye shall not fear the gods of the Amorites, in whose land ye dwell; but ye have not obeyed my voice." (Judges 6, 8:10.)

In the agonizing appeal made by the "man of God" we find an echo to the frequently found Biblical statement that Israel had at that time become a peasant people. This is the dawn of the great prophetic protest against the cult of the Baal. It has always the undertone of the call to a return to the nomad ideal. The feverish anti-Baalic activity of an Elijah, a Jehu, and the pathetic invectives of an Amos, a Hosea, and a Jeremiah are already contained in the appearance of this anonymous and nomad prophet on the occasion of the war against Midian, and in his short but meaningful message which fits in so well with the logic of Hebrew history.

At the time of Gideon, the triumph of Israelite rusticity is accompanied by a feeling of inner strength and unity which leads to a radical change in the political system. The Israelite peasants offer Gideon royal and hereditary rank. But he refuses with the words "the Lord shall rule over you." (Judges 8:23.) Historians believe that, contrary to the Biblical affirmation, Gideon did accept.[16] This would then be the first royal dynasty in Israel. It covered only a few mountain tribes; from the very beginning it led to strifes among jealous tribes, and it collapsed tragically shortly after Gideon's death. Nevertheless it has all the features of a true sovereignty. Gideon transformed his native village of Ophra into the capital city. He installed there a court, a cult, and a harem, and he imposed taxes. Through a political marriage he allied himself with the dignitaries of the still Canaanite city of Shechem (Judges 8:22ff.) This was the first sketch of a kingship which might be compared with that of Saul or David at their beginnings.

But Gideon's refusal has also a larger meaning. It was not put into his mouth by a later antiroyalist writer, but is the testimony of an opinion contemporary with Gideon, which was spread far and wide in many Israelite circles. Jotham's fable (Judges 9:7ff.) proves the existence of

an antiroyalist attitude even among the peasants, and a
persevering will to freedom which could not be entirely
wiped out by the settlement in Canaan. Even if Gideon
did not reject the crown, many of his contemporaries
would have liked to see him do so. This is true primarily
of the prophets. For to reject the regime of the Judges
in order to install a hereditary one meant the denial of the
value of the political charisma. At the midst of an epoch
as charismatic as that of the Judges, when every political
investiture was the manifestation of God's will and
presence, the adoption of a hereditary regime could only
be resented by those who were familiar with inspiration.
The prophets, the Judges, and all those elected by God
considered this an attempt to drive God out of political
life and to entrust the life of the people to men who had
no immediate contact with God.

From the point of view of history, Gideon's refusal to
accept the crown is therefore of the same value as his
destruction of the altar of the Baal. Whether those were
really his own attitudes or not, they were symptomatic of
a spirit which prevailed at the height of the rural civilization in Israel. At that time arose the prophetic protest
against the Baal and the equally prophetic claim that God
is the only King. Those two themes allow of many nuances, but here they are expressed for the first time. From
then on they were to become permanent in prophetic
thinking.

III.

In the Song of Deborah God intervenes as a warrior.
He is the Leader of the battle and consequently takes up
functions which, on the human plane, belong to the Judge.
It is therefore not surprising that in another passage in
the Book of Judges God is clearly called a Judge: "the
Lord, the Judge, be judge this day between the children

of Israel and the children of Ammon" (11:27). But this is not said in connection with the Song of Deborah. It is not the case of a battle but of *arbitration*. The conflict between Ammon and Israel has an ideological background. Ammon contests Israel's territorial claim, which goes back three hundred years. Israel refutes the argument and calls on the God of Israel to be the arbitrator. We have here the beginning of a theological concept about Israel's relations with its neighbors. We observe the vestige of a certain universalism, the idea of a moral agreement valid for all peoples of the Middle East who are Israel's neighbors, an agreement vouchsafed by the God of Israel. We know what range and depth the prophets of the eighth century were to give to what one of them called "the brotherly covenant" (Amos 1:9). We may suppose that, from the time of the Judges, prophetic thinking tended toward that concept of a God who watched over the fulfillment of the clauses of a covenant which He had made with the people whom He had created and whose destiny in history He guided.

This assumption leads to another. The human judge, the image of the Divine Judge, did not only have military and political functions. He actually dispensed justice, established the right, and came to the defense of the oppressed. Thus he accomplished *within* the people of Israel what God was supposed to fulfill among the various nations, namely, the protection of the covenant, the Levitical charter of which, the Torah, had an eminently social character. By assuming the functions of an arbitrator of the law of the Torah—as a protector—and as an advocate of the poor and oppressed, the Judge anticipated the later prophetic attitude. When the Judges gave way to kings, and their charismatic function became an institutional one, the prophets at once adopted the mission which had previously been fulfilled by the Judges. They confronted the political justice of kings and their

PROPHECY IN HISTORY 201

subordinates with the divine right of the charter of the poor. The somber scenes of moral anarchy with which the Book of Judges concludes show that the Judge had many occasions for demanding that people ought to act according to the law of the Torah. Levites and priests are mentioned in the text as aides to the Judge. Later on we shall find these side by side with the prophet, whose place had previously been occupied by the Judge.

IV.

Towards the end of the eleventh century there erupted a crisis in Israel which transformed the political structure of the country and substituted for the charismatic Judge the hereditary King. On the occasion of that crisis the prophets, from then on known by the technical term of *neviim,* appear in great numbers in Hebrew history. Nearly all the actors in that crisis are presented in the Bible as *neviim,* be they temporary or permanent ones. The last of the Judges, Samuel, the counselor of his people and the man who was to anoint the first two kings, is a loyal prophet.[17] The first king, Saul, is seized by the Spirit and transformed into another person,[18] and that change is accompanied by certain prophetic experiences: "Is Saul also among the prophets?"[19] The second king, David, is also inspired, and transported by the divine spirit.[20] In the background we feel the presence of anonymous prophets who must have had a decisive role in the great political events of their time.

In such an atmosphere overloaded with prophetism, we can easily find some of the traits which characterize the prophetism of the preceding epoch. Like Samson, Samuel is a Nazarite. He belongs to the category of the *predestined* ones, those who are entirely consecrated to God and prepared for a fight. At that time the fight was still a military or political one. Samuel repairs the damages

done to a vanquished nation. He stops the invasion of
the Philistines. He proclaims holy wars, and on the occasion of one of these there erupts the conflict between
Samuel and the first king, whom he himself had
anointed.[21] In all of these situations Samuel is a true
Judge, and he remains just that when, with an implacable
intransigence, he follows up a principle which had been
defended by the Judges—the political charisma. The
great prophetic protest against a hereditary royalty finds
in Samuel its most typical incarnation. Gideon's gesture
had only been a sympton, but Samuel's ratifies a dogma.
God is Israel's only King, and it is up to Him to elect His
representative and vicar. That election lasts as long as
the spirit, the *ruach*. When the spirit withdraws, the
king falls.[22] It is characteristic that the people did not
offer Samuel personally what they had offered Gideon.
Thus Samuel holds on to the absolute role of a prophet.
That he himself should become king is out of the question; but the demand for a king must be submitted to him.
He is God's authentic and constant mouthpiece. He makes
a king and unmakes him. These are exactly the functions
which the prophets were to have from then on. In the
future no investiture or dethronement is thinkable without intervention by the prophets.[23]

In the political arena, therefore, the prophetism of
the time of Samuel only broadens previous trends. But
in two other important respects it presents itself in a
new form.

For the first time the prophets appear as a compact
brotherhood. They are led by a *father,* and they themselves are called the *sons of the prophets.* This phenomenon, which is noted in the Bible from the beginning of
the eleventh century on, was to last until the end of the
ninth, and the prophetic brotherhoods of the time of Samuel and Saul are reflected in those of the period of the
Omrides. Only as late as the eighth century did the

prophets resume the individual character of the time of the Judges.

The *collective* character of prophetism is joined by a purely *ecstatic* one. The investiture is not limited to the gift of the spirit but also involves an increase in physical or spiritual powers. Ecstatic phenomena come to the fore, and the spirit is transmitteed by individual or collective suggestion.[24] The enthusiasm leads to a delirium which is accompanied by frenetic gestures, the shedding of clothes, and prostration.[25] Dancing, singing, and music create an atmosphere of exaltation which the charisma of the Judges had not known.[26]

What is the connection, if any, between the collective aspect and the ecstatic form of that new prophetism? Were the brotherhoods schools of initiation, where a mystic discipline led adolescents to a prophetic vocation? This is hardly credible. Several authors have shown that we tend to give the words "father" and "sons," when used in connection with the prophets, a meaning which the text did not have in mind. Though there were prophetic brotherhoods at the time of the Bible, prophetic *schools* probably never existed. A disciplinary institution where members are instructed in precise methods is one thing; a simple association, where people meet because certain occasions call for similar tasks, is quite another thing.

Numerous historians, however, have pointed out that a more reliable analogy can be found regarding the Phrygian, Phoenician, and Greek prophetisms.[27] Phrygian and Phoenician prophetisms are characterized by ecstases, and Greek chresmology by its collective and popular aspect. Therefore certain historians embrace the hypothesis that the Israelite prophetism of the eleventh century, which was ecstatic as well as collective, was part of a great current which, having originated in Phrygia, passed through Phoenicia, reached Israel from there toward the eleventh century, and then extended into Greece.[28]

The prophetism of Israel in the eleventh century would then be something radically new, without equivalent in previous Israelite history. It would rather have been taken over from neighboring countries, and, in a weakened form, it would have yielded in the eighth century to a new prophetism—literary prophecy.

But that theory cannot be accepted without criticism. We have just shown that, at least in certain aspects, the prophetism of the eleventh century was closely related to the one that prevailed in previous centuries in Israel. The permanence of a political charisma and its important repercussions on the question of a royal dynasty established an undeniable continuity between the two prophetic epochs in Israel. It must nevertheless be admitted that prophetism was not entirely new. But even in its original aspects Hebrew prophetism cannot be compared with foreign. One question arises immediately: Since, as the texts of Ras-Shamra show, the ecstatic prophetism of Phoenicia is very old, why should its influence be felt only in the eleventh century, at a time when the Hebrews had already been installed for centuries in a Phoenician sphere of influence? Moreover, Phoenician ecstasis carries an element that is totally absent from the Hebrew prophetism of the eleventh century—the rite of bloody mutilations. Now that rite was indeed adopted in the ninth century by the prophets in Israel, at the time of the Omrides, when Phoenician civilization was officially imported.[29] This means that from the time that cultural exchanges between Phoenicia and Israel are unquestionable, Israelite prophecy remodels its rites according to Phoenician prototypes. Thus we are led to the conclusion that if before that time the prophetic ecstasis in Israel did not have the basic rite of mutilation, the Phoenician influence had not yet made itself felt. Therefore Israelite prophetism is not a direct outcome of Phoenician ecstasis, and if there is at all an analogy between the two it is not based on an

influence but because both of them probably testify to
a prophetism that had been shared at the same time by
many ancient peoples.

We find the same superficiality in a supposed analogy
between Hebrew prophetism and chresmology. It is true
that the Israelite prophets of the eleventh and ninth
centuries wandered around in groups, just as did the
chresmologists. But quite unlike the latter, they are tied
to certain localities. We see them going to and from certain centers which—and this is important—are cultic
places like Nayoth, Ramah, Jericho, Gilgal, and Beth-El.
Thus their freedom is by far not as total as that of the
chresmologists. On the other hand, the brotherhoods of
the prophets are not at all popular, but rather groups of
privileged beings. People are surprised to find that a
peasant as unrefined as Saul is among the prophets. This
is the meaning of the proverb that expresses a certain distrust of, or at least a distance from the people, as re-
gards the prophets.[30] Similarly in the ninth century the
brotherhoods of Elijah and Elisha have something mystical and aristocratic which is totally absent from the
chresmologists.

Besides this, when we mention the collective and ecstatic prophetism, we sometimes have the prophets of the
eleventh century in mind, at other times those of the ninth.
This implies a tacit admission that in the tenth century,
under David and Solomon, prophets had temporarily
disappeared. But why should that have been so? Could
the new conditions created by a stable royalty explain
the temporary disappearance of a religious mentality
which was in no way inimical to the new regime? We
should rather assume that prophetism existed also under David and Solomon, although we shall have to investigate the details. Its appearance in the eleventh and
ninth centuries can be explained only if we admit that it
had also existed in the intervening century.

Prophetism must justly be considered to have been a continuous and homogeneous movement. Its characteristic features cannot be found in the realm of ecstasis but in a domain more in accord with historical evidence. We are here faced with a form of *cultic* prophetism. As mentioned before, the prophetic brotherhoods lived in certain centers that are mainly cultic places like Nayoth, Ramah, Jericho, Gilgal, and Beth-El. Samuel is not merely a prophet and a seer but he also fulfills priestly functions, and his journeys are accompanied by sacrifices and ritual meals.[31] The inspired processions in which Saul takes part have to do with "high places";[32] The most typical episode in Elijah's career is the erection or restoration of an altar and the offering of a sacrifice on Mount Carmel.[33] All the traits which we may call ecstatic originate in, or are accompanied by, cultic rites. Prophetism is not a movement of personal or mystic exaltation, but the inspiration comes from priestly rites to which the prophets subject themselves, as they were nearly always attached to the cult.

Numerous recent studies have thrown light on the importance of cultic prophetism in Israel.[34] There exists with all the people of the ancient Near East a connection between cult and prophecy. This is so also for Israel, and we ought not to neglect this important aspect of the religious life of the Hebrews. On the other hand, we must also not exaggerate it unduly and extend it over the entire history of Israelite prophetism. Cultic prophetism coincides with the prophecies of the *neviim*. Before the eleventh and after the ninth century it appears only sporadically. Historical circumstances explain the importance which prophetism acquired in Israel at the time of the foundation of the royalty.

There are indeed close ties between the rise of kingship and a profound modification in the religious structure of Israel. We witness the disappearance of the *priest-*

hood in Shiloh, the origins of which coincide with those of the people of Israel. Although the details about Israelite priesthood are controversial, all Biblical data stress the fact that the priests, too, were the objects of a charisma, and that at one time a particular family had been chosen in order to assure the service at the sanctuary as taken over from Mosiac legislation. That sanctuary was in Shiloh. With its concecrated objects and the Tent sheltering the Holy Ark, Shiloh symbolized the semi-nomad cult of the desert. Mosiac religion was observed there in its pure form. There is no sign of Canaanite influence. Shiloh was not one of those "high places" where nomad Hebrew forms had come to terms with sedentary Canaanite forms of the cult. The symbol of nomadism was preserved there in all its fascination.

But whereas the texts are silent about the real role that Shiloh and its priests played at the time of the Judges, we are well informed about weakening and the end of the sanctuary and its priesthood in the eleventh and tenth centuries. The capture of the Holy Ark during a tragic military defeat led to the destruction of the sanctuary of Shiloh[35] and the dispersion of its priests. They find themselves involved—sometimes against their own will, but always on the same side of the fence—in the great political strifes which accompanied the rise of the kingship, at which time they were always the victims. Nearly all of those who fled to Nob were wiped out by Saul.[36] When those who did escape resumed their functions under David, they had to join a rival branch that had not previously shown proof of its qualities.[37] The last representatives of the Shiloh branch were finally done away with under Solomon.[38] Thus the newly born royalty led to the fall of Shiloh as well as to the end of its priests.

The prophets reacted in two different ways to those events. At the beginning, right after the destruction of Shiloh, they replaced the failing priests. Although Sam-

uel, the greatest of the prophets of that time, did not
even consider the assumption of regal powers when that
question arose, he quite naturally took upon himself
priestly functions. In a remarkable analysis, Buber described Samuel's profoundly religious intentions.[39] When
the Holy Ark could have been returned, Samuel refused
to do so, which shows that he wished to create a wandering and priestly prophetism that would fulfill the nomad
ideal not only symbolically but through its very existence.
Thus started the cultic prophetism as a brotherhood
which recruited priest-prophets with branches wherever
there were sanctuaries. These groups were well defined
and migratory. They either remained with ancient cultic
places or founded new ones. Whereas Shiloh had only
been an isolated center of nomad Mosaism, prophetism
tried to propagate that nomad Mosaism all over the
country.

When David reinstalled the Holy Ark in his new capital city, Jerusalem took over the centralizing role that
Shiloh had previously occupied. But David had been
anointed by Samuel, and he himself had been initiated
into the cultic prophetic brotherhoods, who accepted his
new religious policies. From then on prophetism was
transformed. It settled in Jerusalem, and, at first near
the Tent of the Ark, subsequently in Solomon's Temple,
it maintained a prophetic atmosphere whose exterior
features faithfully reproduced the prophetism of Samuel's time, for instance the music and the choirs, which
had occupied an important place there, and also collective
inspiration. Those texts that show that the descendants
of Samuel were prophets and Levites in the Temple of
Solomon[40] are not based on fiction, but tell us what became of prophetism: The prophets who had been instructed by Samuel, and their rivals, adapted themselves
to the new religious conditions created by David, who was
one of their own. Thus they became prophets in Jerusa-

lem. In this body of Levites and prophets at Jerusalem the prophetism of the tenth century was realized. It became a permanent body that was to maintain cultic prophetism at David's court up to the period of the exile, and it had a considerable influence on the religious mentality of the Kingdom of Judah.]

But after Solomon's death, the great schism was to break asunder the unity of prophetism, and it is note-worthy that the schism originated with a prophet who had come from Shiloh. Ahijah was among the priests from Shiloh whom Solomon had definitely rejected. The encouragement which he gave to Jeroboam and the fact that he anointed him turned the spiritual and political interests of a certain number of prophets toward the Northern Kingdom. A prophetism was thence installed around the cultic places which Jeroboam had founded. That prophetism existed side by side with that of Je-rusalem, but it had a more dramatic fate. From the ninth century on the dynasty of the Omrides developed a new religious ideology. Whereas Jeroboam and his immediate successors had restored ancient pre-Davidic values, now Phoenician Baalism was introduced. The cult tried to in-tegrate Israelite elements and contributions of the Baals. Prophets who followed that movement were protected by the crown. Under Ahab there were significant brother-hoods that show the same distinctive and ecstatic signs of prophetism. Those prophets went on calling them-selves "prophets of the Lord," but they also accepted compromises with the Baal who was recognized by the court of Samaria. Those prophets who refused to do this became the object of severe persecutions.[41] They survived only because of the extraordinary prestige of Elijah, who was himself a cultic prophet, as is shown in the scene on Mount Carmel,[42] and who initiated secret brotherhoods.

Elijah's merit, however, was not to have prolonged cultic prophetism in the Northern Kingdom but to have attempted, beyond the political cleft, to reconstitute the spiritual unity of the people of Israel. Although the Bible does not tell us much about Elijah's activity, we certainly feel ourselves confronted by a person of great depth. Moreover, certain details enlighten us concerning his bold ideology. When he called on the Hebrews assembled on Mount Carmel to choose between God and the Baal, he built an altar of twelve stones (I Kings 18:31) and he pointed out that the choice made no sense unless it concerned all the people, the twelve tribes, and not only those ten whose representatives stood before him. His journeys took him through the entire country, the south as well as the north. Finally he sent a prophetic message to the King of Judah.[43] That prophet from the North was thus concerned with all of Israel. With him prophetism assumes a new political meaning. It is true that for a hundred years the prophets had not always accepted the split, and a prophet had more than once arisen to remind his people of the profound fraternity of the two kingdoms.[44] But now, when a peace was to be signed between Ahab and Jehoshaphat, Elijah made of that fraternity a spiritual demand. He pointed out that any alliance between Israel and Judah remained artificial unless it was an alliance with God.

Elisha, Elijah's chosen disciple, was not the one who was to continue his master's work. For half a century Elisha's group accepted the task of representing the prophetism of the North. Unlike Elijah, who had only been the "prophet of God," Elisha was also the "prophet of Samaria." The prophets of Elisha's community were the Levites of Samaria. They must have worked bravely and efficiently, since they were responsible for the revolution of Jezreel, the downfall of the dynasty of the Omrides, and the anointing of Jehu, who promised to be zealous for God. But their program was restricted to the North. It is even probable that if Jehu dreamed of adding Judah to his empire, the prophets foiled his project, because they felt that Judah ought to remain the realm of the Levites of Jerusalem.[46]

The true successors of Elijah, those who took up his message and fought for its realization, were the prophets of the eighth century. Some of them were Judeans, others Israelites. For all of them there exists only one Israel, that of the covenant, without frontiers or divisions. They could not have accepted that view if they had not maintained that prophetism and particularism are irreconcilable. The first of them, Amos, said: "I am neither a prophet nor a prophet's son" (7:14). But that break with prophetism corresponds to a new contact with those problems with which the Hebrew spirit was faced in the extraordinary eighth century.

The Literary Prophets

The eighth century was the climax of the political history of the Hebrews. There is an ascending incline and a descending one. The former is characterized by the mounting military, diplomatic, and cultural power under Jeroboam II in Israel and Uzziah in Judah. The latter leads to the progressive disappearance of the two kingdoms, in 722 and 586, respectively.

Literary prophecy—the most complicated and variegated of Hebrew prophecies—was entirely situated on the descending incline. It began in the middle of the eighth century and ended toward the close of the sixth. It seemed to hasten to an abyss with steep descents whose deepest chasms were the catastrophes of 722 and 586. Even when the political situation improved toward the end of the Babylonian exile, literary prophecy exhausted itself in putting things aright, although politically speaking the level of the eighth century was not reached again.

The fact that literary prophecy coincided with a political decline gave the former a deep internal unity beyond the apparent diversities. From the eighth century on, the prophets witnessed one of the harshest periods —a country going to ruins. Although the fall did not occur in any one single moment, yet the intermissions gave history only a chance to take a breath before disappearing into the abyss. Sometimes circumstances changed, and yesterday's enemy became today's ally.

But the reversal of situation did not change the massive weight of the events that led the country further and further down. The end had to come, and this fact characterized the literary prophets in comparison with their predecessors, who had lived in a state in which history had many possibilities, where reversals were considered to be of a temporary character, where enemies were of a normal stature—in short, where foreign policy was an incident without grave repercussions. The entire weight of politics remained within the country. This is how the prophets experienced things, and to them the great interventions of God were internal revolutions, changes of dynasty and regime, and "reforms." Ahijah had been sent forth to end the crisis of Solomon. His political program was the schism, a purely interior affair. In order to solve the crisis of the Omrides at the end of the ninth century, Elijah, Elisha, and Jehu had overthrown the dynasty and its Baalic ideology. It had again been an interior affair. The wars with Aram had only played an episodic role, and the prophets had indeed connected them with what went on in Israel itself, but it did not touch the essentials. It was in the state that the evil arose, and there the salvation had to be found.

The prophets of the eighth century and their successors, on the other hand, faced a threat from the outside. First it was Assyria, and then Chaldea. By these giants the Hebrew state was to be broken. The political destiny of Israel no longer depended on itself but on the wish of powers that were immeasurably stronger. The catastrophe was unavoidable.

We may well ask ourselves[47] whether that certainty was the sole property of the prophets, who had received it through an intuitive look into the future, or whether by applying some clarity and clairvoyance, the common man in the street could not foresee the tragical denouement. Whatever the case—whether the prophets simply represented a strong fraction of public opinion or whether they were alone in their conviction—they manifested it with great stubbornness unlike anything to be found with their contemporaries. Their very prophecy was oriented toward the downfall.

This is the first fact that must be properly appreciated, for it explains why the literary prophets fought so vigorously against the political optimism of their day. They were convinced of the futility of resistance against the colossus that destroyed all surrounding states. Opinions to the contrary were merely cowardly assumptions or perverse ambitions. The political enemies of the prophets were of all shades, according to the various facets of the struggles the prophets had to wage against optimists of all kinds. First of all they mistrusted *reforms*. The prophetic panacea that preceded the eighth century now stirred up the skepticism of the prophets. The reformers are kings and priests of the type of Hezekiah, Hilkiah, and Josiah. They tried to lead Judah back to the right path, but the prophets refused to see in that attempt a decisive means of salvation. Though they encouraged reforms, they considered them to be insufficient, not because they were not followed up strongly enough—a reproach that would not have been justified—but rather because a mere reform could not avoid the catastrophe. At best, it could provide a breathing spell. This is quite clear from the answer which the prophetess Huldah gave Josiah (II Kings 22:14-20) and which Isaiah gave Hezekiah (Isaiah 39). Isaiah and Huldah (and also Jeremiah, whose lukewarm enthusiasm for the reform of Josiah is typical) not only did not initiate the reforms but when they became effective they fought them because of the inevitability of the catastrope. Isaiah's attitude teaches us where the prophets saw salvation: in a miracle, which means in God's immediate intervention. For the miraculous end of the siege of Jerusalem by the Assyrians appeared to Isaiah to be the sign of a definitive salvation, and he embellished that event with the themes of a Messianic redemption, while scolding his contemporaries for not accepting it as such. Like all other prophets, Isaiah expected salvation to come from God and not from men. Therefore the prophets experienced another radical form of mistrust concerning the prophets of *peace* and *happiness*. Those who spoke of peace were not only reproached by the prophets for harboring a wrongly applied optimism and for shirking their responsibilities. They could not admit that the optimistic message was divinely inspired and eventually they identified it with false prophecy.

The scene which brings Jeremiah and Hananiah together is typical (Jeremiah 28). The theory of false prophecy which is developed there rests at first on ethical arguments. If Hananiah preaches peace, he entertains the illusion that everything is all right, so that the Judeans will not repent, whereas Jeremiah, by preaching impending disaster, makes an appeal for repentance. But we have the feeling that this cannot be Jeremiah's last word. For that theory makes a distinction between a prophecy which works and that which does not; it does not distinguish between true and false prophecy. If the prophecy of the disaster is true, it is not because its practical consequences lead to something good but because it derives from God. On the other hand, the prophecy of peace is false because it cannot come from God. Good

fortune and misfortune, peace and war, are realities
planned by God who in His sovereignty made a choice between them. The certainty of the catastrophe led the
prophets to some boundary situations. Isaiah denounced
the mentality of the military who gave themselves up to
enjoyment at the very eve of death (22:13f.) Jeremiah
did not want Jerusalem to defend itself against the Chaldeans (21:8f.) He did not find that criminal optimism
only with the leaders who were without scruples but he
also blamed the guards, who only fulfilled their strict
soldierly duties. To him the obligation to rebel and to
commit treason was more important than to obey and
to be patriotic. The catastrophe called for demands which
overthrew the list of political values. Attitudes like those
of Jeremiah show how seriously the prophets evaluated
the catastrophe.

But the literary prophets were not only sure of the
catastrophe. They had another certainty which was as
strong, although it did not move on the political level but
on that of redemption. That certainty had to do with the
other side of the political reality, a subjective and eminently religious side. It spelled out hope and salvation. It
was a conviction which was based first of all on the idea
that God was mightier than all the powers, that the center of gravity of the universal forces was not to be found
in Assyria but in God, and that Assyria and Chaldea
themselves were only creatures guided by God. This
then is a theocentrism which could have remained pessimistic and which could have granted the final victory
to God only at the price of the disappearance of all of
mankind if it had not been compensated by an Israelo-
centrism, which made it obstinately optimistic. God's
victory was tied up with Israel's survival. Those are indeed vague connections, which neither reason nor politics
could explain, and which, far from being lessened by the
final catastrophe, were even strengthened by it. It is as

if Israel's fall had been indispensable to its survival, as if the pessimistic outlook were needed for the ascent. It is also as if the entire world rested on God and Israel, and as if all the problems of its existence were contained in that polarity, and which shows as in rough outlines the meaning of the covenant. The literary prophets looked at the history in which they lived under the aspect of the covenant. They finally reduced it to the naïve connection between God and Israel. Nothing else counted, since God and Israel, to them, meant everything. The influence of that prophetic thought has been an extraordinary one, since it was largely owing to that idea that the Hebrews were able to survive the catastrophe. We must investigate how, from one epoch to the other and from one prophet to the other the double certainty of the downfall and the salvation has expanded within the framework of the covenant.

II.

With Amos, the first of the literary prophets, the theme of the downfall has a somewhat halucinatory character. Although his message does not call Assyria by name, it is alluded to, and we sense its presence (5:27). The misfortune is impending, and in a nightmare atmosphere we hear the prophet intone the funeral plaint over Judah, and we see the gestures of his mourning. "The virgin of Israel is fallen, she shall no more rise" (5:2). " . . . if there remain ten men in one house, they shall die" (6:9). But even the mourning heart gives rise to the theme of the salvation: "Seek ye me, and live" (5:4). Life as well as death is in the hands of the people. Fate has not been decided upon but offers a choice. It is up to them to avoid the disaster.

We might therefore be tempted to place Amos in a line with his predecessors, since Elijah, too, had cried out:

"If the Lord be God, follow Him; but if Baal, follow him." (I Kings 18:21). Thus even in the choice of words Amos seems to follow the ancient plan. He, too, suggests a decision between God and the Baal, only that he does not mention Baal by name, so that the choice is really one between God and—nothing. To him, life is good, and death, evil. He reviles Israel in terms of religion and ethics. Salvation can be attained by substituting the cult of God for the cult of the Baal, by rejecting injustice and immorality and adopting justice and righteousness. There is even a purely political note in Amos' message: the fall of Jeroboam and his descendants is a condition of salvation. Like Elijah before him, Amos announces the end of a dynasty which he himself was not to witness. Perhaps he hoped that the disappearance of the evil sovereigns and the installation of a regime loyal to God ("the tabernacle of David that is fallen" 9:11) would by themselves assure salvation. All this might well suggest that Amos believed in the efficacy of a moral and cultic reform, and that such a reform, if it were only followed up energetically on the religious and political level, would prevent the catastrophe.

It might surprise us to see a prophet as intransigent as Amos stake so much on a reform about which, as we have noted, Isaiah, Huldah, and Jeremiah were doubtful. Did Isaiah and Jeremiah then not recognize the obligation of a choice? But a comparison of their formulas with that of Amos shows that a choice is not necessarily an ethical option. Perhaps a moral plan underlies Isaiah's words: "If ye be willing and obedient, ye shall eat the good of the land; but if ye refuse and rebel, ye shall be devoured with the sword; for the mouth of the Lord hath spoken" (Isaiah 1:19-20.); although this sounds more as a summons to a divine court than an appeal to a moral choice. Unlike Amos, Isaiah does not call on his people to seek the good, to avoid evil, but to obey or to refuse. The object is not clear. God's word, *whatever its contents may be,* demands obedience. Only later (16f.) we are told of obedience to moral principles. But Jeremiah clearly separates the choice from ethics: "And unto his people thou shalt say: Thus saith the Lord: Behold, I set before you the way of life and the way of death. He that abideth in this city shall die by the sword, and by the famine, and by the pestilence; but he that goeth out, and falleth away to the Chaldeans that besiege you, he shall live . . . " (Jeremiah 21:8-9)

It is hard to imagine a situation less ethical than this one. Following Deuteronomy, Amos identifies life with the good, and death with evil.[48] But to Jeremiah life is flight, and death means the will to stay in Jerusalem. Such definitions shock ethical instincts, since to remain in a city besieged by an enemy is at least a sign of patriotism and solidarity. But according to the prophet it implies death! Under such conditions flight would be cowardly and treacherous; but according to the prophet it is the way to life! We must not even talk of a political choice inspired by ethical considerations, as had been the case with Elijah and Amos. For Elijah and Amos had called for the condemnation of an evil dynasty and its replacement by a government of pious and loyal people (descendants of Jehu or David).

But in what respect were the Chaldeans of Nebuchadnezzar ethically superior to Zedekiah? How are we to assume that, from a moral or cultic point of view, the substitution of the Chaldean regime for the dynasty of David was good and desirable? Furthermore, was not the choice placed equally before all the members of the people, including Zedekiah and his functionaries? Like all the citizens of Jerusalem, the royal household felt sure they would survive and, as is implied in the text, preserve a semblance of power, as if in order to be saved the evil government of Judah only had to be cowardly and treacherous! Thus we see that the choice cannot really be translated in terms of ethics or politics. In order to understand it we must turn to another language, to a frame of reference which has only to do with God. The roads to life or death are here marked off by the will of God, and the demand for a choice is based entirely on that will. However scandalous that divine demand may be, and even though it may be diametrically opposed to natural morals and political ethics, it must be heeded because it comes from the absolute, from God.

Here we must ask ourselves whether, after all, Amos' choice ought not to be understood in the language of the absolute rather than in that of a cultic or political ethics. More than anyone else, Amos has clearly experienced and expressed the absoluteness of the divine call. As he stated in a famous formula, his acceptance of the divine message did not depend on the content of that message but on the simple fact that it came from God: "The lion has roared, who will not fear? the Lord God has spoken, who can but prophesy?" (Amos 3:8).

God's word is as compelling as the roaring of the lion; it is imperative; it must be spread the way it is, without any consideration for what is outside of it. It is thus that to Amos, as to Isaiah and Jeremiah, the ethical or political choice is not all there is to the divine message. There remains an important latitude where the choice can only be made in an immediate relation with God. The result is a *devaluation* of ethical or political reforms, which cannot have the last word. When ethics and politics have had their say, everything has not yet been said, since beyond that God is still talking. It is the same God whose voice should have been detected within ethics and politics, since these are not autonomous.

Amos treats that "devaluation" of the reform in two ways. He shows that if Israel refuses to reform it is not necessarily doomed to disaster, but has to be prepared to meet the God whom they had wished to evade: "Yet have you not returned unto Me . . . Therefore thus will I do unto thee, O Israel; because I will do this unto thee. Prepare to meet thy God, O Israel" (4:6-12).

He does not spell out what the goal of such a meeting would be, a last chastisement or reconciliation. Only the meeting itself is important. The refusal to "return" does not remove Israel definitely from God. On the contrary, they will come close to each other, and this is achieved through the divine will, which is put into effect in spite of Israel's refusal.

As we see a little later, a reform was no absolute guarantee for salvation: "Hate the evil, and love the good, and establish justice in the gate; It may be that the Lord, the God of hosts, will be gracious unto the remnant of Joseph." (5:15).

"It may be!"[49] This means that the choice between ethical evil and good, the fulfillment of a positive moral and social reform, are not enough to bring about forgiveness. Repentance does not automatically lead to certain repercussions, and the reform has no obligatory consequences. A mysterious door, through which disaster may enter, remains open. Only God's will controls that access. Quite aside from human attempts, salvation depends on God.

These perspectives of Amos are quite clear in spite of their discreteness. He does not believe blindly in the efficacy of reforms, and this attitude was to be expressed even more clearly with the literary prophets who followed Amos. His twofold certainty—that of the fall and of salvation—is not basically tied in with an ethical reference but with a theocentric one. Death as well as life depends on God. To avoid death and to choose life does not mean to solve the problems posed by history in terms of ethics, but to be aware of the fact that these problems are inherently divine ones. The option is thus not a moral or political one but a prophetic one.

III.

Hosea's prophecy sounds like an accompaniment to that of Amos, whose contemporary he was. Like Amos, he foretold and expected the fall of the descendants of Jehu and that of Samaria (14:1); likewise, he foretold and expected a righteous government incarnated in the person of a descendant of David (3:5). But, again like Amos, the moral and political reform did not appear to him to be sufficient. He stressed the theme of the grace of God, which Amos had called *chen* (5:15), whereas Hosea used an ancient expression of the covenant, an expression to which he gave a particular meaning: *hessed.* We shall have to analyze that term further on. He, too, does not see salvation simply as a reward for man's ethical efforts but as a voluntary act of God, in His appearance before Israel. That theophany of which he dreamt is more plastic than that seen by Amos. It is a kind of violence which God commits against Israel, which He seduces just as a husband uses force against his disloyal and stubborn wife: "Therefore, behold, I will allure her, and bring her into the wilderness, And speak tenderly unto her." (2:16)

But Hosea excelled Amos in his feeling and expression of the mystery which exists in the connection between the catastrophe and salvation. He was eminently pathetic. His vibrant sensibility allowed him to be open to the secrets of the divine intention. He knew that the movement which led to salvation was an interpretation *post facto,* an inner overthrow of the movement of the catastrophe, and he observed that this "return" and repentance presented a mysterious paradox.

Hosea does not try to analyze that paradox, but he

experiences it in a simple and primitive belief, expressed in images and symbols. One of those images allows us to recognize the scope of the paradox. Hosea has a first-born son whom he calls Jezreel. This is an ambiguous name, since it has a historical as well as a biological meaning. In history Jezreel stands for the valley or the city where Jehu had defeated the dynasty of the descendants of Omri.[50] Those events had taken place about seventy-five years before Hosea, and while he flourished, a descendant of Jehu always occupied the throne of Israel. But even if the fight of Jehu at Jezreel had originally been a magnificent battle against Baal and for God, history subsequently proved that all those massacres had really been nonsense, a tragic mistake. The descendants of Jehu were in no wise better than those of Omri. They, too, had to disappear. The "day of Jezreel"[51] was one of a terrible error, and in order to indicate how fatally it led to the catastrophe of the successors of Jehu and of Israel, Hosea was to call his son Jezreel: "And the Lord said unto him: Call his name Jezreel; for yet a little while, and I will visit the blood of Jezreel upon the house of Jehu, and will cause to cease the kingdom of the house of Israel. And it shall come to pass at that day, that I will break the bow of Israel in the valley of Jezreel." (Hosea 1:4, 5)

But etymologically Jezreel means "God will sow," and this biological meaning applies also to the name of Hosea's son. " . . . in that day they shall respond to Jezreel, and I will sow her unto Me in the land . . . " (2:23)

This meaning runs counter to the historical value of the term. The political decay is not the cause of the catastrophe but an element of salvation, just as the grain cannot sprout before it has disintegrated in the soil. Jezreel stands for depositing the grain in the earth. Condemned to death, the grain will revive. Thus does the catastrophe prepare the germ of salvation.

Other images in Hosea's prophecies do not connect the salvation with the catastrophe so clearly through a causal nexus, yet they too insist on the unavoidable continuity of the catastrophe and salvation. Repentance, "the return," is the passage from one to the other, the crossing of the abyss which confronts and also separates them. Life becomes then a jump across death:

"Come, and let us return unto the Lord; for He hath torn, and He will heal us,

He hath smitten, and He will bind us up. After two days will He revive us,

On the third day He will raise us up, that we may live in His presence." (6:1,2)

Here there is no choice between life and death, but a penetration into the mystery of the connection between life and death, of death being overcome by life: "I will ransom them from the power of the grave; I will redeem them from death: O death, I will be thy plagues; O grave, I will be thy destruction. . . . " (13, 14) The catastrophe makes an end to its own defeat and prepares salvation.

It seems that Hosea brought this idea of a "return" to a climax in the symbols of the first three chapters of his book. The moment which separates the catastrophe from salvation corresponds to a break in history, and the "return" is the overcoming of the instant of historical void. Suddenly history jumps into an abyss in order to disappear there, and a slice of nonhistory allows the rise of a new history. Perhaps the third chapter of Hosea is in its entirety built upon that concept of a nonhistory, the prelude to a new start: " . . . the children of Israel shall sit solitary many days without king, and without prince, and without sacrifices, and without pillar, and without ephod or terephim; afterward shall the children of Israel return, and seek the Lord their God, and David their king . . . " (3:4-5.) The reconciliation seems to follow a long period of suspension of political and religious ac-

tivities in Israel. However that may be, the first chapter
clearly expresses the idea of a nonhistory. In the course of
time, Hosea has three children. As we have seen, the firstborn, Jezreel, symbolizes the end of the historical frame
of Hosea's life, the fall of the dynasty of Jehu's successors. The name of the daughter born next is lo-Ruhamah,
meaning, "she has not obtained compassion." She symbolizes the end of God's love for Israel. The third child
is a son named lo-Ammi, meaning: "Not my people." He
symbolizes the end of the covenant. Instead of mentioning
the future catastrophes by suggesting, for example, the
death or the banishment of the children, Hosea depicts
the children themselves as destroyers of the future. The
last two represent by their very names a negation. It is
noteworthy that after the last one is born, God, too, appears in a negative form: "For ye are not My people, and
I will not be God to ye." (3:9) This daring formula
which describes a nondivinity and which is reserved for
idols in Deuteronomy 65 is here being applied to God by
Hosea. History is thus absolutely denied. Between God
and Israel there is no longer any question of love or of
anything else, for that matter, for the word "between,"
so characteristic of the covenant, makes no sense any
more. Through this denial of history the relationship between the divine and the human is being abolished. But
the nonhistory is in itself only the introduction to a new
history, where everything becomes positive again. Jezreel is the seed which will create the germ of the future.
Lo-ammi becomes Ammi, and lo-Ruhamah becomes Ruhamah. God is acclaimed once more, and it is He Who
denies the demands that the denial of history be denied:
"Say ye unto your brethren: Ammi, and to your sister:
Ruhamah." (2,3)

Between the catastrophe and the salvation, both of
which are unavoidable, there is the mystery of nothingness.

IV.

There is a good reason for studying the problem of political prophetism in the Bible in connection with Isaiah.[53] For here the problem of God's place in the state is posed in unmistakable terms. When prophets had heretofore addressed sovereigns, they saw in them moral persons. Gad, Nathan, Elijah, and Elisha did not consider the virtues and sins of the kings as praiseworthy or blameworthy because of their political interventions, whose success or failure was in the eyes of the prophets conditioned by their personal conduct. When kings did consult prophets about a political or military affair, this was done in very limited cases, such as an expedition. But Isaiah—by his own initiative or challenged by Achaz— recommended to his king a policy of a wider scope—the cancellation of the treaty with Assyria.

Isaiah's demand substitutes God's will for that of the king in a state affair. This will of God's is no longer satisfied with a king who is loyal to God in his religious and moral life and who buys that loyalty with a certain political freedom. The political domain, too, is part of the covenant. God is the absolute sovereign of the politics of the Hebrew state, just as He is its absolute religious and ethical sovereign. This is the limit of the all-important idea of the covenant, according to which God is King and the Hebrew society is His kingdom. That idea had been in existence for a long time.[54] Isaiah is taking over the Messianism of the prophecies of Nathan, Amos, and Hosea. All of them hope for a descendant of David, who is not only the servant of God but His authentic deputy. But the idea has grown in the meantime, and what had previously been "King David" now takes on gigantic forms. His royal anointing comes to him from the Spirit of God, which implies six gifts: wisdom, intelligence, counsel, might, knowledge, and the fear of God. He is the

Messiah because he is a prophet. The divine inspiration guarantees his rank.

Following this analysis we might be able to show that Isaiah's "theopolitics" is accompanied by the belief in a miracle which is without equal among other literary prophets. No other prophet after the eighth century accepted the miraculous atmosphere in which he lived so naïvely. Certan miracles, like the birth of Immanuel and the cure of Hezekiah, were called into existence by Isaiah himself. Other miracles were witnessed or announced by him, like lifting the siege of Jerusalem and the miraculous pacification of the world by the Prophet-Messiah. The miracle is here the basis of the theopolitics, which tries to insert God into the politic reality, and the miracle is the instrument of this inclusion. In every miracle God is visibly on the verge of interfering and of penetrating the state. For this reason Isaiah believed in miracles. His belief in God's kingship leads to his faith in the miracle. Every miracle made an epoch in God's kingship concrete. It is for the same reason that, on a certain solemn occasion, Achaz refused to *tempt* God by accepting the challenge that Isaiah should perform a miracle.[55]

The king had well understood the prophet's psychology, and he knew that a miracle performed by Isaiah was a radical proof of the royal authority by means of divine authority. Actually, when Isaiah went beyond Achaz's refusal and did announce the "sign," it consisted of the birth of Immanuel. It does not matter whether Immanuel is the child Hezekiah or the anticipation of the future Messiah. His vocation is clear. According to the meaning of his name, he is the man of the covenant, through whom all men will feel that "God is with us." In the state, he must occupy the place of the king, since only he can show that God is king in the state. At Immanuel's birth Achaz must disappear. Perhaps Isaiah himself had his doubts concerning the identity of Immanuel. Was he simply a man or was he the Messiah? If that latter hypothesis was the only true one, Isaiah's attitude would mean a turning point in prophetism. He would then have been the first *Christic* prophet in the sense we have given that word earlier. He would have been the first prophet to believe himself a contemporary of the Messiah. We must therefore not be surprised to observe that Isaiah's prophecy remained the main support of all future Christians. The disciples of Jesus were to read that text avidly and to see in their master a confirmation of Immanuel.[56] Some Jews, on the other hand, were to say that since the Messiah was born at Isaiah's time he also died then, and thus "the days of the Messiah were consumed under the rule of Immanuel-Hezekiah."[57] Others never stopped waiting for the future "days of the Messiah," since they contest the "christism" of Isaiah. Immanuel would then be only a surname of Hezekiah, lacking any Messianic pretensions, nor would Isaiah have believed that his predecessors witnessed the birth of the Messiah.

Through his belief in miracles Isaiah remains loyal to the theocentrism of Amos and Hosea. He simply underlines their practical range, which the prophets of the eighth century had neglected for the benefit of theoretical demands. Perhaps that practical concern, that accent on the demands of the day, of the immediate situation, explains another aspect which distinguishes Isaiah from Amos and Hosea. The polarity of the catastrophe and of salvation is no longer expressed, as in the eighth century, in terms of a sequence: first disaster, then salvation, but it is rather inscribed in reality. Isaiah feels that he is a spectator of the downfall and the return. These two alternative paths concern him simultaneously.

Hosea had begotten *non-children,* who sooner or later became *children* again. With Hosea, this was the meaning of the *return*—the passing from the negative to the positive, the appearance of something where nothing had ex-

isted before, the resurrection after death. Isaiah creates
two beings. One is a *non-child,* called "the spoil speedeth,
the prey hasteth," the other one has become a child again,
named " a remnant shall return." But neither of them
is really a child. The first one is not so any longer, he has
been banished, destined to die, as his name indicates. The
other is not yet a child, but he will be. As his name tells
us, he is destined to live. These two sons express the imminent ambiguity of Israel's fate. Hosea sees all of Israel
transcend death to attain life. Isaiah sees some go to
their death, some will live. The segregation of the dead
and the living is not the consequence of the succession of
a lifeless time and a living time, but it operates within
living time itself, condemning some to death, allowing
others to live. Thus we understand the very impressive
picture of Isaiah's prophecy, which imposes itself on his
spirit from his first message on: " . . . as a terebinth, and
as an oak, whose stock remaineth, when they cast their
leaves" (6:13).

Salvation does not follow the catastrophe but is well
within it. Within Israel itself there are both: the trunk
which will be eaten up, and the holy seed which will survive:

"If there yet be a tenth in it, it shall again be eaten up;
but the holy seed shall be the stock thereof." (*Ibid.*)

The Messiah himself is a branch which will come out
of the seed of Jesse, a shoot emerging from his roots
(11:1). Like the people as a whole, the Davidic lineage
undergoes that double current of death and life. The tree
will come down, but the trunk and the roots will remain.

This basic image is mirrored in the intellectual and political idea of the *remnant:* " a remnant shall return."
This symbolic name of Isaiah's son attaches the *return*
to a *remnant.* Here lies the important difference between
Isaiah's *return* and that of Hosea. Whereas the latter is
universal, the former is limited. At least at the beginning,

Isaiah wanted perhaps to discriminate between the Kingdom of Israel, which had been lost, and the Kingdom of
Judah, which had been saved. This is also shown by the
exegesis which he gives to the catastrophic name "the
spoil speedeth, the prey hasteth." He applies this to Sa-
mariah (8:4). Furthermore, he make a connection between the miracle which saved Jerusalem from Sennac-
herib's attack and the Messianic vision (chapters 10f).
But he is sure that the idea of the *remnant* will furnish
his most important attitudes even after the fall of Sa-
mariah. He then introduces that idea in Judah itself,
where it develops into a real doctrine of salvation. Since
it affects only a few, we see a community of chosen ones
arise around Isaiah. They are his disciples, the *limmudim,*
who are mainly recruited among the "humble," to whom
he confides secret teachings:
"Bind up the testimony, seal the instruction among my
disciples. And I will wait for the Lord, that hideth His
face from the house of Jacob, and I will look for Him.
Behold, I and the children whom the Lord hath given me
shall be for signs and for wonders in Israel from the Lord
of hosts, who dwelleth in Mount Zion." (8,16ff)
Micah, that great contemporary of Isaiah, also announced the ruin of Judah in harsh terms: "Therefore
shall Zion for your sake be plowed as a field, and Jerusalem shall become heaps, and the mountain of the house
as the high places of a forest." (Micah 3:12)
With this too, he associated the idea of a remnant:
"And the remnant of Jacob shall be in the midst of many
peoples, as dew from the Lord, as showers upon the grass,
that are not looked for from man, nor awaited at the
hands of the son of men." (Micah 5:6)
But we know from Jeremiah (26:18) that Micah's
prophecy led to a moral reform in the entire state. Nothing like it is indicated with Isaiah. Only within his intimates does he try to form a "sacred tenth" destined

for salvation, after having been exposed to a secret discipline.[58]

V.

Although to Isaiah the catastrophe and the salvation are simultaneous and not successive events, they are meant for the future, since he does not see them unified in his own persons but in his children, tomorrow's generation. He is the prophet of the birth of a destiny, and Jeremiah and Ezekiel are the prophets of its fulfillment. Neither of them had any children. Jeremiah had to remain a bachelor,[59] and Ezekiel lost his wife without perhaps ever having had any children.[60] To them, destiny does not concern the future, but has threatened them in their very persons. Both of them have witnessed the ruin of Jerusalem, the burning of the Temple, and the end of the state. In their own existence they have reached the lowest point of the history of Israel. This makes their spiritual experience of the "return" and of salvation even more remarkable, for among all the efforts of Hebrew prophecy, this is the most difficult one, a dizzy ascent.

In spite of the notable difference in their personal lives, Jeremiah and Ezekiel experienced the unavoidable necessity of the catastrophe in an identical manner. Herein they are equals. All they differ in is the hope of salvation.

Jeremiah had been a prophet long before Ezekiel, but just like Jeremiah, Ezekiel witnessed the two events which, from the time Josiah mounted the throne, prepared the downfall of the kingdom of Judah. Both prophets saw five kings disappear, not by natural death, but by violence and catastrophe. Two—Josiah and his son Joyakim, succumbed, pierced by arrows, defeated on the battlefield. The other three—Joachaz, Joyakin, and Zedekiah, all of them Josiah's sons or grandsons, died or were to die as exiled prisoners of war.

How blindly did destiny work when it made those five

kings disappear! We have the feeling that an obscure and fatal force guides history here and brings human will to naught. For those kings, who are linked together by the tragedy of their denouement, are utterly unequal. They differ in character, in politics, and in the conditions of their existence. One of them, Josiah, is a model of piety; another, Joyachim, is rotten to the core through vice and sins. Some of them are proud and arrogant; others weak, undecided, and sluggish. Some rule for decades and thus have enough time on their hands to develop cunning or bold policies; others rule only for three months, so that as soon as they realize that they have become kings, they are already dethroned. But history laughs at such differences. It takes them up to play with them. In this way they do become equals—united in the same final disaster.

At that time Jerusalem was a buffer between two great rival powers—Egypt in the south and the Chaldea of Nebuchadnezzar in the north. At certain times Jerusalem turned to one of them, at other times to their opponent. But it always bet on the wrong side. The puppets who shared six months of rulership were separated by an interval of eleven years. In that span of time, history is made, and men have the time to break up alliances. Joachaz is the puppet king of Pharaoh Necho, and Joyachin the one of Nebuchadnezzar. One symbolizes the success of Egyptian propaganda in Judah, and the other that of Chaldean propaganda. But both are crushed by the same fate. In those eleven years both are taken off the throne in the same city of Jerusalem and led into exile in chains. The only difference is that one dies in the south, in Egypt, and the other finds his end in the north, in Babylonia.

No political wisdom and no human will can oppose the fatal force of the disaster. The five kings disappear, and each of them takes a part of the state with him. When the last of them, Zedekiah, disappears before Nebuchadnezzar, this means the irrevocable end.

Jeremiah and Ezekiel emphasize that history with the full weight of their prophetic conviction. They foresee the catastrophe, they announce it, and they prepare for it. Rarely have prophets used a more variegated and suggestive technique for forging their idea. Both prophets ornamented the theme of the catastrophe with moving variations. They see it in hallucinatory visions. Jeremiah hears the sound of the hoofs and the neighing of the horses of the enemies who enter Jerusalem (4:29); Ezekiel sees the Holy Ark and the cherubim leave the defiled Temple (10:18). They announce this in passionate words, and they even act it out: for months on end, Jeremiah walks around in the streets of Jerusalem, a yoke around his neck (chapter 28). Ezekiel remains pinned down to his bed, and eats his own excrements (chapter 4). The sword, fire, slavery, banishment, and death appear again and again in the visions and prophecies, in the very lives of these two prophets.

Jeremiah fights within Jerusalem itself. He remains in the city to the very last moment, a prisoner of his own prophecy and of the people. When the siege begins, he takes up his conviction of the upsetting alternative between capitulation and resistance. Those who resist the Chaldeans were to die, and those who surrender were to remain alive (21:8f.). So bitter is the reality of the catastrophe, so rotten is the political existence of Jerusalem, that salvation can be had only by the radical rejection of all politics, even if this means cowardice and treason. King Zedekiah and his tortuous diplomacy, his ambitious armies and venal functionaries, the false prophets of peace, the priests of the ritual and of the devout and hypocritical piety, and, finally, the masses who howl with the wolves, are faced with Jeremiah's one and absolute demand—God. Whatever the human consequences of the choice may be, it is inevitable. To be heroic and loyal means to be with God, even if the alternative is cowardice and treason.

Ezekiel is among those who, eleven years before the fall of Jerusalem, had been exiled to Babylonia together with the young King Joyakin. But there he fought the same battle which Jeremiah had fought on the national soil. The small exiled community lived under a double illusion. Some of them believed that the fall of Chaldea was imminent. They remained united with the Jerusalemites, not in thoughts alone but by direct and important contacts, and they supported the politics of alliance with Egypt that Zedekiah had practiced. They were convinced that the salvation of Jerusalem and their own return depended on a speedy and decisive military encounter between the Pharaoh and Nebuchadnezzar. The others stood by Joyakin whom even in prison they considered their legitimate king. They even believed that once Nebuchadnezzar fell, Joyakin would enter Jerusalem in triumph, and Zedekiah, that puppet of the Chaldean will, forced to abdicate. They were animated by a confused Messianism. Salvation will not only come by weapons but by the victorious liberation achieved by a loyal descendant of the house of David.[61] Within that exiled community both groups have their own propagandists and prophets. Ezekiel faced them with the whole force of his personality, and announced in his visions, words, gestures, and even silences, that neither Zedekiah nor Joyakin twould triumph, but that the catastrophe was unavoidable. In this he was assisted by Jeremiah, who, in the famous letters which he sent to Babylonia (chapter 29) spoke up against the illusion of an imminent return. Indefatigably, Ezekiel and Jeremiah confronted the prophecies of peace which, in Judah as well as in Babylonia, denied the catastrophe with the absolute certainty of the fall. They differed only in the perspectives of the salvation.

The chapters of the Book of Jeremiah that deal with joy and salvation are very touching. There are many of them, and they are scattered all over the book, like grains of seed disseminated in the ground. It is typical that Jeremiah's Book of Lamentations is a separate book and not included in the fifty-two chapters dealing with Jeremiah's life. But Jeremiah's cheerfulness is the very core of his book. Isaiah had the serenity that comes from being far away from a disaster which they might have avoided or overcome. Isaiah did prophesy the disaster, but for a distant future. Ezekiel, who witnessed the catastrophe, escaped it, and built a new life on the rivers of Babylonia. His happiness comes from the fact that he has been saved. The joy of Isaiah and Ezekiel is the outcome of a miracle —the former did not have to live through the catastrophe, the latter escaped. But Jeremiah did not live through a miracle nor did he escape. He was a victim. His trial illuminates that impossible justification, the rejection of the miracle (chapter 26). Jeremiah wanted to convey God's word to the Temple. They were words of threat, of disaster, and an appeal. The priests, the professional prophets, and the mob seized Jeremiah, took him before a tribunal, accused him of lies, and demanded his death. Thus Jeremiah was at the very brink of disaster. He needed a miracle more than Isaiah had, since in the latter's case the miracle would only have shown the prophet's word to be true. In Jeremiah's case it could have saved his life. But not only was there no miracle but Jeremiah did not even think of piercing God's silence. That is what he said to his accusers:

". . . I am in your hand; do with me as is good and right in your eyes. Only know ye for certain that, if ye put me to death, ye will bring innocent blood upon yourselves, and upon this city, and upon the inhabitants thereof; for of a truth the Lord hath sent me unto you to speak all these words in your ears." (26:14f.).

Jeremiah did not die in Jerusalem. He disappeared as an exile in Egypt, without having been able to reconstruct his own life there. Together with others, he has been engulfed, and his joy resounds only on the cliffs and reefs.

Jeremiah's joy does not deny suffering or tears. It feeds on trials and resignations. Its strength comes from the torture which animates and exalts him. This chorus of joy and of hope can only be shared by those who, like the prophet, had known suffering, this means the poor and forsaken, the disinherited and famished, those who die in the wilderness and stay awake in their graves:

"A voice is heard in Ramah, lamentation, and bitter weeping, Rachel weeping for her children; she refuseth to be comforted for her children, because they are gone. Thus saith the Lord: Refrain thy voice from weeping, and thine eyes from tears; for thy work shall be rewarded, saith the Lord; and they shall come back from the land of the enemy. . . . Behold, I will bring them from the north country, and gather them from the uttermost parts of the earth, and with them the blind and the lame, the woman with child and her that travaileth with child together; a great company shall they return hither. They shall come with weeping, and with supplications will I lead them; I will cause them to walk by rivers of waters, in a straight way wherein they shall not stumble." (31:7-9, 15-16).

That song of joy ends with this confession of Jeremiah: "Upon this I awaked, and beheld; and my sleep was sweet unto me" (31:25). This is a touching confession—Jeremiah's joys had only been dreams. It is the joy of a morrow which Jeremiah had never known, whose dawn he had never perceived, and of which he knew only that after the dark night it had to come, since it was past midnight.

Past midnight—this is the feeling Jeremiah has regarding his prophetic destiny. By passing midnight with twin realities in his soul—the catastrophe and the dream

of salvation—Jeremiah forces the actual terror to be
ended by the consolation of the future, and thus to be
justified. He has actually entered the days of nothingness
that Hosea had foreseen. But he was not to come out of
those days. By entering them, he has obtained the immovable certainty of resurrection.

One of the most important moments of that attain-
ment is told to us in Jeremiah 32. The prophet is already
surrounded by the night. He is in prison, and well he
knows that this is his final prison, since for two years
the Chaldean army has besieged Jerusalem. The assail-
ants are already close to the walls, the battering rams
strike the gates, and their heavy sound can be heard
through the streets, where the people, plagued by famine
and pestilence, expect the final assault at any moment.
At this hour Hanamel visits the prophet in jail. A cousin
from Anatoth, he wants Jeremiah to take back his field.
Jeremiah draws up the contract, seals it, and deposits it
in an earthen vase so that it can be preserved for a long
time. How is that? Is Anatoth not occupied by the Chaldeans, and has Hanamel's field not been trampled on by
the hoofs of the enemy's horses? Is not the nation lost,
and together with it its soil? What can such an absurd
gesture mean as the background of such a terrible catastrophe? It means that "again—one day—people will buy
in this land houses, fields, and vineyards" (verse 15).
This is God's answer to Jeremiah's question, for it is
God who has sent Hanamel to Jeremiah, and Jeremiah
agreed to commit that absurdity. God tells him: "Behold,
I will give this city into the hands of the Chaldeans . . .
they shall come and set this city on fire, and burn it . . .
however, I will gather the inhabitants of this city and of
this land from all the countries, whither I have driven
them in my anger . . . and they shall be My people, and
I will be their God . . . Men shall buy fields for money, and
subscribe the deeds, and seal them, and call witnesses, in

the land of Benjamin, and in the places about Jerusalem, and in the cities of Judah, and in the cities of the hill-country, and in the cities of the lowland, and in the cities of the South; for I will cause their captivity to return . . ." (verses 28, 37f., 44).

"*However.*" This word reverses the impossible, sweeps away obstacles, and creates the future. *However!* This world clearly accepts all difficulties, all stumblingblocks, and crushes them through hope. It pierces all the walls of time and wipes out all distances. Two events, separated from each other by months, years, centuries, millennia—the catastrophe and the return—coincide *however,* they are close to one another, intimate, simultaneous. Two feelings separated from each other by a contradiction—pain and joy—are *however* united. If Jeremiah had not heard that word *however* from God's own mouth, it would merely be an obstinate wager. In this *however* Jeremiah's theocentrism reaches its climax. The divine absolute which Amos had seen only vaguely, which Hosea had experienced as grace, and Isaiah as a miracle, is identified by Jeremiah with the absurd.[62]

This is the point of departure for Jeremiah's typical and total transvaluation of all values. Heroism and loyalty change signs, and now they are to be found exactly where people see only cowardice and treason. When God mentions Nebuchadnezzar, that hammer of the peoples, that gigantic club, the mighty blasphemer, He calls him "My servant"[63] as He had called Israel in the covenant. The Temple—God's residence, where all those close to Him could find Him—the Kingdom of David, that incarnation of God's tangible intentions in history, the land flowing with milk and honey and full of promises for God's intimates—everything crumbles away, everything is swept away, everything is burned. But Israel lives on. Since the covenant is not inscribed on any outside sign, every Hebrew carries it on himself, engraved on his very heart.[64] To Jeremiah, the distance from God is an intimate closeness: "From afar the Lord appeared unto me" (32:2). "Remember the Lord from afar" (51:50). "Am I a God near at hand . . . and not a God far off?" (23:23).

Here is where the transvaluation assumes its essentially prophetic significance. Whatever is exterior, extended and spatial, is relative; only time is absolute. God may be far away in space, yet He is close in time. The state and the Temple can be destroyed, but the covenant remains, through the very existence of every Hebrew. At times God had been Israel's space. With Jeremiah He becomes again their time.

With Ezekiel, on the other side, God enters space again. Here lies the essential difference between Jeremiah's expectation and that of Ezekiel. Both of them had gone down to the lowest point in history, but each of them dreams of a different ascent. Jeremiah's dream is a pure rhythm—nothing delineates the future, unless the *movement* of the return, men and women *on the march*, an immense start for *coming back*. Ezekiel's dream concerns space. It is a plan—utopian though it may be, where all lost elements are found again and put in their proper places. Those Jews who returned from Babylonia with Jeremiah's spirit must have been possessed of the rhythm expressed in Psalm 126. There everything is tender, animated by a rhythm which substitutes joy for tears, harvest for sowing, the return for the departure. That return, however, remained a dream, as is shown by the very first verse of the psalm. Its reality consisted solely in the fact that it reflected the departure like a wave that returns to its source, but it had no practical application. Those, however, who returned with the spirit of Ezekiel have a valid constructive plan. Not that everything is usable; but everything is clearly outlined and can serve as a sketch for something real—the Temple, the cult, government, and administration. Although Ezekiel's plan[65] has never materialized, it offers a complete system of references for the new religious state of the Hebrews.

There are many causes for this fundamental difference between Jeremiah and Ezekiel. As mentioned above, there is first of all the fact that Ezekiel had escaped. Whereas the catastrophe of the year 586 seems to have broken Jeremiah's energy, since the people did not wish to listen to him either in Jerusalem or in Egypt, it created in Ezekiel a greater prophetic tension. The catastrophe affected the community of the exile only in their spirit, and not in their flesh, as had been the case with the community of Jerusalem. After the month of Av, 586, those around Jeremiah had to fight for their very lives, whereas for those around Ezekiel nothing had changed, except that people were spiritually exhausted.[66] Jeremiah could not grant security to his brethren in misfortune, whereas Ezekiel did have the means to rebuild the exiles morally, and this he undertook with great energy.

But even aside from these conditions which were so favorable to receiving prophecy, Ezekiel differed greatly from Jeremiah in character as well as in temperament. Although both men were prophets and priests, Jeremiah was more passive than active in this double vocation. He apparently never fulfilled a priestly function. He is a prophet against his will; he suffers from it, he wishes to get rid of the heavy burden God has placed upon him. His personality is identical with his human condition, and he is a prophet and a priest besides. Ezekiel, on the other hand, seems to have accepted his prophetic vocation and his priesthood voluntarily. He firmly believes in the efficacy of his double mission, and some of his plans have to do with his personal intervention. Like Hosea and Jeremiah, he mentions the subject of resurrection. But whereas those two note it only briefly, as a secret to which God alone has the key, Ezekiel paints a broad picture, in

which God tells him to play a major role. It is at the call
of the prophet that the Spirit arises from the four corners
of the earth in order to revive the dry bones (37:10).
The resurrection is an act of prophecy, and the prophet
is God's agent. Likewise, the Temple plan does not remain an abstraction, but on the day that it will be in-
augurated Ezekiel will offer up the first sacrifices
(43:18). Thus Ezekiel's priestly vocation occupies as important a place as does his prophetic vocation in the
vision of the dry bones. Among all loyal priests he is the
chosen one. The purification of the Temple depends on his
priesthood.

This belief in his own person explains why Ezekiel
projected his prophecy into space. He was the architect
of a work in which he was ready to take his own place.

There is no conceit in this psychology. Ezekiel takes
all the implications of his mission in utter seriousness,
not only those which enhance his prestige, but also those
which weigh him down. No one has emphasized more the
idea of personal responsibility. Ezekiel knew that as a
prophet he was a guardian and that therefore the life of
his people was entrusted to him (chapters 3 and 33).
The slightest neglect of his function as a guardian causes
him deepest grief. There is a distension of the human
value which sometimes tones down the very value of God.
In his prophecy God is often the mystical knight who
leaves it to his prophet to intervene on earth. Whereas
the dialogue between God and the prophet is well per-
fected, the one between God and His people is not.
Moreover, Ezekiel's concept of a meeting between God
and Israel is not very original, since earlier prophets had
already formulated his theocentrism. In an important
chapter, in which he spells out the return as an absolute
divine demand, he comes back to the ideas of violence
and of a gratuitious divine act: "In spite of you, by force,
will I be king over you." (20:33)

These ideas had been introduced by Hosea into Hebrew religious thinking, and Ezekiel takes them over without any change.

VI.

At the time that Ezekiel again found the spiritual atmosphere of Hosea, another prophet appeared, who had many similarities with Isaiah. The critics call him Deutero-Isaiah, and his message is found in the second part of the canonical Book of Isaiah. The spiritual harmony between the two Isaiahs is so great that the canonical tradition refuses to see in the second a different one and attributes to the prophet of the seventh century the entirety of a message the last part of which is not only "prophecy" but "foreknowledge."

One of the two sons of Isaiah who symbolized the future of Israel had fulfilled his destiny. The booty of Jerusalem had been taken, the city had been plundered, the state had gone to pieces, the Exile was a fact. The time had come for the fulfillment of the destiny of the other son. Cyrus' decree can be formulated in that name of Isaiah's son: "A remnant shall return." It is the return of that "remnant" which Isaiah alludes to in his speeches of consolation.

But he foresees it in his own perspective, in an atmosphere saturated with miracles. There is an absolute theocentrism in his announcements which turn an exact political event into a divine affair. It is not only the people who will return from banishment but God Himself. For Him the roads are marked out and all obstacles removed: "Hark! One calleth: Clear ye in the wilderness the way of the Lord, make plain in the desert a highway for our God." (40:3)

He is the vanguard and the rear guard: "The Lord will go before you, and the God of Israel will be your rearward." (52:12)

But if the return is above all a divine return, we are not talking of just *any* god but of *God.* The theocentrism

is emphasized in a monotheism whose affirmations have
hardly ever been so radical. Violent speeches against idolatry occupy an important place in this message and underline the idea that God is the only One. As against the
dead divinities, He is the Living God. He is the Creator;
"He has the whole world in His hands," and He can do
with it as He pleases. He can destroy it and re-create it.
Nowhere else has the divine absolute—holiness—been
proclaimed with so much force. One finds this accentua-
tion again when Isaiah affirms God's threefold holiness:
(6,3)

". . . ye shall know and believe and understand that I
am He; before Me no God existed, neither shall any be
after Me. I, even I, am the Lord; and beside Me there
is no savior . . . I am the Lord, your Holy One, the Creator of Israel, your King . . ." (43:10f,15)

This Holy One, this Creator, this King is the only One
to inspire all events and creatures: "Thus saith God the
Lord, He that created the heavens, and stretched them
forth, He that spread forth the earth and that which
cometh out of it, He that giveth breath unto the people
upon it, and spirit to them that walk therein . . ." (42:5)

By a sovereign decision of His will *new things* are
created, and in this chapter they are insistently compared
to *childbirth*.[67] There are two predominating ideas in that
image of the childbirth: there is first the unknown, the
unforeseeable and surprising element which is typical of
the newly born child, whose character nobody can foretell. But we are also certain of the resemblance to his
parents, of a connection with those who begot him. This
is exactly the case with Isaiah—the "remnant" (which
could not be identified) erupts out of a group, and thus
the *new* thing cannot be identified at the time of the Return, yet it is intimately tied to the *old* and comes out of
its depths.

For the epoch of the return there develops thus a

prophetism which accepts suffering as an unavoidable condition of life. Messianism is conceived of in the pangs of childbirth. Whether the Messiah is a man, a people, Cyrus (who allowed the return), a prophet well acquainted with God's plan, Zerubabel the descendant of David, or Israel as a whole, God's witness—all we do know is that the Messiah is a *servant*, and God must be able to refer to him as His servant. From the very first he figures in God's plan, and he takes the only good route, the one which God has marked out, and on which Israel has advanced from the beginning. He bears the signs of humility and suffering which can also be found on Israel's face. He is the child of Israel's history, born of Israel's pain.

By further preparing the road of Israel's history Biblical prophecy is being achieved. The last prophets—Haggai, Zechariah, and Malachi—are modest artisans who try to make the new State prophetically valid. They furnish it with new elements in order to fulfill its ancient destiny. The Spirit and the Word cease at the very moment when the inscription of the *new* in the *old* seems to be achieved (Malachi 3:22ff.)

But at the very time when this achievement allows the covenant to go on, another aspiration is born in Israel—not to go on but to be content with the achievement. One wants to see the Messiah in order to stand outside of all time by entering his own time. People want to pierce the mystery of the Messiah no matter how, provided this is the *last* channel. So far the path of the covenant had been the *only* one; now it becomes the *last* one. If it takes too long, one can always invent games to decipher the mystery. Messianic expectation becomes a science, and one lives only in the expectation of that science to become affirmed. This then is the theme of the Apocalypse.[68]

The Apocalypse takes us out of the time of the covenant, since it is based on the concept of cyclical time. The circle closes at the moment of the "revelation." One thing

had definitely been achieved, and another thing begins.
A great break is made in history, and according to that
all things are arranged.

Biblical prophecy has rejected the Apocalypse. Looking out toward the future, prophecy is fulfilled in the
continuity of the expectation. How are we to explain that
rejection, this orientation which is so typical of prophecy? The *historical* aspect of prophecy cannot account
for it. We must now investigate literary prophecy in its
spiritual essence. As witnesses of a history the literary
prophets felt that they are responsible for the *covenant*.
But they are not limited to that feeling. They have enriched the idea of the covenant with contributions of their
own, in width as well as in depth, and in this *extension*
the contents of prophetic *thought* can be found.

Notes

1. Moses (Exodus 3:4); Samuel : (I Samuel 3:6); Jeremiah (1:11);
   Amos (7:8).
2. See above, p. 103, for a definition of "knowledge" in prophetic experience.
2a. (See Martin Buber: Abraham the Seer, in: *Judaism* vol. 5 no. 4, Fall,
   1956) Tr.
3. Jeremiah 42:1ff; Ezekiel 20:1.
4. For Samuel see I Samuel 9; for Ahijah see I Kings 14:1ff. Elijah,
   Elisha, and Isaiah have often been "consulted" by individuals.
5. This is but a change in consciousness but not a tear in it, as Hegel
   would have it. See J. Hyppolite: *Les travaux de jeunesse de Hegel,*
   1935, p. 552. See also André and Renée Néher: *Histoire Biblique du
   Peuple d'Israel,* Paris, 1962, I, p. 17f., 53f.
6. Max Weber: *Das antike Judentum.* p. 20.
7. Thus Saul told his soldiers to fast (I Samuel 14:24); David's com-
   panions observed abstinence (*Ibid.* 21:6). See Max Weber, *op. cit.,*
   p. 99.
8. I Samuel 4.
9. I Kings 18.
10. A recent account of this has been made by A. Lods: *Histoire de la lit-
   térature hébraique et juive,* Paris, 1950, p. 36.
11. I Kings 18:31.
12. Verses 4f.

13. Verses 20f.
14. The original meaning of the Hebrew "am haaretz" is countryman. At the time of the kingdom, it was used for "people" in general, and later on it assumed different meanings again, like "assembly," "ignoramus."
15. In Mosiac times the Midianites lived in the Arabian desert, and at the time of Gideon in Transjordania. Later on they migrated further north.
16. A. Lods: Israel, Paris 1930, p. 397.
17. I Samuel 3:20.
18. *Ibid.*, 10:6, 9.
19. *Ibid.*, 10:12 and 19:24.
20. *Ibid.*. 16:13.
21. *Ibid.*. 1–15.
22. *Ibid.*, 16:13f.
23. Note Ahijah's role in the post-Solomonian schism, the one of Jehu ben Chanani in the fall of the house of Baacha (I Kings 16:1ff.), the one of Elijah and Elisha in the fall of the house of Omri, Joyadah's in that of Athalia, and Amos' in that of the descendants of Jehu.
24. II Kings 2:9; I Samuel 10:10ff; 19:22ff.
25. I Samuel 19:22ff.
26. *Ibid.*, 10:10ff; II Kings 3:15.
27. This question is being dealt with by A. Jepsen: *Navi,* Munich 1934.
28. *Ibid.*
29. The prophets of the Baal practice mutilation in the scene on Mt. Carmel (I Kings 18:28). The false prophets of God did probably the same (chapter 22).
30. The context speaks for that meaning (I Samuel 10:12).
31. I Samuel 9:12 and 16:2.
32. *Ibid.*, 10:5f.
33. I Kings 18:30.
34. Engnell: *Studies in Divine Kingship,* 1943. Haldar: *Associations of Cultic Prophets among the ancient Semites,* 1945. A. R. Johnson: *The Cultic Prophet in Ancient Israel,* Cardiff, 1944. Martin Buber: *The Prophetic Faith,* 1949.
35. The destruction of the sanctuary of Shiloh is implied in the account of the First Book of Samuel. It is mentioned in Jeremiah 7:12ff and 26:6. See also Psalms 78:60.
36. I Samuel 22.
37. *Ibid.*, verse 25. where Zadok is mentioned side by side with Ebyatar of Shiloh.
38. I Kings 2:26f.
39. *The Prophetic Faith,* p. 61.
40. I Chronicles 25:1.

41. I Kings 22 and *passim,* in the last chapters of that book.

42. *Ibid.,* chapter 18.

43. II Chronicles 21:12.

44. Shemaya I Kings 12:22ff, and Azarya ben Oded II Chronicles 15.

45. II Kings 2:24 and 5:3.

46. See my book *Amos,* p. 185.

47. This question has been dealt with in various ways by E. Troeltsch: *Das Ethos der hebraeischen Propheten Logos* VI, 1916–17, *and F.* Weinrich: *Der religioes-utopische Charakter der "prophetischen Politik,"* 1932. See also Wilke: *Die politische Wirksamkeit der Propheten Israels,* 1913, and Karl Elliger: "Prophet und Politik," *Zeitschrift fuer die Alttestamentliche Wissenschaft,* 1935.

48. See my book *Amos,* pp. 108ff: "The Deuteronomic scheme of the choice."

49. The Babylonian Talmud (Haguiga 4b) insists on the fact that we have here only a possibility. Do not righteousness and justice guarantee the salvation? Rabbi Assi cried when he read that verse in Amos.

50. II Kings 9ff.

51. Hosea 2:2.

52. Deuteronomy 32:21.

53. See the fine analysis of Isaiah's "theopolitical hour" in Buber's *The Prophetic Faith,* pp. 126ff. On the same question see also: Staerk: *Das assyrische weltreich im Urteil der Propheten,* 1908. Kuchler: *Die Stellung des Propheten Jesaja zur Politik seiner Zeit,* 1906, and the books mentioned in n. 47 of this chapter.

54. M. Buber, *Das Koenigtum Gottes.*

55. Isaiah 7:10ff.

56. Matthew 1:23.

57. Babylonian Talmud Sanhedrin 99a.

58. Isaiah 7:3; 8:1, 3.

59. Jeremiah 13:1.

60. Ezekiel 24:15f.

61. See M. Noth: Un catastrophe de Jérusalem en l'an 587 avant J. C. et sa ignification pour Israel. *Revue d'histoire et de philosophie religieuses.* 1953, 2, p. 86.

62. See A. Néher: *Jérémie.* Paris, 1960. p. 218.

63. 25:9; 27:6; 43:10.

64. Jeremiah 31:32.

65. Chapters 40–48 of his book.

66. Those deported to Babylonia considered themselves uprooted and desperate (Ezekiel 37:11), while those in Egypt counted on the benevolence of foreign gods (Jeremiah 44:15f.)

67. 54:1 and 66:8.

68. The Book of Daniel deals fully with this subject.

2

Prophetic Thought

Matrimonial Symbolism

I.

Matrimonial symbolism, the nature and scope of which we shall now investigate, is one of the favorite themes of Biblical prophetism. In an original and profoundly lyrical form it tries to allude to the love between God and His chosen people. Jewish as well as Christian commentators easily recognized God and Israel in the Song of Songs, wherever a beloved one or a betrothed one is mentioned. In numerous passages the prophets use the same terms in a clear reference to God and His people. Thus in Isaiah's famous song (chapter 5) there is a dialogue between the Beloved and His vineyard. Verse 7 states in express terms that God is indeed Israel's Beloved.[1] The same prophet (62.5) also says that God feels for Israel the *joy of a bridegroom over his bride.* Jeremiah (2:2) uses the same word, bride, for Israel, when he states that God remembers "the love of Jerusalem's espousals," which means the time when Israel was God's "bride." Again in the Book of Ezekiel we are told of "the time of love" between God and Jerusalem (16:8). Finally Hosea, who beyond betrothal speaks of marriage albeit an unhappy one, does not hesitate to call God the husband and Israel His wife, following the terminology of Genesis (2:23). These are his words: "She is not my wife any longer, nor am I her husband" (Hosea 2:4),

247

and after the reconciliation of the unfortunate couple: "On that day, says the Lord, you will call me "my husband," you will no longer call me "my master." (verse 18).

Entire chapters in the Bible use that matrimonial symbolism consistently, and with the help of such symbols they trace the love of God and Israel from its origins to its peaceful or tragic denouement. This is particularly the case in Ezekiel 16. Here the prophet tries to describe Israel's unfaithfulness to God, and he does so step by step, the development of the wife's love from birth unto death. The prophet underlines the following stages: birth (verse 4), puberty (7), betrothal (8), marriage (8), unfaithfulness and prostitution (15-35), punishment and death (40).

Another example for a systematic application of matrimonial love can be found in Jeremiah (2:2). This piece is a rather short one, but it is precise enough to offer the outlines for a frame of matrimonial experience: youthful love, engagement, and marriage.

In the second chapter of Hosea the love theme is treated within two aspects: normal matrimonial love, fulfilled or desired, and violent and illicit love. The stages of normal love are: birth (5), youth (17), marriage (21 f.) matrimonial encounter (22).[2] The passionate catastrophe is indicated by these terms: prostitution (7), seduction (16), violence (16),[3] and repentance (9).

In addition to these great scenes the prophets return, less systematically yet very regularly, to the matrimonial symbolism in order to describe the noteworthy aspects or the incidents of love between God and Israel. Thus before "knowing" God, Israel is a virgin (Amos 5:2; Jeremiah 8:13, and 31:3 and 20; Isaiah 54:4). After the wedding, which is expressed in different terms, comes the period of fecundity, when the *children* of God and Israel are born (Ezekiel 16:20; 23:4): "Thou hast taken thy

sons and thy daughters whom thou hast borne unto me;
Ohola and Oholibah—Samaria and Jerusalem, which
means the Kingdom of North and that of the South—
were mine and had sons and daughters of their own."
Sometimes such children are the fruit of sin, since Israel
got them through adultery (Hosea 5 :7 and Isaiah 57 :4).
Isaiah mentions the lost and found children (49 :20 f.,
54 :1). Israel the adulteress is accused by Jeremiah (3 :9
and 13 :27) and Ezekiel (16 :18 and 23 :45). Almost always Israel's unfaithfulness is real *prostitution* and well-
known invectives chastise that unpardonable violation of
marital love (Hosea 1 through 4; 9 :1; 4 :15; Jeremiah
2 :20 and all of chapter 3; Ezekiel chapters 16 and 23).
Various catastrophes put an end to that love betrayed:
abandonment or repudiation (Hosea 2 :4; Isaiah 54 :6);
divorce (Jeremiah 3 :1 and 8; Isaiah 50 :1); the death of
the children (Isaiah 47 :8f.; 49 :20f.), widowhood (Jeremiah 51 :5; Isaiah 47 :8f.) Finally, certain prophets com-
bine the mention of Israel's return and redemption with
elements of matrimonial symbolism. The "return to God"
then becomes the equivalent of a reconciliation between
the separated mates or a new marriage.[4]

That symbolism can also be found in a certain Biblical
attribute of God which, though often misinterpreted, can
easily be explained in the perspectives of a marital covenant. When the Bible mentions a "jealous" God, it does
not particularly refer to God's jealousy concerning idols.
The principle of that idea is not necessarily a monotheistic
one. What is meant is rather the zeal by which God is
animated when Israel becomes unfaithful to Him. Like
a husband who is alerted by the first signs of infidelity,
God watches jealously over his wife and tries to prevent
future acts of betrayal.

Let us first point out a number of Biblical passages
where the matrimonial symbolism does not concern Israel
but other nations. Thus Egypt, Bablyonia, and Sidon are

called "virgins" just like Israel and Zion (Jeremiah 46:11; Isaiah 47:1; 23:12). On the day of wrath God "repudiates" Ashdod, the capital city of the Philistines (Zephania 2:4) or Egypt (Ezekiel 31:11) as He repudiates Israel (Hosea 9:15). These instances, though small in number, show that the Bible does not reserve matrimonial symbolism to the relationship between God and Israel. Just as the covenant has a universal character—does the account of the deluge not imply the idea of a covenant valid for all of humanity?—so do the symbolic modalities of the covenant apply outside of Israel. God is the Father of all men (Malachi 2:10). Nebuchadnezzar and Cyrus are His servants. The language of love is common to all men in their relation to God.

II.

What is the significance of that "language of love," that matrimonial terminology which the Bible uses as one of the most typical expressions for the covenant?

It means first of all that the *knowledge* granted by the spirit is not only intimate and penetrating like any other sexual knowledge. Since here we are dealing with a divine-human encounter, the "knowledge" is of a marital order, and its symbol has to do with two ideas: to the constant fidelity of two beings of different sex is added the equally constant link between two beings who may temporarily be separated by time or the disharmony of their feelings. One of the differences between marital love and simple sexual love is that the former persists beyond the actual encounter. Even when the mates are separated by endless space or time, they "know" each other by the same force of love, and even if the love of one of the two should weaken, the relationship remains the same as long as the other party's love has not diminished. Thus the matrimonial symbolism does not only allow us to describe a covenant, which means a communication between two beings, but a true dialectic of the covenant. For, on the one side, the covenant unites two beings who necessarily differ as sexual partners but who are constantly alike by virtue of the love they feel for one another; on the other hand, the marital relationship implies an interplay of closeness and distance, of energy and weariness, of knowledge and unfaithfulness, so that the covenant seems to be constantly in motion. This motion, or, if you prefer, that dramatic character of the matrimonial symbolism, is decisive for the adoption of that symbol in the Bible, which finds therein a device for expressing what in its general *Weltanschauung* is essentially dynamic and dramatic—*history*.[6]

The matrimonial symbolism is historical first of all because it places a value on the *past*. When the eighth-century prophets begin to make use of that symbolism, it is because they feel the need of discovering a divine intention in the already prolonged history of Israel. Whatever the true reasons for the prophets' *looking back to history*, they could best express it in the matrimonial symbolism, since thus they could tell of the past as well as draw conclusions from it. Usually that symbol is quite clear, and almost always the prophetic account of the love between God and Israel has an obvious meaning which the listener can understand without difficulty and without exegetical effort. Every single period of love corresponds to a certain epoch in history. The pathetic moment of love—the wedding or, more precisely, the first marital encounter—takes place in the wilderness, after the Exodus, before entering Canaan. This localization is clearly stated in some texts, whereas in others it is only implied, and the shadings depend on the personal temperament of each prophet. Thus Amos and Hosea see in the wilderness a social as well as a religious experience. Jeremiah emphasizes its moral aspect, and Ezekiel connects it with the revelation of the Torah.[7] But whether we are dealing with a nomad ideal, with faith or the Law, the localization is the same with all prophets: the great period of encounter is the wilderness. Following this landmark the other data of the symbol can be easily portioned out. Birth, youth, virginity, and betrothal characterize the beginning; the patriarchal period, the sojourn in Egypt, and the Exodus. By entering Canaan Israel becomes God's wife, and then starts the real marriage, with its successes and disappointments.

In that actual union the criteria of love must be the same as in the past. In its youth Israel had given ineradicable proof of its love by having faith in God, by following Him in the wilderness, and by allowing herself to be guided by Him. A similar confidence should always animate Israel in actual history and prepare it for a new divine revelation. The prophets develop the great themes of *faith* by making frequent use of the matrimonial terminology. But that faith does not simply mean that the expectation of God is a mere idea or a feeling but rather the direction which must be taken by an existence which has been affected by time. "Prepare thyself, O Israel, to meet thy God." This call of Amos (4:12) is stylistically the tone addressing a young married woman. But at the same time it is an appeal to an *immediate* religious and moral regeneration.

Beyond the past and the immediate present, the matrimonial symbolism looks at the *future*. Once unfaithfulness has been experienced and reognized, it has to be overcome. This can be done in various ways.

It is of the very essence of the matrimonial symbolism that the actual union has a future. It is in the *children* that that future is incarnated, for they extend the love in time and testify to its reality. Often the prophetic symbol applies to the children rather than to the parents. As the prophets see it, Israel is actually represented by the chil-

dren, the product of the love between God and Mother
Israel. Thus the couple retreats to the past, and the
prophetic announcements do not directly concern the
two. If there is to be a drama, it will break out over the
head of actual Israel, namely, the children. Thus Ephra-
im is called God's child, and Israel the mother who has
brought forth the rebellious son.[8] Here we meet again
the symbolism of the *generations* mentioned previously,
and which serves to express history. Within the matrimonial symbolism, and as if derived of it, the symbolism
of the generations is used by the prophets for sketching
the future. The crisis of unfaithfulness will be resolved,
for better or for worse, without a change in the love that
ties the Husband God to His spouse Israel. The *children*
will be the object either of a punishment (death, for the
wife Israel will be "deprived of children," but perhaps
it is only a question of exile)[9] or by a trial followed by
repentance and return.[10] The "return of the children"
allows for the continuation of a history which had become a tragedy by their own obstinacy.

But sometimes the denouement of the crisis has to do
with the couple itself. The marital tie can be broken
through divorce or repudiation. The prophets, however,
foresee such a possibility only in order to reject it immediately. Nothing can really destroy the love of God
and Israel, and a separation can only be a temporary one.
Reconciliation is always possible.[11] The wife is not di-
vorced forever, but she will find her Husband again, if
not through repentance then at least by way of the dis-
illusions she will have experienced during her unfaithfulness or through boredom and idleness. These themes
are developed in the second chapter of Hosea, and they
represent a surprising effort to maintain an optimistic
concept of history. Everything is based on a linear concept of time. If history is truly the work of God, it must
have a perfect ending, and all accidents must be taken in

stride, either through a repentance deep enough to correct the failures of the past, or, outside of ethics, through God's undeserved intervention. We have shown how in one continuous line the literary prophets from Amos to Ezekiel insisted on the reality of God's interfering in history, through grace, through the absurd, or through violence.[14] These are the prophets who tremble with the matrimonial theme. To them that theme opened wide the doors to the future. It was not a new history that began after the catastrophe but a continuation of the old.

III.

The matrimonial terminology is the most remarkable variation which the prophets have attempted towards a description of the covenant. All expressions of the covenant are thus formulated in a new language. This is a bold effort to grant *love* its fullest significance.

We have defined the love of the covenant as a dialogue which goes on between God and man in man's heart. The matrimonial terminology insists that that love should be experienced as a marriage, which implies first of all a sexual encounter. Rarely has *holiness,* as demanded by the Torah, been practiced with more courage. In the matrimonial symbolism there is hidden a strong acceptance of the entire sexual life, an insertion of sexuality into metaphysical servitude, an outstanding example for sanctification. The same root, *yadoa,* stands for the act of union between man and wife, and also for the knowledge of God. In this way the prophets give *knowledge* an entirely new definition, deprived of intellectual perception and moral progress. It is an immediate experience, penetrating and expanding, involving one's whole being in a sudden and total revelation. We get thus also a new definition of *history,* not only because history is enriched by love but by *marital* love. That marital rela-

tion between God and Israel gives the time of the covenant a new meaning. We have found earlier[12] when we
investigated ritual agrarian time, that the time of the
covenant could deal with it only by changing possession
into loyalty, and loyalty is indeed the sign of marital love.
We will also see that only faith can raise righteousness
into loving-kindness. Finally, as will be shown immediately, when we discuss cyclical and mystical time, matrimonial symbolism prevents the tarnishing of Biblical time.

Prophetic History and the Cycle

Biblical time cannot be reduced to cyclical time, if only
for the reason that the latter does not bestow any meaning upon history, whereas Biblical time is joined with
history. The basic differences between Hebrew and Greek
thought have been pointed out frequently. It can also be
illustrated by the fact that the theme of God's being
married to a man is absent from the Greek but present
with the Hebrews. As we have mentioned before, the internal logic of the matrimonial symbolism demands a
future for the actual union. This future is incarnated by
the children, since they extend love in time and testify
to its reality. We have thus in Hebrew religion a principle
of fertility as against the sterility found in Greek religious thought. Greek time, as a metaphysical dimension,
cannot bring forth anything; it is not the source for any
progress. It can be reflected only in perfectly similar
images, whereas Hebrew time re-creates itself through
births in an unforeseeable future. Through birth the time
of the children depends on the time of the parents, yet
it has a physiognomy and a content of its own. Hebrew
time does not start all over like Greek time but it begets
something. The fact that Biblical time could be described
with the word "generations" shows that the Hebrews
saw in history a power to give birth. From this derives

a whole perspective of progress and maturation, opposed to the theme of degradation which cyclic concepts enforced upon the Greek. Thus Plato shows in his *Republic* that the logical law of political institutions is not growth but corruption. Decadence marks the history of governments. That law of degradation is inherent in humanity itself, and while Plato limited it to state institutions,[12] other Greek thinkers applied it to the world as a whole, the cosmos as well as man, and this is the direct result of their concept of time. Aristotle's *Physics* furnishes a remarkable juxtaposition of circular and destructive time: "Can time ever be exhausted? This is impossible, since movement is never-ending. Does it then change, or is it the same in different forms? This evidently depends on the movement, so that if the movement remains the same, so does time, and if not, time too changes. Now the moment is not part of time but rather the end of the past and the beginning of the future (just as a circle is concave and convex at the same time.) Likewise, time itself always ends and starts, and therefore it is apparently always different. Now since all change is naturally destructive, and everything is created and annihilated in time, therefore some call it all-wise, whereas to the Pythagorean Paro it is ignorant. The latter is right, since in time we forget everything. Thus we see that time is the very cause of destruction rather than of generation, since change always means destruction. Whenever time is the cause of generation and existence, this is a mere accident."[13] Here Aristotle lays down what all Greek philosophers since Heraclitus had felt vaguely—compared to the immovable, motion is a decrease. To accept time means to lower oneself. As Claude Tresmontant has remarked,[14] in that concept all becoming seems to stand under a negative sign. All ideas which have to do with growth, like creation, development, and generation, are considered corrupt, and may even be expendable. On the other hand,

concepts like fall, flight, and evasion become basic ideas
in philosophy and ethics. It seems that this idea finds its
culmination in the revelation which Hesiod announced
in his myth of the cycles: the Golden Age is behind mankind, and the further we get away from it, the more mud-
dled we become. Tresmontant writes: "The Greeks seem
to have been struck above all by the movements of corruption and dispersion. . . . The Hebrews watched passionately the process of fertility and maturation. The
Greek symbol for becoming is the river with its irretriev-
able water, or else the light, which vanishes in darkness.
The Hebrew symbol of becoming is the tree—it grows,
and out of one seed comes a multitude of fruit."[15] We
would rather say that marriage is a more typical image
than the tree. For though it is true that sometimes the
Hebrews compared their history to the blossoming of a
seed, they refused to restrict themselves to a passive role
in a purely vegetative history. Therefore the symbol of
marital love, as rich in images of development, maturation, and fruitfulness as that of a tree, allowed them to
emphasize the active role they assumed in history. The
wife is not only a provider but a participant. History is
the achievement of the joint efforts of both spouses. As
opposed to the Greek passivity in the face of time, the
Hebrew symbolism of marriage manifests a whole-
hearted acceptance of time. The Greeks permitted time
to die in endless cycles. The Hebrews brought time to life
by constructing on it the unforeseeable and constantly
fruitful history of their marital alliance with God.

We must therefore not see in the Biblical idea of the
"return" a derivation of the cyclical concept of time,[16]
for the return is one of the phases of marital history. We
have already pointed out that the separation of the
spouses—in symbolical language divorce or widowhood
—does not mean the end of their love. Separation is only
temporary and does not affect the essence of the marital

alliance, which has an eternal character. *Return* is therefore always possible. The wayward wife will find her Husband again. Widowhood, too, will end, either through a repentance deep enough to overcome death, or, beyond ethics, through God's own free will. "Death, where is thy message?" This is the theological challenge implied in the idea of the *return*. It had been launched by Hosea (13:14), the same prophet who gave that idea its deepest Hebrew meaning, and who, for that very reason, was furthest removed from any cyclical perspective. In Biblical thinking the *return* is not history beginning anew but the continuation of a history whose sequence seemed to be impossible. If the idea of the *return* is the least tragic concept in Greek thought, one through which it clears a path toward eternity and stability, it corresponds in Hebrew thinking to the exact moment when Biblical time, in spite of its dramatic character, becomes tragic. Whenever it appears in Greek thinking, it solves a question. But when it comes up in Hebrew thinking, a problem arises, namely, that of the continuity of history. If the last prophecies of the Book of Isaiah belong to the period of the *return,* they show with what faith and optimism Biblical prophecy approached the problem in its ultimate manifestations. *New* history means the revival of the *old,* or, in the terms of that matrimonial symbolism which the author uses so profusely, the kiss of mates who meet again after a long and painful separation.[17] But we need only think of the general rhythm of prophecy until Zachariah and Malachi and to their constant references to the matrimonial symbolism in order to feel that Biblical prophecy rejects a break in history. The end of prophecy does not mean the end of history. As long as there are men, the dialogue of love and faithfulness between God and man will persist.

This dialogue is perpetuated by the existence of Jewish man, while Christians perpetuate it through their *mystical* union with God. In a brief parenthesis we must show how Biblical time, as taken up by the Jews under the symbol of marital love, differs from Christian time, as seen in the experience of mystical love.

Prophetic History and Mysticism

When the great Christian mystics describe love, they take into account the essence of mystical experience, which is without extension and strives toward one point only. This central point is the encounter between God and man, their very fusion.[18] It is the magnetic point of the universe, and it attracts whatever moves in the spiritual sphere. As long as love has not reached this aim, it has not been consummated and remains wish, nostalgia, and yearning. Once the goal has been reached, love becomes really itself but in an irrevocable way—it is as eternal and immovable as the God into whose intimacy it penetrates. Once the union has been established, it remains forever —it is enduring, permanent, and indestructible. In the experience everything is concentrated in the Only One. The encounter between God and man lasts only a moment, but it is God's eternal moment. Mystical love is love *in God*.

Married love in the Old Testament, on the other hand, is love *with God*. It is not limited to a point but has an extension; it is not immutable but mobile. It is basically evolving and goes through phases which change it without suspending it.

It is true, however, that in mystical experience, too, we find the idea of a developing love. There is an entire terminology which insists on the movements of love which describe the pathways of the soul, its stages and mystical progress.[19] But all this is only an ascending line. The soul moves upward. When it meets with resistance, it bends back into a spiral, yet it never relinquishes the impetus that animates it and leads it constantly higher. It is noteworthy that the image most frequently used by the mystics in order to describe their voyage is that of a *ladder*. We find it almost everywhere in mystical biographies, and it occupies an important place in the writings of Richard de St. Victor, who was one of the first to outline the progress of the soul in precise forms, to give us the framework for an "evolution" of love, as most mystics have accepted it from him. The mystical voyage is an ascent. The soul rises by climbing "the four rungs of the steep ladder of love: betrothal, wedding, union, and fertility."[20] We see here clearly the sketch of a plan which is common to all mystics. Married love goes through different phases, yet they are all on the way up.

The mystic has taken the image of the ladder from the Old Testament. Jacob's dream (Genesis 28:12) is really a metaphor of the covenant, and the ladder, too, symbolizes the relation between God and man. But in the Old Testament it does not have the same meaning as the symbol of married love, and thus the mystics were wrong when they united these two symbols into one. The least we can say is that the symbol of married love loses its primordial meaning when it is too closely associated with that of a ladder.[21] For though the ladder describes the meeting of the divine and the earthly, it does so in a *dream*. It is quite another thing to say that in an ecstasis man can have relations with the divinity, which implies tensions, an effort, an ascent, and finally an alliance, but all this involving a literally ecstatic man, a man "beside himself," a who had to give up many essential elements of his condition, and before all else the very consciousness of his own effort.[22] In contrast to this, the metaphor of married love in the Old Testament describes man in his *reality*. The narrator of Genesis could use the symbol of the ladder only by incorporating it with a dream. When the prophetic narrators make use of married symbols, they assign to them a place in man's consciousness but never in a vision, although some prophetic visions include images closely related to that of the ladder. There are apparently two different concepts of the alliance in the Old Testament. To one of these, the alliance with God is an ideal which man can see vaguely in an ecstasis by overcoming himself. To the other, it is a reality to man's life, when he remains himself, and the content of which he can experience through married love. These two conceptions stand side by side and supplement each other, although they differ in the means of expression and in symbols. The symbolism of one of the two systems rarely takes the meaning of the other into account.

In the Old Testament the terms "husband" and "wife" have a substantial meaning, so that married love not only refers to the soul but also to the body. Marriage is essential to Biblical love, because it opens up an adventure which is at once spiritual and physical. Therefore man is entirely involved in that adventure, body and soul. On the other hand, man's physical fate can be tied in with a spiritual destiny which involves the presence of God. The encounter between the transcendent and the immanent finds an adequate symbol in married love, since the description of that love calls for two equally indispensable expressions if the symbol is to retain its proper force—a physical expression which suggests a carnal union, and a sentimental one which appeals to passion. In other words, if the metaphor of married love permits a tie between God and man without disobliging God, even more so it permits a union of man and God without sublimating man. The variegated and rich virtue of a marriage allows us to think of man in his nakedness even in the face of the Spirit. When the alliance between the divine and the earthly is symbolized by a marriage, man is invited to present himself in a perfectly human identity, without renouncing anything of his human condition.

Many terms of the *covenant* (love, holiness, righteousness) defined that condition. The prophets, however, have chosen the term *hessed* by giving it a new meaning which is impregnated with the marital symbolism. To them the real human condition is that of the man who shares in *hessed*—the *chassid*.

Hessed

Hessed is first of all a moral or legal tie between people who are associated in some way.[23] That association can be of different kinds. Close members of a family are tied to each other by the duties of *hessed* (husband and wife; Abraham and Sarah (Genesis 20:13); parents and children: Jacob and Joseph (Genesis 47:29). In a wider sense, the family includes hosts (the spies who have enjoyed Rachab's hospitality must show her *hessed* (Joshua 2:12 and 14); this applies also to a divine messenger in regard to his host Lot (Genesis 19:19). It includes furthermore those who have been taken back into the family by "redemption." Therefore there is *hessed* between Boaz and Ruth (Ruth 3:10). In this case the word does not denote any feeling of love, since at that point we do not know anything about the sentiments Boaz and Ruth will experience for each other later. The word is also applied to the legal and moral relation between the "redeemer" and the widow he is supposed to "buy back," which means to lead back to her family. Between friends and allies, the faith vowed to one another is a *hessed:* David and Jonathan (I Samuel 20:8, 14, and 15; II Samuel 9:1, 3, and 7); David and Chanun, King of Ammon (II Samuel 10:2). Chushai pretends to betray the *hessed* he owes his friend David (II Samuel 16:17). Subjects owe *hessed* to the legitimate dynasty (Joad acted with *hessed* toward the young Davidic king Joas (II Chronicles 24:22). On the other hand, the children of Israel did not show *hessed* to the dynasty of Gideon (Judges 8:35).

In all these cases *hessed* is basically synonomous with *brith*, the covenant. It is a covenant which imposes on the parties a number of moral and legal duties. The scope of those duties depends on the character of the covenant in question. It does not go beyond the limits of normal demands of family, friendship, or authority. Without *hessed*, social relations would remain anarchic, while through *hessed* they are solidified, and the ties between the associated individuals become real, so that by practicing *hessed*, they simply manifest that the covenant is not an empty word but exists in fact.

Hessed, however, has an additional meaning which is not juridical but is entirely related to the emotions. It is a sympathy witnessed spontaneously, without having become natural or necessary between two individuals by an earlier association. Thus Joseph asks the butler not to forget him but to exercise *hessed* on his behalf (Genesis 40:14). This in spite of the fact that the butler owes Joseph only the interpretation of a dream and the promise of an early deliverance. But Joseph takes no active part in all this, except for his proper interpretation. Therefore the *hessed* which he expects of the butler is a free act of friendship. There is no "covenant" between Joseph and the butler, but everything belongs to the domain of the emotions, everything depends on the butler's good will. The inhabitants of Yabesh-Gilead have certainly not forgotten the service which Saul rendered to them in coming to their assistance; but the *hessed* which they show to Saul's body goes beyond a moral obligation. It is a profound sentiment of humanity and respect for the dead which makes them brave dangers in order to give the last honors to their deceased and vanquished sovereign (II Samuel 2:5). It is a voluntary act of goodness, the kind that the Hebrews practiced, again as *hessed*, when they spared the life of the young inhabitant of Luz (Judges 1:24). Also, the kings of Israel were known

for being kings of *hessed* (I Kings 30:21), and that word
implies their magnanimity and goodness. Esther inspires
hessed in the presence of all those who see her (Esther
2:9 and 17), and her personality evokes a radiating
sympathy.

In this new meaning *hessed* is no longer a synonym for
the covenant, but it is rather an equivalent for *chen*
(grace) and *ahavah* (love). It is spontaneous grace, love
beyond the call of duty. In these new examples *hessed* is
a notion derived from social relations, something intuitive, and a feeling rather than an obligation.[24]

Biblical theology has paid special attention to this
second meaning of *hessed,* and this is one of its most
original aspects. A covenant between man and God is as
much a *brith* as a covenant between men and men. But
the *hessed* of that *brith,* the manifestation of its existence, cannot be only a legal one and not even exclusively
a moral one, but contains something emotional and intuitive. In the covenant with God, the *hessed* has immediately
the meaning of grace or love. When God grants men a
covenant, this fact is in itself grace, since it is somehow
exorbitant and incomprehensible. Therefore the marital
metaphor suggests itself forcefully and logically as a description of that covenant. Between God and Israel there
is the same *hessed* as between a man and his bride (Jeremiah 2:2) or between husband and wife (Hosea 2:21;
Jeremiah 31:2). The marital relationship as interpreted
by the prophets is not exhausted by the marriage contract
nor in the faithfulness of the mates, but in *knowledge,*
(Hosea 2:22), which means a meeting of love and fertility. This is the *hessed* of the lovers. When the prophets
applied this to God, they underlined and tried to emphasize the fact that in the encounter with God there is something infinite, irreducibly mysterious and sometimes even
violent. Election by God is an act of partiality. God
chooses, and man cannot evade the choice (Amos 3:2).

He who is the object of God's *hessed* is so forever, since God's *hessed* is as infinite as God Himself (for which reason in the Psalms *hessed* is so often side by side with *olam,* eternity).

One sees how improper it is to speak of the "ethical monotheism" of the prophets. The single notion of mercy, in the sense given it by the prophets, suffices to make known whatever would have been incomplete in limiting to its ethical aspect the *covenant* of which the prophets speak. Prophetic monotheism is essentially religious. The alliance with God is conceived by them not as an exchange of rights and duties but as an unhoped-for grace. In the theology of the prophets, the *mercy* of God is not his justice, his ethic, but his love, his infinitude, his mystery.

It is to this mystery that men whom God has blessed with his mercy should respond. For there is perpetual reciprocity of mercy among the members of an alliance. In the divine alliance, God grants mercy, but he exacts it equally from men.

(Hosea 6:6): "I prefer *hessed* to sacrifice, and the knowledge of God to offerings . . . (12:7): Now return to thy Lord, observe *hessed* and righteousness, wait constantly for thy God . . . .(Micah 6:8): You have been told, O man, what is good, and what the Lord demands of thee: to do justly, to love mercy, and to walk humbly with thy God. (Jeremiah 9:24): Let him who wishes to glorify himself, glorify in this: to understand and to know Me, that I am the God who practices right, *hessed,* and charity on earth, and desiring all this, saith God. . . .

This *hessed,* which man owes God, cannot be defined through strict laws or ethical rules. It is rather a sympathy which comes before God's will and is beyond its expressions. It knows how to arouse what is infinite in man's soul, and it puts unknown and always new resources of human actions into the service of participating in the divine covenant. The contrasts and comparisons mentioned in the verses above are very typical. As a demand for an inner piety, as a disposition of the heart, *hessed* is opposed to sacrifices. *Hessed* completes righteousness and charity by crossing over "the strict line of justice."[25] In the covenant there are two kinds of piety: that of the *tsaddik*, which corresponds to God's *tsedek*, and that of the *chassid*, which corresponds to His *hessed*. Thus the analysis of the idea of *hessed* leads us to the human attitude of the *chassid*, an attitude which manifested itself in Hebrew society at a time when it had become familiar with *hessed*, which means precisely during the period of the prophets. We must indeed take it for granted that the type of *chassid* came into being at the same time as the development of the idea of *hessed*. The more consistent the theme of the *hessed* became, the more it became accepted by the people, inspiring their attitudes and creating a style of life. Those who agreed to practice *hessed* and to place its doctrine into their very lives were called *chassidim*. But their practical experience of the *hessed* made them give it certain variations and even new meanings. In this manner a reciprocity between the *hessed* and the *chassid* was established. The *chassid* is the source as well as the object of the *hessed*. He benefits by the *hessed*, but he is also its creator. Now whereas we cannot possibly fix the origin of the idea of *hessed* in Hebrew thinking, we know at least the moment of its greatest intensity, the time when the *hessed* found in Hebrew literature its most meaningful expression and when therefore the existence of the *chassidim* can be considered highly probable. It is the period of the great literary prophets, the eighth century, when Hosea and Micah gave the *hessed* a typical and fruitful meaning. We must not suppose that either of the two prophets was a *chassid*. But everything leads us to the belief that their fiery way of preaching the *hessed* was sufficiently convincing to create around them movements of *chassiduth*. The eighth century and the two that followed seem to have been eminently favorable to the existence of *chassidim* within a people who, through prophetic preachings, had become more and more familiar with the value of *hessed*. We must now investigate whether those Biblical texts which mention *chassidim* support our hypothesis.[26]

II.

Almost all of these texts come from the Book of Psalms. Several psalms give a systematic and picturesque description of the *chassidim*. The real existence and the thoughts of the Biblical *chassidim*, however, cannot be discovered in these chapters, since they have mainly a literary character. Here the figure of the *chassid* is entirely ideal, parallel with the aspirations of the *chassidic* milieu, but without giving us an assurance that the *chassidic* type described in these texts had ever found its equivalent in real life. This is especially the case with Psalm 149, which is often quoted in support of the "Maccabean" thesis of Biblical *chassidism*:

"Hallelujah! Sing to the Lord a new song, may His praises resound in the assembly of the *chassidim*. May Israel rejoice in their Creator, may the sons of Zion jubilate in their King. May they glorify His name in dances, may they celebrate it with drums and lyres. For the Lord takes pleasure in His people, He crowns the humble with salvation. The *chassidim* exult in honor, and sing songs on their beds. With hymns of God on their lips, a double-edged sword in their hands, they take revenge on people and inflict chastisement on nations. They tie kings and noblemen with iron chains. They execute judgment on them according to the law. Glory to all His *chassidim*, Hallelujah."

Some want to see in this psalm a realistic picture of the patriotic *chassidim* who assisted Judas Maccabaeus in

his struggle. But we would then have to forget how artificial and stylized this psalm is. The brave warriors of
whom this psalm sings existed perhaps only in the imagination of the inspired poet. Similarly, the idyllic picture
of "those who fear the Lord" (Psalm 128) may be attributed to pious idealism:

"Happy is he who fears the Lord and walks in His
ways. When you eat the fruit of your hands, you will be
happy, and all will be well with you. Your wife will be
like a fruitful vine in your house, and your sons like olive
trees around your table. Thus is the man blessed who
fears the Lord. May the Lord bless you from Zion. May
you see the happiness of Jerusalem all the days of your
life. May you live to see your grandchildren. Peace over
Israel."

The Biblical *chassidim* were no fighters on the battle-
fields, nor were those "who fear God" humdrum fellows.
Those two psalms are the diptych of the Hebrew ideal, as
it could be conceived by opposing temperaments. The
militant spirit of certain centers created a martial vision
of Hebrew man, so that people wished that all *chassidim*
were brave soldiers of God. On the other hand, there was
a pacifist concept, which placed the ideal life of those
who fear God within the limited frame of the family
and of a rural profession. These two paintings help us to
recognize the *"Sitz im Leben"* of certain pietistic tendencies, but they are too abstract to give us indications
as to how such tendencies were put into practice. These
are rather scattered in other Biblical texts, and we must
gather them up there as a spontaneous and concrete testimony, not blunted by any literary plan.

These texts tell us first of all of the intimate relationship between the chassidim on the one side and the Levites and prophets on the other. Like the poor, the desti-
tute and the *yereim,* the *chassidim* belong to those who
keep close to the Levites and the prophets in every day

life, and with whom they are always concerned. It looks often as if the main function of the Levites and prophets was to share the lives of these popular elements, to educate and to encourage them, and to announce and support their claims. But as far as the *chassidim* are concerned, we have sometimes the impression that they were not only related to, but identical with the Levites and prophets. At least two texts speak of such an identity. Deuteronomy 33:8 sees in Moses God's chassid and the leader of the brotherhood of the Levites. When the prophets who instituted David's royalty are mentioned (Psalm 89:20), they are called *chassidim*. Thus, at a certain moment of Biblical history, the tradition connected the Levitic investiture and the election of the Davidic dynasty with the idea of a chassid. A *chassid-prophet* is said to have founded the order of the Levites, and *chassidim*-prophets had from the beginning pointed out the Messianic destiny of the House of David.

These general facts support the hypothesis of a close relationship between the chassidim, the Levites and the prophets. We shall see that they fulfilled certain functions together, and that they joined in working out a great number of concepts.

The first joint project is education. Like the Levites and the prophets, the *chassidim* teach ethics for which they either use the Levitical terms Torah (teaching) or *Mussar* (instruction) or the prophetic terms Derech (way) or *Davar* (word). Torah and Mussar are lessons inspired by tradition, while the Derech and the Davar are rules of life elaborated at a certain moment following a popular decision or a call from God.[27] The Levitic aspect predominates in the ethics of Torah and Mussar, whereas a prophetic attitude can be seen in the Derech or the Davar. Both aspects seem to have been adopted by the *chassidim*.

We are in a position to determine the content of the

ethics of the *chassidim*. It insists first of all on repentance, whose regenerative power is always underlined. In this concept, sin is something infinitely serious, which must be wiped out, if man wants to remain before God. But repentance is stronger than sin and can wash it off entirely, thus giving man an enitrely new and fresh purity. The *chassidim* see this passage from sin to innocence on the ritual level—here they come close to the Levites, and on the spiritual one—which relates them to the prophets. The technique of repentance as described and used by the *chassidim* depends on the liberty of the human soul as well as on the rigidity of a rite of passage. It calls for efforts and resignations which only a courageous will can agree to —humility, the acceptance of insults and even ataraxy, corporeal and spiritual asceticism and confession[28]—these are disciplines which must be valued highly. They are animated by the spirit of repentance which we also find in prophetic appeals. But that discipline is at the same time an automatic one. It cannot be stopped, nor can its efficiency be doubted. The prophets call on people to repent, but they do not know whether God will accept that will to return. There hovers a "perhaps" over the prophetic perspectives, and it emphasizes the illusory character of all human certainty, even if it is upheld by the highest purity. The *chassidic* discipline of repentance, on the other hand, is in spite of its inner wealth no less strictly dogmatic in its results. It is certain that sin can be wiped out. Herein lies an imitation of the Levitical doctrine of the ritual, where purification through sacrifice is automatic. Through the purity of its demands and the certainty of its results chassidic repentance reveals the complexity of its prophetic as well as Levitical sources.

The ethics of the *chassidim* mention prayer besides repentance. Prayer is certainly one of the techniques of repentance, but one strange circumstance sets it aside from all other prayers of Biblical times—the prayer of the *chassidim* is preferably offered at night.[29] The *chassidim* stay awake, and many such hours are devoted to songs, prayers, and examination of one's conscience. Nocturnal prayer may have to do with the asceticism of the *chassidim*. But it is more natural to think of Levitical or prophetic influences. It was the Levites who had to stay awake at the Temple of Jerusalem. We have many proofs of this with regard to the time of the Second Temple, and it may have been the same at pre-exilic times.[30] We also know from various sources that these wakes were accompanied by prayers and meditations. This is particularly evident from Psalm 134. a song apparently recited at the relief of the night watch at the Temple:

"Bless the Lord, all you who are the servants of the Lord, who stand in the house of the Lord in the night. Lift up your hands toward the sanctuary, and bless ye the Lord . . . "

Among the Levites there were bound to be many *chassidim*, and these kept up the practice of nightly watches and nocturnal prayers even outside of the Levitical service. But the inclination of the *chassidim* for the night can perhaps also be seen as an effect prophetic influences. The night is best suited for dreams, and it is at that time that the prophets get their dreams and visions.[31] The practice of prophetic experiences made the prophets approach the night with certain silent devotions, since every night could become the source of a revelation which was offered in the form of a dream in the midst of the sleep. The prophets-*chassidim* mentioned in Psalms 89:20 know of a vision which is preferably communicated during sleep. Therefore it could have been the experience of prophecy as well as Levitical activity which gave the nights of the *chassidim* its meditative and mystical character.

Although the instruction of the *chassidim* is valid for all, it is preached only by a small minority. This is another basic aspect where the *chassidim* meet the Levites and the prophets. The minority character of the Levites and prophets derives from the hereditary and charismatic character of their orders. A Levite was born, a prophet was chosen. There is nothing comparable in the purely ethical doctrine of the chassidim. Their exclusiveness can only be explained by the fact that they themselves did the enlisting, which was, at least at the beginning, done among Levites and prophets, and that they applied to their community the principles of a religious order or a chosen sect. But once they were constituted, the chassidim gave a new meaning to the fact that they were so small in number. In Levitism and prophetism the minority aspect is manifested mainly by the increase in individual Levites or prophets. Since the Levites and prophets are only a few, some of them stand out from the group and reveal a strong personality. This is a very remarkable fact for the prophets, since more and more they give the impression of fighting the whole world. The solitude of a Jeremiah, whom God does not even permit marriage or family establishment is the best proof of the fact that the prophets were a minority and unique. At certain moments of their existence Moses, Elijah, Amos, Hosea, Jonah, and Ezekiel were nearly as alone as Jeremiah, showing in various ways that the prophets were a minority. Also, in the most typical documents (Judges, Deuteronomy) the Levite appears in the singular (Deuteronomy 14:27 and 29; 16:6; Judges 17:7ff.) He absorbs the entire Levitism in his own person and proves that Levitism is not the choice of a mass of people but of certain rare individuals. With the *chassidim*, on the other hand, the community never disappears in favor of the individual. The *chassidim* always form a group, and this group, in which individuals cannot easily be distinguished, considers itself always as a minority. When the community of the *chassidim* goes into action, it clashes with others who are sometimes called "evil" (in which case the *chassidim* are considered righteous), or else "the multitude, the mob, the children of men, or the children of Adam," which means all mankind.[32] In this latter case the contrast is not a moral one any longer but it derives from the fact that the *chassidim* are aware of being a cosmic minority. Their existence as a minority is tied up with the salvation of the world. In this connection lies the mystery to which the *chassidim* must respond.

Noachism

It is more probable that the prophets embellished that *minority* with the theme of the *remnant* than, as one unlikely hypothesis claims, that the *remnant* was at first the kingdom of Judah after the disappearance of the Northern Kingdom; then the community of the exiles of Joyachin Babylonia, as opposed to the false remnant of the Judeans of Zedekiah; and finally the community of the returning at the end of the exile.[33] According to the prophets the remnant does not consist simply of survivors but of those who know that they are different from the masses, available for other tasks, chosen by a particular grace and for a special destiny. Again a marital metaphor has a role in the concept of the remnant—the faithfulness of the *remnant* can only be compared with the *partiality* of the One who had planned it all. The *chassidim* accepted that partiality, that *hessed,* as a given fact of their destiny. For that reason, theirs was a greater meaning than that of other minorities. The Levites were a minority by virtue of their blood; the *chassidim* were a minority by choice. The segregating power manifested itself in them as a will. They were aware of the fact that they stood in opposition to the whole world, but they also knew that that opposition was necessary to the world.

The prophets define Israel's relation to other people in terms of the *hessed*. The *chassidim* furnish them with the most fitting image for assigning a place to Israel. To the prophets the Hebrews are the chassidim among the *children of Adam*. They are those whom God loves, on whom He counts, through whom He makes history work. Without them God is alone. Through them, the entire world is with Him.

A *chassidic* Psalm summarizes that *universalism* of the *chassidim*:

"The Lord God speaks, He calls the earth from sunrise to sunset. From Zion, the center of beauty, the Lord appears. Our God marches forth, He does not stop, fire is in front of him, and trumpets sound around Him. He calls the heavens above and the earth to judge His people. Gather for Me My chassidim, those who have concluded My covenant through a sacrifice. The heavens proclaim His righteousness, for God is the Judge. Selah. (Psalms 50:1ff.)

Everything in this psalm proves its antiquity—its style, the breaks, the images. The theophany resembles that of the very earliest Biblical poems. There, too, everything is universal, the heavens and the earth are invited to judgment. But the cosmos has Israel as its axis. Zion is the center of the theophany, God's place; the covenant is the beginning of God's time, and through it Israel has begun to be God's people. And that Israel, thus placed between the heavens and the earth as the axis of God's judgment and acquittal, that Israel is God's *chassid*. The use of that term is quite remarkable. In order to arrive at righteousness (verse 6), God uses the *hessed* of His people, who are allied to Him through the covenant.

I have selected this psalm in order to show that the so-called "universalism" of the prophets is in reality a Hebrew idea deeply embedded in the covenant. All the prophets have introduced is the idea of *hessed*. They have given the particular value of Israel's election within a universal election its most mysterious as well as its strongest meaning.

For the idea of a universal election, of a covenant concluded by God the Creator with the entire mankind, has from the very first been part and parcel of Hebrew thinking. The election of the Hebrews is presented in the Bible as a progressive and historical segregation. From Noah to Abraham, from Abraham to Isaac, and from Isaac to Israel, a selection is at work. One child is chosen among others, and that choice receives the meaning of its existence and its value from those others. "Ye shall be My own treasure among all peoples, for Mine is the earth." (Exodus 19:6) The *others* have their own law, even before Israel existed and could have had a law of their own. As soon as mankind had been saved through Noah, he and his children receive a *law,* which completes the covenant, which God makes with them. As said above, the Hebrews could not imagine that mankind could have existed in any other way than through a covenant with God, and through the observance of a law. Noachism is not an intellectual fiction which the Jews of rabbinic times introduced into Biblical doctrine. It *is* in the Bible and characterizes its religious system.[34] Through Noachism the prophets arrived at universalism. Their universalism expresses first of all Hebrew Noachism—Adam's children, Noah's children, and all men are allied with God. The *covenant* with Noah is the *law* of humanity.

Noachism explains that the prophets did not receive messages for Israel exclusively but for all peoples and even at first sight independently from all relation to Israel. The case of Jonah is typical. God calls on him to prophesy over Nineveh. But his case is not an isolated one. Jeremiah is installed as a *prophet of the nations* (Jeremiah 1:5) and the "servant" mentioned by Isaiah as *"a light to the nations"* (49:6), and many prophecies stated by other prophets concern mainly other nations.[35]

Noachism explains also why the prophets interpreted certain historical events in a language common to Israel and all others. There is not only *one exodus* (Israel's leaving Egypt) but many of them, all started by the same God who, in order to fulfill the same promise made to the same Father, Abraham, had taken the Arameans out of Kir, the Moabites and Ammonites out of the valley of the Arabah, the Edomites, the Amalekites, and the Midianites out of the desert, the Philistines out of Crete in order to leave them on the edges of Canaan—the promised land—so that every one's territory was guaranteed together with its boundaries. God was the arbiter of their conflicts, the witness to their doings, and the judge of their works.[36] Perhaps in the eyes of the prophets Syria and Palestine were a piece of the earth that could serve as a reference and as a model to the whole world. The moral and religious problems of mankind were not treated by the scale of humanity as a whole but rather by the dimension of that small space which could be grasped at one look but which political circumstances—the situation between two great empires of that time, Egypt and Babylonia—gave a remarkable diversity of structures and events. By applying to those people the language of history or rather that of a common historic destiny, namely, the exodus, the prophets equally applied to them the language of the covenant with all its moral implications. Just like Israel, all nations are responsible to God. They, too, are the *children* of the Father, the *servants* of the Master, and we have seen that, when referring to them, the prophets even use the language of marriage, albeit in a stereotype form. The symbolism of the covenant involves the Noachidic covenant as well as the covenant with Israel.

Nevertheless, the prophets know also that in the background of the Noachidic covenant the covenant with Israel has a meaning of its own, and that this meaning cannot be reduced to that of Noachism. It seems that the prophetic contribution to the *particular* idea of Israel is more important than their contribution to the universalism of the Hebrew religion. For while on the level of universalism they simply used Noachism, they opened up new problems on the level of particularism. Hebrew thought attributed to Israel a complementary dignity— among all the children of the Father, they were the *firstborn* (Exodus 4:22); also, among all the servants of the Master, they were the *priests* (*Ibid.* 9:6). That dignity implied responsibility, vocation, and a mission. A clearly intelligible program traced Israel's route, and one could notice that one day the Noachidic responsibility would be mixed up with that of Israel. Considered to be first fruit (Jeremiah 2:3) Israel spoke of a universal harvest; and instead of being priests, they speak of a universal priesthood. Traces of this catholicism can be found with the prophets, who, however, strongly insisted on Israel's singularity. To them the election of Israel was not entirely clear. It was a free act of love, *hessed*. In revealing Himself, God had taken hold of His chassidim. Then he kept them in an act of real love. The catholic conception was based on the idea of a whim. It is true that God had chosen Israel one day, but by and by that election had to be considered a mere bet. The *prophetic* conception, on the other hand, rests on the *seriousness* of the divine love of Israel. The dramatic struggle which is illustrated by the symbolism of marital love, the pathetic and dialogical encounter of God and Israel, gave universal history a meaning. The history of mankind *receives its meaning* by the intimacy of God and Israel.

In this perspective God's work in the world does not come to an end when all nations will be united into one but, on the contrary, with the individual preservation of every nation in the conscience of their responsibilities to God. Israel is neither the *firstborn* nor the *priest* but the *witness* (Isaiah 43:12). By the solitary experience of its love shared by God, Israel testifies to the truth of similar experiences. It guarantees the individuality of every people and of history. The prophets have said little about a concrete definition of that guarantee. They were only interested in stating that it existed. By making it inaccessible to a clear understanding, they underlined its irreducible mystery. The prophets have forever placed Israel in a particular destiny by making it the axis of history.

Notes

1. For the vineyard of the Lord of Hosts is the house of Israel, and the men of Judah are the plant of His predilection.
2. In these two verses the roots *arass* and *yadoa* must retain their technical sense of "acquiring a wife at the price of a dowry" and of "having carnal knowledge with a woman." The logic of the marital symbolism explains the strict precision of these terms. If the prophets see a marriage in the union of God and Israel, no false shame can prevent them from describing that union through whatever constitutes a marriage, and first of all through a marital encounter, the summit of love and source of fertility. All attempts to reduce Hosea's "yadoa" to an intellectual knowledge of God (Nowack: *Handkommentar zum Alten Testament, Kleine Propheten*, p. 23. Van Hoonacker: *Les douze petits Prophètes*, p. 29) destroy the "logical perspective" of the marital symbolism in that chapter of Hosea. (P. Humbert: *"La logique de la perspective nomade chez Osée,"* in: *Vom Alten Testament. Karl Marti gewidmet*, p. 166).
3. Contrary to Paul Humbert (*op. cit.*, p. 164) it seems to me that v.16 implies violence and not softness. The root "pth" has almost always the meaning of a forceful seduction (God *forces* the prophets to speak by seducing them and by breaking down their resistance Jeremiah 20:7; Ezekiel 14:9; I Kings 22:21. The mob hopes to seduce Jeremiah and to triumph over his resistance Jeremiah 20:10. Exodus 22:15 is doubtful, since we do not know whether the girl consents or not). The expression *"daver al lev"* always follows an act of violence; it is the comfort which a man gives his victim after having inflicted on him some punishment (Isaiah 40:2) or after having abused her (Genesis 34:3).

4. Isaiah 61:10; Jeremiah 31:2; Hosea 2:17.

5. See Heschel: *Die Prophetie,* p. 169 (Translator's Note: See also Heschel: *The Prophets,* 1962, p. 83, and Chief Rabbi Hertz's commentary on the Pentateuch, on Exodus 20:5).

6. See my essay: Le symbolisme conjugal, expression de l'histoire dans l'Ancien Testament. *Revue d'Histoire et Philosophie Religieuses,* 1954, I, pp. 39ff.

7. Jeremiah 2:2; Hosea 2:17; Ezekiel 23:3, 8, 9, 21, where Israel's youthful years are placed in Egypt. The "wedding" takes place in the wilderness, which is to Ezekiel the time of the giving of the Torah.

8. Jeremiah 9:13.

9. Isaiah 47:8f; 49:20f.

10. *Ibid.,* and 54:1.

11. Jeremiah 3:8 (verse 10 makes up for the threat in v.8). Isaiah 50:1.

12. Comp. M. Nedoncelle: *De la fidélité,* Paris, 1953, p. 130.

12a. *Republic* 442a, 546a.

13. *Physics* IV, 222b.

14. See Tresmontant: *Essai sue la pensée hebraique,* Paris, 1953, p. 35.

15. See Thorleif Boman: *Hebrew Thought compared with Greek,* Philadelphia, 1961, Part III. (Tr.)

16. See G. Pidoux: La notion biblique du temps, *Revue de Théologie et de Philosophie,* 1952, II, p. 120.

17. "Fear not for thou wilt not be humiliated. do not be afraid, for thou wilt not be put to shame; for thou wilt forget the shame of thy youth, and thou wilt not remember the dishonor of thy widowhood. Thy Creator will be thy Husband, the Lord of hosts is His name. The Holy One of Israel will by Thy Savior, He is called the God of the whole earth. For God has recalled thee like an afflicted and abandoned wife, and like the companion of one's youth who cannot be forsaken, this is the word of God. I have abandoned thee for a short moment, but with great tenderness I shall gather thee again. In overflowing wrath I had hidden My face for an instant, but now I shall love thee without limits, saith Thy Redeemer, the Lord." (Isaiah 54:4ff.)

18. A remarkable formula by Catherine of Genoa takes this incarnation of the individual in God into account: "My I is God, and I do not know any other I than this my God." (*Via mirabile,* Padua, 1743, XIV, 3).

19. The "progress" of Theresa of Avila, the "ascent" of St. John of the Cross, the "stages" of the pietists.

20. See *De quatuor gradibus violentiae charitatis.*

21. This error has been made, for instance, by Richard of St. Victor, who associates with the symbolism of the rungs of the ladder a verse of Isaiah which is based on the symbolism of childbirth.

22. The inner silence, the dark night, self-denial and self-hatred—these

are frequent themes expressed by the mystics. They point to a denial of the will and of conscience.

23. See Nelson Glueck: *Das Wort "hesed" im alttestamentlichen Sprachgebrauch als menschliche und goettliche gemeinschaftsgemaesse Verhaltungsweise*, 47, 1927.

24. Translator's note: See also Norman H. Snaith: *The Distinctive Ideas of the Old Testament*, ch. 5.

25. "*Lifnim mishurat hadin.*" This is one of the attitudes of Talmudic *chassidism*, as against the strict fulfillment of one's obligations, the *din*. See Babylonian Talmud Baba Kamma 103b and *passim*.

26. The history of *chassid* as a word and as an idea is well known. When the great modern movement of Chassidism arose in Poland at the beginning of the eighteenth century, the idea was not new. The word was purposely chosen because it is linked with the traditional evolution of Jewish life. From the sixteenth century on the mystic milieu of Safed was chassidic. It generated the Messianism of Sabbatai Zvi, which was counteracted by the Polish chassidism of the Baal Shem Tov. In the thirteenth and fourteenth centuries there was in Germany a popular *chassidism*, though less eclectic and ascetic than the one of Safed. Its ideal is recorded in the Sefer Chassidim (The Book of the Pious), where influences of Christian medieval mysticism are visible, without, however, lessening the authentically Jewish foundation. (See now: Simon G. Kramer: *God and Man in the Sefer Chassidim*. Tr.)

Chassidism is vastly represented in Talmudic literature, although it has as yet not been systematically appraised. In the Talmud we must distinguish between the community of the First Chassidim, who are certainly related to the Maccabean *chassidim* and to the sectaries mentioned in the Dead Sea Scrolls and, on the other side, the *chassiduth* which flourished after the events of the years 70 and 135. Then the *chassid* was not any longer an isolated figure but the hero par excellence of Jewish piety. For post-Talmudic *chassidism* see G. Scholem: *Major Trends in Jewish Mysticism*, 3rd. edition 1954 and L. Gulkowitsch: *Die Bildung des Begriffes Hassid Tartu*, 1935. The classical works which deal with the period of the Second Temple contain chapters or information concerning Maccabean Chassidism. These must now be supplemented by a bibliography of the Dead Sea Scrolls. Numerous essays have been written about the meaning of *hessed* in Biblical times, but usually they neglect the hypothesis of the existence of *chassidism* before the Second Temple. The studies of L. Gulkowitsch: *Die Entwicklung des Begriffes hasid im Alten Testament*, Tartu, 1934, and of Eerdmans: *The Chassidim, Old Testament Studies* I, 1942, p. 176, are exceptions. (See also: I. I. Mattuck: *The Thought of the*

Prophets, 1953, and O. J. Raab: *The Theology of the Old Testament,* 1949, p. 127. Tr.) But Gulkowitsch reduces the chassidim to a purely cultic community, and Eerdmans discovers them even in texts which do not mention them at all. The chassidim should be investigated where they are mentioned, but in the full meaning which the Biblical text gives them. They go beyond the narrow frame of a cult and at the time of the Bible they constitute a human group which is defined through its connections with the word *hessed.*

27. Psalms 32:8 and 50:7; Amos 2:7.
28. Psalms 4:3; 22:7; 32; 37:8; 69:11f.
29. Psalms 4:5, 9; 16:7; 22:3; 30:7; 42:9.
30. Mishna Tamid I.
31. Typical situations: Jeremiah 3:25; Job 33:15.
32. Psalms 4:3, 4, and 7; 12:1, 9; 25:16, 19.
33. See J. Meinhold: *Studien zur Israelitischen Religionsgeschichte,* I, *Der heilige Rest,* Bonn, 1903. R. de Vaux: *Le reste d'Israel d'apres les prophetes, Revue Biblique,* 42, 1933, p. 526. Franz Rosenzweig: *Der Stern der Erloesung,* end.
34. See Elie Benamozegh's article on Noachism, translated by Wm. Wolf in *Judaism,* vol. 13, nos. 2 and 3 (Spring and Summer 1964).
35. Jonah, Nahum, Obadiah.
36. This is the spiritual background of the second chapter of Deuteronomy and of the first two chapters of Amos. The fact that all those nations are related to one another through their common ancestor Abraham is spelled out in detail in Genesis 19:25, 36.

3

Prophetic Existence

The Scandal

To the Biblical prophet living means to share the mystery of Israel. It means, then, not to know the ultimate secret of the divine intention, even if one experiences the violent outburst of a partial revelation. Even when the prophets gave history and Hebrew thinking their true meaning, they hid at the same time the absolute kernel of that meaning. This they could discover only in themselves, in an intimate experience which was accessible only to those Hebrews who were, like the prophets, ready to serve the absolute and to become allied to it. Between the Hebrew prophets and laymen a dialectic is established and a dispute concerning Biblical times. To the prophets, that time was unfinished and had to be built at every instant. To the others, the building had already been finished. In all its pages the Bible shows that prophecy was an invasion into the edifice of Hebrew time. There it was felt as an interference and a scandal.

This scandal, which was born out of the conflict between two periods, erupts in the lives of certain prophets of whom we know only that they were accused and persecuted, as if their entire lives had had only that basic meaning of being a scandal.

In the ninth century two prophets dominate all others in the depth of their personality and importance of their message. They are Elijah and Michayu. What do we know of them? It seems that they emerged from the night and went back to it for some brief moments in a particularly tragic light. Elijah is hunted down by Jezebel, who has sworn to have him killed. He must flee to the north or to the south, running and hiding all his life. He is not only hated by the queen, although she is the most ruthless of his persecuters. He finds support only from some isolated and courageous individuals.[1] The majority of the people are obstinately neutral, and in order to impress them, Elijah must perform spectacular miracles, whose effects are not nearly as spectacular. Even after the scene on Mount Carmel,[2] Baal goes on to be worshipped in Israel. If the people are not openly against Elijah, they are at least not much for him. Michayu[3] appears only in order to vanish in the jail in which Ahab most probably let him die a miserable death. When we follow the story we feel how Michayu, too, has been persecuted and probably kept under surveillance even before receiving his final penalty. The scene takes place at the gates of the capital of the North. Ahab, the King of Samaria, has a famous visitor, his ally Jehoshaphat, King of Jerusalem. Ever since the schism, it had been a rare occurrence that the prophet addresses both kings at the same time. Even if Jehoshaphat is sympathetic toward Michayu's message, he does not protest when his royal colleague has the prophet put in chains. This shows that even to Jehoshaphat, who was a loyal servant of the Lord, a prophet was out of principle a defendant. But these two kings are not Michayu's only antagonists. The messenger who comes to fetch him expresses the popular opinion when he tells him in no uncertain terms to yield to the royal intentions. We are aware of the fact that the anonymous masses, whose interpreter the messenger is, are opposed to the obstinate exaltation of the prophet and want that obstacle to the pacification of the country to be removed. Finally, numerous prophets, functionaries at Ahab's court, rise against Michayu. To Michayu they are false prophets, and he tells them so. One of them slaps him in public. This brutal act illustrates the hatred which the false prophets felt toward Michayu, and also the prestige which they themselves enjoyed when they pretended to be the authentic spokesmen of God. Michayu did not only feel insulted but greatly pained for being suspected to be a liar by the very people of whom he knows, in an obscure but profound conviction, that they are the real liars.

Michayu was not the first prophet who ended up in prison. The precedent of Chanani the Seer is even more remarkable, since the king who persecuted him was not, like Ahab, a Baal worshipper, but a man loyal to God: Assa the King of Judah, and Jehoshaphat's father. Although in the Book of Kings the incident of Chanani is passed over in silence, Jehoshaphat's attitude in the scene of Michayu lets us understand the story as it is told in the Book of Chronicles.[4]

In the same book we read that in the ninth century it happened for the first time that a prophet was murdered in Judah. The murders ordered by Jezebel came from a wholesale oppression in a supercharged political atmosphere. But Zechariah became the victim of a trial for high treason in Jerusalem. Here is indeed a distressing circumstance: He is the son of the high priest Joyada, the protector and teacher of King Joas, who has him put to death.[5] Zechariah inaugurates the tragic series of Judean prophets who ended through assassination. According to a legend, Isaiah belongs to them.[6] The Biblical text specifically mentions Uriah. He had escaped to Egypt, but King Joyakim obtained his extradition and had him executed in Jerusalem.[7] Jeremiah, who had been persecuted at the same time as Uriah, succeeded temporarily in avoiding condemnation by hiding in Jerusalem itself.[8]

When Amaziah, the priest of Beth El, denounced Amos

as a spy to King Jeroboam, it was certainly done so as
to make him suffer the supreme penalty. That scene took
place in the midst of the eighth century.[9] The fact that
this is the only biographical element in the prophecy of
Amos emphasizes that his very life was at the mercy
of a capricious king. On that day Jeroboam had more
urgent concerns. If he had had the leisure to take up the
case of Amos, the prophet would not have escaped with
a mere sentence of banishment. Amos was accused of
grave offenses. He was said to have started a conspiracy
against the King of Israel, in complicity with the King of
Judah. The political climate of the days indeed favored
both of these accusations. For had not Amos announced
the speedy fall of the dynasty of Jeroboam, and this in
the name of God? Such prophecies were bound to excite
popular passions and personal ambitions. In the past several dynasties had fallen to pieces as a consequence of
prophetical interventions. It had been easy for the prophets to find accomplices among the dissatisfied. Ahijah had
broken the unity of the kingdom of Solomon by talking
Jeroboam I into revolt.[10] Elijah and Elisha had prepared
the ground for the insurrection of Jehu.[11] When Amos
proclaimed that God would raise the sword against the
house of Jeroboam, he encouraged thereby his anonymous
listeners to think of themselves as God's swordbearers.
Amos' Judean nationality made his gesture even more
grave and intolerable. Amaziah pointed out that Beth El
was the royal sanctuary of the North, an establishment
of the dynasty of Jeroboam.

It was evident that by prophesying in the religious
capital of the north, Amos had taken a great risk. It
meant hitting those loyal to Jeroboam where it hurt most,
it meant insulting the king in his own residence. It also
meant that the prophet exposed himself to immediate
retaliation. Amaziah could not imagine that Amos' courage came solely from his prophetic inspiration. As an ex-

perienced politician he saw behind Amos not God but the King of Judah that shrewd rival of the King of Israel. Just as in Israel, there were prophets in Judah who "ate the bread" of those for whom they prophesied.[12] Their oracles depended on how much money they received. Amaziah saw in Amos one of those venial prophets. He was a spy and an agitator paid by Judah to start troubles in Israel, and that is why when Amaziah did not succeed in having Amos arrested, he sent him beyond the frontier of Judah: "Seer go away! Return fast to Judah, and eat thy bread there, and there shalt thou prophesy!" (Amos 7:12).

The new feature of this scene is that the prophet's main antagonist is no longer the king but the priest. It is true that the priest is a royal functionary but the influence of the king himself seems to have been a moderating one. In previous instances the prophet had stood face to face with the king. Now the latter remains in the shade. It is not he that stirs up the prophetic scandal but the priest. This change is the more profound, as already in the past the king had had substitutes in his fight against the prophets, but these had been other prophets. Elijah had to face the prophets of the Baal, Michayu the false prophets of the Lord, and one of them assaulted him. Now for the first time we have a contrast between the prophet and the priest. So far those functions had been spiritually associated with each other. Zechariah, the first martyred prophet, was a prophet and a priest at the same time. Those who accuse him are princes and lay ministers. Now we have a double conflict within the religious field: besides the antagonism between true and false prophets there is a rivalry between the true prophet and the priest.

This observation is important for the following centuries, when the priest can be found constantly among the prophet's adversaries, with this important difference: often the priests and the false prophets unite their efforts in order to subjugate the true prophet, while the priest Amaziah seems to mistrust all prophets, true and false alike.

In Jeremiah's fate the prophetic scandal assumes its sharpest form. The prophet has been completely isolated. He faces the whole world. He describes himself as "a man of quarrels" (15:10), and his word is a perpetual source of shame and insults (20:7f.) He is an object of laughter; everybody disgraces him. His behavior exposes him to sarcasm, to contempt and hatred, and finally to torture and death. From the very first moment on, he had seen in his mission a fight against all:

"From this day on I will make of thee a fortified city, an iron pillar, brazen walls against the entire country, the kings of Judah and its princes, the priests and the people of the land." (Jeremiah 1:18)

This list was to become literally true. Jeremiah had to break with his family and his friends at Anatoth, who pursued him with their jibes and slanders and nearly killed him with their own hands (11:21). In Jerusalem he finds opposition from kings, princes, prophets, priests, and the people at large, and he heaps upon himself all the castigations that had been experienced only partially by other prophets. Michayu had been beaten by a false prophet, and Amos had been insulted by a priest. Jeremiah was both beaten and insulted, and the ill treatment came to him from a priest[13] and a false prophet.[14] Elijah had been forced to go into hiding, Michayu was thrown into prison, and Zachariah was condemned to death. Jeremiah spent twenty of the forty years of his career in prisons of different kinds. Sometimes it was the cell of a political prisoner, a suspect, and other times the dungeon of a traitor. Sometimes he was chained in jail like a criminal, with a crust of dry bread and a jar of water; and other times it was the cistern of man condemned to death, standing in mud up to his waist, and saved only at the last moment.[15] Jeremiah spent more than ten years in hiding. He owes his escape to the protection of a notable man of Jerusalem, so that he does not share the fate of the unlucky prophet Uriah.[16]

It is meaningful that it was the family of Shafan who protected Jeremiah. This was a family of well-known people. Shafan himself was the secretary of King Josiah;[17] his grandson Gedaliah was to become governor of Judea after the fall of Jerusalem.[18] On other occasions, too, we notice that well-known people were concerned about Jeremiah's fate.[19] This confirms a fact which, although not new, is stressed in the Bible only from the time of Jeremiah on; if the prophet is understood at all, it is by the great, whereas the common people oppose the prophet. Side by side with kings, false prophets, and priests, the anonymous masses occupy a place among those who resist the prophets. This had already been evident from the passive attitude of those who surrounded Elijah. It is clearly shown by the aggressive and almost hysterical attitude of the people toward Jeremiah. To them prophecy is a scandal.

The masses were equally scandalized by Ezekiel. It is true that those who were exiled to Babylonia did not have the means to attack the prophet himself (at least after the conquest of Jerusalem; before that, letters sent to Babylonia denounced Jeremiah to the authorities of the Temple.[20] But they met Ezekiel with distrust, incredulity, and sometimes even cynicism. They "rebel" against God's word—this is the subject of Ezekiel's reproaches.[21] They did not want to admit that *there was a prophet in their midst,* and when they did hear him speak, they compared him with an artist or a poet.[22] The armed conflict became thus a spiritual one, and this had always been the basis of the previous forms of opposition between the prophet and the people. When circumstances made physical violence impossible, the people still maintained a moral hostility against the prophet, who felt this to be as painful as violence. It shows that when we speak of "masses" we must think of a collective mentality rather than of a social group. Prophecy was opposed by a certain attitude, in which we easily recognize the influence of "wisdom." Together with the kingdom and the priesthood, wisdom was among those spiritual forces against which prophecy had to wage an endless battle. We must now analyze the details of those conflicts.

Prophecy and Royalty

In the community of the covenant God alone is King; for a human king can take over only by giving up the essential part of his reality, which is his power. The prophets over and over again repeated this demand for resignation, and thus they got into a conflict with the royal person himself as well as with those who shared his power. The situation of the prophet in the state follows from his situation in the covenant.

Metaphorically, "King" is one of the terms for God in the covenant. But this human expression, when applied to God, always involves a dramatic possibility. This drama erupts in the vision of the prophets, and they describe it with a grave yet naïve obstinacy. When the prophet says: "God is the Father," "God is your Husband," he says at the same time, "God loves you." That love changes according to circumstances and even undergoes adventures. In the love of God and Israel there are sudden turns of fortune just as such changes can be found in the relations between a father and his children, and between a husband and his wife. As a *child,* Israel is not only the young and pure adolescent, surrounded by his father's care.[23] He is also the miserable and naked infant, forsaken by his mother, picked up and adopted at the roadside if some should pass by.[24] He is also an orphan.[25] As a child he is rocked to sleep, comforted, and hurt. He is a *child* in all the variations of a smiling or cruel destiny. Likewise, as God's *wife,* Israel is not only the partner in a pathetic dialogue of love but also the virgin concerned about the future, taking a risk with her first step;[26] the savage adulteress;[27] the arrogant prostitute,[28] and the widow.[29] She is always a woman, but sometimes with caressing gestures, at other times fighting; her voice may be that of seduction, of threats, of defiances or of sighing.

The same drama can be found in God's *kingship.* In at least two instances of Biblical history God's royal attribute is clearly outlined and has a precise meaning. First of all, we have a gesture of retreat at the time of Samuel. God agrees that a king be proclaimed in Israel, that a being of flesh and blood should carry the royal attribute which heretofore had belonged to God alone. The acceptance has many shadings. We see indignation ("Is not God your King?")[30] and resignation ("They have despised Me as their King").[31] But when all is said the final result is an abdication. God seems to have given up His royal function in favor of man. Later, at the time of Ezekiel, God claims that same fuction in an authoritarian manner. God is and will be Israel's King, whether they agree or not ("In spite of you, I shall rule over you").[32] This is a reaffirmation of God's royal power, a gesture of reintroduction which corresponds inversely to the retreat at the period of Samuel. The co-existence of these two movements shows a sudden turn in fortune, a divine-royal drama, which can be compared to that of God-Father and God-Husband.

But a closer look reveals a great difference between these dramas, between the adventure of God's royal power and that of His love.

For when God says: "I am your Father, I am your Husband," this is purely *symbolic* affirmation. It does not prevent Israelite children from having their actual father, nor does it prevent the encounter of lovers. It is true that the affirmation has applications in the real life of Israel. Thus, God's Fatherhood leads to the brotherhood of all men. Since God and Israel are linked to each other like husband and wife, Israel must not commit "adultery," by worshipping other gods. But the *reality* of fatherly or marital love remains in its *human* form. But in the case of God's *Kingship* the exact opposite takes place. When God says: *"I am King,"* this affirmation has a *concrete* meaning. God cannot tolerate a flesh-and-blood king as a substitute. God is the absolute King, and the state must take this primordial fact into account. The governmental form—the constitution—can only have the unique character of incarnating the *Kingdom of God*. When a human king arises, he has a provisional and unsteady character, and he is but a sign and a symbol. This has indeed been the role of the kingdom in Israel: a temporary and accidental role, in no way tied up with the essence of the state.[33]

The prophets were well aware of the fact that Hebrew royalty was merely accidental. In the northern state they were the vanguard of the great insurrections against the royal power. In the south, they seem to have been more tolerant toward the dynasty of David, since it was more loyal to the principles of the covenant than the sovereigns of the north. We must, however, not forget that the schism had been caused by the prophetic intervention of Ahijah, a schism which constituted the most tragic and lasting disturbance of the Davidic kingdom. Nor must we forget that the last Davidic kings were severely reprimanded by Uriah and Jeremiah. In the state which Ezekiel had in mind, David occupied only a modest place, and above all he does not bear the title of King but of Prince, and the latter metaphor is never used to designate divine power.[34] The Messianism of the prophets is no proof for their attachment to the Davidic dynasty. The opposite is true: since prophetic demands were constantly opposed to royal initiative, only an amended and corrected and sublimated David could survive history in order to live forever. He is a shoot,[35] a plant,[36] a prince, but not a king. Only by becoming a symbol could a human king be integrated in prophetic history. In order to live, David had to become the Messiah. Only God is the King of history. This defiance which the prophets launched against the person of the king also involves the entire state, since the idea of God the King implies that the state with its foundations and institutions must be available as the *Kingdom of God*. But one group sometimes claimed to be God's substitute in the state and was therefore the object of prophetic disapproval. They were the priests.

Prophecy and Priesthood

Can the violent contrast between the prophet and the priest be reduced to the antinomy between two religious tendencies, to the irreducible opposition between legalism and inspiration, between ritual and the spirit? Does not the history of Israel present here the particular illustration of a general problem that has to do with the very roots of a religious attitude? Did it have the merit of presenting the spiritual claim under a form of outstanding value, and did it subsequently make the mistake of weakening that claim and inserting it into a legal and ritual concept? Did the prophets in their fight against the priests already battle against the Pharisaism to come, which then falsified and parodied the teachings of their instructors?[37]

To set such evident contrasts into motion would be too simple. It would be too easy first to reduce the law to formalism, and then to show with what holy indignation the prophets arose against such formalism. We must never forget that he who observes the law is as much opposed to legalism as is the prophet. Just because of his lifelong intimacy with the law, he mistrusts legalism all the more. His vigilance is prehaps less spectacular than that of the prophet, but it is as sincere and unending. After all, a historian is not a showman, and therefore he must not put all kinds of pieces together in order to get a picture of the Pharisee, then bestow on him whatever his fancy can produce in terms of shabbiness, dryness, and barrenness of soul, furnish his empty heart with the sordid cupidity of a Shylock, endow such an automaton with all the exterior accessories of piety, tie him to his phylacteries, dress him up in fringed clothes, and then contrast this scarecrow with the heroic, vibrant, and passionate figure of the prophet. For the historian knows well that Pharisaism is much more complicated than commonly supposed and that although sporadically some Pharisees could be presented in the guise of a Shylock, there are many others among them, some extremely human, and others with an exceptionally deep religiosity. We might be tempted to call these Pharisees "pure" if the doctrinal book of the Pharisees, the Talmud, did not suggest that we call them "true," as opposed to the masked ones who are but *false* Pharisees.[38] To the Talmud, the "pure" Pharisees are not better legalists than the others, but they are the only authentic legalists. Therefore he who contrasts the prophet with the false Pharisee turns his back to the problem of the relations between the prophet and the law, since the false Pharisee is not in the law, neither through his person nor through his life. Not only the prophet but the true Pharisee rises against the mask of the false one, who, in the eyes of the true one, is not only a fallen partner and a bad accomplice but an absolute imposter. The same contrast which exists between the true and the false prophet obtains also between the true and the false Pharisee. Both are "false" but in the case of the Pharisee the implication is that he is not that, ever! To fight against the false Pharisees is not a fight against Pharisaism as such but with its usurpers, just as the fight against false prophetism is not a battle against prophetism but against its usurpers.

Now those priests with whom the prophets clashed were false Pharisees, since they have misused the law.

It is clear from the Biblical texts that the priests were not attacked by the prophets because they were priests but because they were not so any more. They are mentioned together with their sins. That list is like a nomenclature of usurpations and betrayals. Those priests who are mentioned by name—a small number—are particularly invidious. Either they are miserable rakes, like the sons of Eli, who were condemned by the prophecy of Samuel,[39] or else flunkeys of the royal power like Amaziah and Pashchur, who were harshly rebuked by Amos and Jeremiah.[40] Amaziah's case is important, since he is accused by his own words, stating that he is not in the service of God but in that of the king. According to him, Beth El, "the house of God" is a "royal house."[40] No other expression can underline better that sacrilege. The will of the state is substituted for that of God. Amaziah profanes his priesthood voluntarily—he merely wants to be considered a devout functionary. Amos rises against such a profanation. We must add that Amaziah is the type of priest found in the temples of the north. Their political servility goes hand in hand with ritual flexibility which distorts the Law. A syncretic spirit rules in their sanctuaries. At Beth El and at Dan bullocks of the Baal represent the God of Israel. On the other hand, ever since Jehu and the laws forbidding the Baal cult, the liturgy, though officially devoted to the God of Israel, turns secretly to the Canaanite idol.[41] Amaziah is not a priest of the divine Law but he adapts the laws of several gods to political demands. Amos versus Amaziah—this is not prophetism versus priesthood but Hebrew tradition versus clerical opportunism.

Amaziah's counterpart in Jerusalem is Pashchur. The temple in which Pashchur is the High Priest is the very same which is described by Jeremiah and Ezekiel in all its stupefying horror.[42] It is a robbers' den, a meeting place for speculators and hustlers; a place of fornication and idolatry; there the sun is worshipped by people who turn their backs to the Holy One; people bemoan Tammuz and pray to the Queen of Heaven. All the rites of the Orient are observed there together with the ancient Canaanite liturgies. There are orgies and human sacrifice. This well justifies the prophetic opposition. But this is not all. For Pashchur and his priests, the Temple of Jerusalem with all its paganism and excesses remains the Temple of God. The name of God is mingled with all those things to which He is diametrically opposed and seems to justify such a scandalous situation. "The Temple of the Lord!"[43] This is the sacred invocation on Pashchur's lips. It means that after having discarded God in the religious area, people cling to Him alone in the political arena. He personifies the national traditions; He represents the hopes of the people; His presence in the Temple is a sign of prestige and trust. At a time when the Assyrian menace is clear, the slogan "the Temple of the Lord" takes on all its political meaning. The Lord in the Temple—this is the banner of victory and of peace. The tortuous diplomacy of the last kings of Judah bears His name, and the Temple priests give it the impressive support of the official religion. It is not the priest who slaps Jeremiah and has him arrested, but a member of the staff. Just like Amaziah, Pashchur is a tool of the Crown.

Side by side with the sons of Eli, with Amaziah and Pashchur, there are many anonymous priests. The prophetic texts are full of grievances against them, but nobody scolds them for being priests. The entire prophetic violence is directed against abuse and neglect. Not referring to the innumerable priests of the false gods, the others—in Jerusalem and elsewhere—claim to belong to the Lord, falsify His doctrine or turn it upside down. They permit orgies next to the altars;[44] they favor the wealthy and encourage social exploitation.[45] They accept bribes and offer God a mere pittance.[46] They do not ask "Where is God?"[47] But they certainly ask: "Where are the people who will fatten us?" They have no conscience, only a spirit of caste and of opportunism. Such is the swarming mass of the priests whom the prophets take to task. It is not hard to understand why in such circumstances prophecy is considered a scandal in the eyes of the priesthood. The prophets speak in the name of the Law, the Torah, when they instruct and practice with such monotony.

In the charter of the Hebrew covenant, priesthood is as valid as Levitism and prophetism. It was supposed to be Levitic, but it was so only rarely. Like everywhere else, the Israelite priests abused their rights and were ignorant of their obligations. The priestly families attached themselves to a cultic place which was quite limited in space. Their ambitions did not take them beyond local prestige. Their destiny was one with that of the Temple. They had to defend certain interests, and when those were taken over by a political authority, they did not distinguish between the spiritual and the worldly. As everywhere else, in Hebrew society the priests became subordinates. They were no longer the mouthpiece of the divine law but of the will of the state. When they pretend to represent God in society, they abuse their power.

It must be pointed out, however, that a Levitic priesthood had its legitimate place within the covenant, and Hebrew history has frequently known loyal and therefore authentic priesthoods. The best among the priests were profoundly disturbed by the abuses of the priestly functions, and the constant and almost regular *reforms* in Biblical history prove that there existed the will to improve an institution which had frequently taken to the wrong road. The history of Biblical priesthood does not exhaust itself in Amaziah, Pashchur, and their acolytes of the north and the south, but it comprises equally the priesthood of Shiloh up to Eli and Samuel, the pietists of Elijah's time, Hezekiah and his people, Josiah and his co-workers, so many humble and kind servants of the Law and of the cult, none of whom had ever been the object of prophetic attacks. Quite the contrary, the prophets supported and intensified the work of maintaining the religious covenant and of reforms. In this they did not stand alone, but the true priests aided them. Often priesthood and prophetism were united in the same person. Thus Samuel, Elijah, Zechariah, Jeremiah, and Ezekiel were priestly Levites and prophets. That unity emphasizes the spiritual identity of priesthood and prophetism, wherever both of them were authentic.

But this restatement of historical facts must not hide the real difference between priesthood and prophetism. As far as religion is concerned, the two terms are not interchangeable; each stands for a particular attitude toward God. However, we must investigate the contrast in the authentic forms of those systems, where they try to reach God, and not where one of them is cut off from Him. The prophet is not a Don Quixote, sent forth to fight windmills. Nor are his enemies simply hypocrites and masqueraders. In order to chase the false priests and Pharisees out of the Temple, no prophets were needed but good priests and honest Pharisees, who could wield a good broom. The prophets could be put to good use in such tasks, but they did not have to waste their efforts in such situations. They had to be concerned with more important things—the law and a priesthood inspired by God. The debate between prophetism and priesthood is held within the framework of the covenant, and here two divine words meet face to face.

In principle these two words are identical, and in deed they are so in their common effort towards *sanctification*. But since this is but an effort, there is a wide margin of unfinished tasks. The law and prophecy supplement each other because each of the two wishes to realize what the other one cannot attain. This mutual tension has all the aspects of a fight since the realization of the one indicates the failure of the other.

Undeniably, prophetism is not mainly concerned with ritual but with ethics. But this is only true for the pre-exilic prophets. From the Exile on, prophetism assigns to rituals and their religious meaning an important place. Must we assume that this is a decadence of prophetism and an abandonment of its true vocation? No. For in reality Biblical prophetism covers two very distinct periods, separated by the destruction of the Temple in 586. Before that date, prophecy was faced with an essentially ritual type of religion. After that, it addressed itself to a nonritual religion. This difference is of the greatest importance for the understanding of prophetism. In the ritualized religion before 586 the prophets make moral and spiritual claims. They insist that when rites are atrophied and mechanized, they do not fulfill the covenant. The covenant makes a universal demand, and prophetism strongly points out that side of the covenant which had been neglected. But after 586 prophetism speaks as obstinately and as vigorously of the ritual, whose existence was threatened by an abstract spirituality after the fall of the Temple. The prophets thus became the builders of the Temple. Ezekiel became its ideal architect, and Haggai, Zechariah, and Malachi its real ones. Therefore in its last phases prophecy had a ritual orientation. The last songs of Biblical prophecy mobilized the Jewish energies for the service in the Temple. Where Joshua's priesthood and Zerubabel's temporal authority had failed, prophecy succeeded; the Temple was rebuilt, thanks to the appeals made by prophets.[48] Here again prophetism brings to the fore the neglected side of the covenant. It supports spiritual faith with ritual.

But the ethical significance of pre-exilic prophetism and the ritual meaning of exilic prophetism must not obscure the universal character in all prophetic efforts. It is clearly evident from all the prophecies of Ezekiel, Haggai, Zechariah, and Malachi that they did not see in the Temple the only condition for a religious life. As we shall see instantly, the prophets of the Exile had a unique spiritual view of the Temple. To them the Temple was a necessary but meager sign of a universal reality, which, in the form of the covenant, was the religious destiny of Israel. On the other hand, pre-exilic prophecies never radically condemned the rituals or the Temple but only their deviations or mechanizations. When Elijah appeared on Mount Carmel, he did so as a priest, and he linked the important choice between the Lord and the Baal to a cult. Isaiah had his first call at the Temple of Jerusalem. The grandiose scene shows that to him the Temple was the rightful abode of the Lord and His angels.[49] But the same prophet strongly opposed the cult and its mechanical rituals.[50] Before Ezekiel was banished, he probably had priestly functions at the Temple in Jerusalem, and he assumes solemn ones in the rebuilt Temple of his dreams.[51]

In both periods of existence prophecy thus aimed at the total sanctification of the life of Israel, just as did the law. For this very reason it turned against priesthood. For if both prophecy and the law may be equated with Biblical time, priesthood runs the risk of abandoning Biblical time through some of its implications.

These implications may be of a minor character but

they are all-important. Since priesthood is a discipline of the sacred, it may confound purity with holiness. Approaching God assumes a material meaning which eliminates man's problem before God. The religious debate goes on between a man and his conscience, so that repentance and sacrifice are more important than prayer. Metaphysical demands can be met by man himself, and no longer by God. Therefore the priest is surprised when he notices that God appears suddenly, and in a prophetic manner. The religious content of a priest's life was derived from disciplinary habits. His life thus did not move in Biblical time, which calls for a dialogue between God and man, whereas the priest talks to himself. His sacred partner is not God but priesthood

On the other hand, the complexity of the ritual tasks directs the priest's spirit towards a ritual vocation. He gets used to interpreting life's problems only in ritual and immutable terms. The historical content of time pales before its mythical content. Time is no longer experienced in the Biblical dimension of history in concentrated moments that are heavy with meaning, and that repeat themselves at regular intervals. In the covenant the priest does not prepare a future. The turning points of a reconciliation are impossible, since the discord does not recognize turning points. If sin is not canceled through rites, it cannot be eliminated altogether. To refuse to serve God means to disappear. The covenant is reduced to servitude. It knows nothing of love and its dramas.

But the major implication has to do with the fact that priesthood is connected with a certain place. This spatial condition of priesthood is not only the source of most of its abuses, like pride, bribes, and submission to power, but through its very essence it places priesthood outside of Biblical time, since priesthood has nothing to do with time but with space. We have noted earlier that the settlement in Canaan gave the Israelites for the first time the problem of space and time. Now, by the way of priest-hood, the problem presented itself once more. As the prophets had fought against the land, they now battled against spatial priesthood. Neither the land nor the Temple were for them the places of the covenant but the elements of marital adventure which they saw in the *brith* between God and Israel. They took the land and the Temple out of space and inserted them in time. Here we find the most important reason for prophetism's op-position to priesthood.

Did certain prophets clearly foresee a universal priest-hood and a cosmic Temple? Such an idea—the disinte-gration of priesthood and of the Temple and the dis-persion of their elements all over the world—appears with Jeremiah[52] and the Isaiah of the Consolation.[53] It does not at all imply a "spiritualization" of Hebrew doc-trine but simply a desperate effort to break the intimate link between priesthood and space.

The most remarkable effort in that direction was made by the most priestly of prophets, Ezekiel. Nowhere else was there a better separation between the Temple in space and that in time. On the one side we have the Temple in space, well established on Mount Zion, proud of itself and its permanence, and brutally destroyed on the ninth of Av in 586.[54] On the other side there is a Temple im-pregnated with historical life, where the angels leave the divine throne and return through the eastern gate, where their exile had begun;[55] a Temple forsaken by God and recaptured by Him; in short, a Temple which is not God's spatial residence but His companion in fate. As if to underline that the Temple exists only by virtue of the history linked up with God, its destruction deeply affects the prophet, so that his wife's death symbolizes the fall of the Temple.[56] This is a very moving transpo-sition of the theme of married love as part of the cove-nant. The mates are united in love beyond death. Likewise, God loves the Temple even after its destruction. As long as it stood, it symbolized God's joy. When it ceased to exist, it symbolized His mourning. It is not necessary for the Temple to *exist* but to *signify* in its presence or in its absence the history of the marriage of God and Israel.

Prophecy and Wisdom

Kingship and priesthood have metaphysical connotations. They assume sacred vocations, against which prophecy protests either by denying them or by pointing out their limitations. But wisdom, *chochma,* is secular. It is proud of its human origins and remains loyal to its earthly horizons. As a product of education and culture, and not of a vocation, *chochma* is not at all concerned with the absolute. If it does meet the absolute on its journeyings, it explains it or utilizes it. Wisdom has made God practicable and placed Him within reach of honest people. The conflict between wisdom and prophecy is the least glorious and most dangerous episode of the prophetic scandal. When the prophet stands face to face with the state or with priesthood, he risks his life. Confronted with wisdom, prophecy risks being adulterated, and the prophet himself may be classified, together with his God, as being on the right side, religiously speaking.

In the Bible there is no concrete conflict between the prophet and wisdom; there is no great scene which confronts them with each other, but there is a perpetual contrast of ideas and methods, a constant struggle, not between two religions but between an authentic one and a corrupt one.

First, let us see the contrast of methods. The *sage* is characterized by a contemplative or educational discipline, a work which goes on within himself and which helps him in the fashioning of his spirit. The prophet, on the other hand, is spontaneously inspired in a sudden outburst. One may rely on the instruction or the theory of a *chacham,* a sage, but not on a prophetic message, since it is unforeseeable and changeable. There is no prophetic "doctrine," but the prophet's lessons are given on the wings of history, sometimes resembling each other, at other times entirely contradicting each other. One cannot even talk of "lessons," since these can only be imagined in a serene atmosphere, in an assembly where an organized discussion can develop according to the rules of courtesy and logic. But the prophet speaks neither in a school nor in an academy nor in an assembly. He delivers his message in the overcharged, emotional and passionate atmosphere of the masses. His cry is answered only by other cries. He does not give lessons but orders. He does not seek discussion or objections but obedience or rejection. The counsel given by the *chacham* is an advice, which links the effect to the cause.[57] The counsel of the prophet is a secret, which links man's action to God's will.[58]

The contrast of ideas corresponds to that of the methods. The painful dialogue between Job and his friends is an example of the contrast between prophecy and wisdom. With scrupulous obstinacy the friends try to convince Job that everything is perfectly clear, that Job, his mourning, and his leprosy and his dunghill are the result of divine calculation, that Job and his God are in the clear, that there is no reason for any more questions, that one must turn over a new leaf. But Job with his leprosy, his mourning, and his dunghill stubbornly remains there and cries to heaven. So does his God. The meeting of God and man is not by calculation. Job is right; after all the arguments of "wisdom," there remains an ultimate possibility wherein man's destiny brings him face to face with God.

We meet the same conflicts in the meditations of the author of Ecclesiastes. He seems divided within himself, being Job and his friends at the same time. Although he pleads for prudence, he suspects it of being treacherous. He chooses the golden mean, but suddenly he finds that it is misleading. He transforms God into the good God, but he also hears the Lord's growling in his heart. He looks for *his* time, but after having discovered it, he finds himself caught in the snare of the time of the absolute.[59]

The prophets constantly live within the critique of the *chochma* as put forth by Job and Ecclesiastes. They mistrust the *maskil*, the intelligent person who keeps silent when he ought to speak and speaks when he ought to keep silent.[60] They become indignant over the preacher of *shalom*, peace, of the man who is satisfied with his achievement and to whom everything is clear. Those who howl for peace are evil in the eyes of God, and He encounters with His "No peace!" Isaiah, Ezekiel, and Jeremiah take "no peace" as the motto for their action.[61] For the peace of wisdom is but a hypocritical sleep, recommended so that misery and injustice cannot be heard. It is a metaphysical anesthesia, the dimming of the divine light above man's pillow. The cry "no peace" of prophecy is a bewildering alarm, a call to listen and to behold, to discover whatever has neither been explained nor resolved. Prophecy is therefore a revolt, a nonconformity whose demands, however, manifest the dominant appeal of a mystery.

Those modern thinkers who wish for a restoration of prophecy usually see it only from the limited viewpoint of a revolt. To them the prophet is the rebel par excellence. Out of his mouth they expect an absolute, intransigent, and revolutionary claim for a just world, and they believe they will find the authentic rhythm of prophetic inspiration in those great movements which, from the eighteenth century on, have led humanity toward greater justice in the social structure.[62] It is true that the legitimate ambition to reconstruct the world on the basis of justice would find considerable support if we had among us prophets whose growling voices and wild wrath would doubtless help us to avoid many dangers. But this image of a revolutionary prophetism can at this time be conceived of only because we live in societies and states whose structure and organization are essentially rational. It is easy to assign to the prophets a seditious role in a society in which order as well as disorder represents human effort. But we would be greatly embarrassed if we had to admit that there is a natural difference between disorder and order; if the established social order which we wish to change were itself the outcome of human will, while the revolt preached by the prophets presented a will outside of man. And this is exactly where Biblical prophecy comes in. It confronted human *chochma* with a different one, coming from God, and man's rational wisdom with the divine and irrational one. In order to bring on absolute disorder, prophecy makes use of an existence in the service of the absolute. Prophetic revolt is the revolt of a man in chains.

Servitude

The Change

Prophecy does not restrict itself to opposition from the outside world and to the questioning of social, religious, and intellectual institutions and traditions and thus expose the prophet to persecutions and suffering. By rising up against the prophet, prophecy places anguish into his very soul. Prophecy is not only a scandal to the world but to the prophet himself. It is his foremost adversary, most terrible because it is so intimate, and most menacing because it is absolute.

The anguish of the prophet begins with a *change*—he

becomes a *different* man. He is torn away from his family, his milieu, the conditions of his life, his mentality, his temperament, and thrust elsewhere. He is removed from his very self and transformed to such an extent that he no longer recognizes himself. He is confronted with himself, so that he says what he has never thought, and announces what he has always dreaded. His existence becomes a paradox of his being.

A peasant of the tribe of Benjamin loses some donkeys and sends his son in search of them.[63] When he finds them, he loses his son, for on his return he is not recognized by those who know him. He is a different man. His father is no longer his father. He obeys a higher paternal power, which is obscure but inexorable. He has become a prophet.

The history of Saul is a typical example of prophetic change. The themes which are elsewhere found individually are here admirably combined. The acquisition of the royal crown is only one episode of the drama of Saul, which is entirely based on his prophetic election. A peasant of the tribe of Benjamin—this is a man attached to his inheritance, a man with limited horizon, with honest and average mental habits. To make him a king might be a rather dangerous trial. But Saul is faced with a different ordeal. Even before he is anointed, we see him plodding behind his plow, his thoughts unlike those of mere peasants. His prophetic election has changed him. He is ready to fight for justice and liberty, to sacrifice his life and to demand the same of others, and to free the inhabitants of Jabesh-Gilead (I Samuel 11:7). From that moment on he serves the absolute. He has, at least morally, broken all ties with his family. He does not belong to his tribe any more. As his parents observe with amazement, he is among the prophets (10:12), those wandering dreamers who cannot adjust to an agrarian community. He joins them in a foolish adventure. Whereas all

reasonable men say "No" and send the messengers of
Jabesh-Gilead back to their homes and to their cares,
Saul says "Yes." And just like his new friends, the prophets, he wants to impose that "Yes" on the entire world
(11:7). He is only satisfied when his furious exaltation
has been made known to all. Like the prophets, he leaps
into action in the name of an intransigent and absolute
call.

But the acceptance of the absolute is the source of
his misery. Every facet of the Biblical account insists on
the naïvité and simplicity of Saul's religious mentality.
He bows humbly before the agents who send man on the
way to God. He offers sacrifices and makes others do the
same, and to him this is a means of making God listen to
his request (13:9). He consults the priestly oracle, which
seems to him to be God's ear and mouth (14:18). Saul
knows that among the paths which lead to God there are
some that are forbidden, and he avoids them. He has an
acute sense of what is pure and what is not. His fight
against magicians and necromancers is equaled only by
his absolute respect for traditional sacrifices and authorized ritual (28:9). His observance of the cultic means to
approach God is scrupulous in all details. Then he is
chosen. He becomes a prophet, and now he no longer
faces institutions and the men who personify them but
the absolute. Saul remains baffled before the unilateral
reactions of the absolute. He accepts them without understanding them. Fright enters his naïveté. Overwhelmed
by the demands which he does not question although he
does not understand them, he is terrified to note that he
must submit himself entirely, and the slightest hesitation means the rejection of the whole. Saul participates
in an entirely different order, which he cannot integrate
with his own. This knowledge reaches its climax after the
batle against Amalek (chapter 15). As in the fight for
Jabesh-Gilead, Saul has accepted the absolute demand.

But in taking up the cause of Jabesh-Gilead, he had saved unfortunate victims of a barbaric tyranny, and the demand of the absolute was in accordance with moral instinct. The fight against Amalek, on the other hand, offended that instinct, since it involved innocent women and children and herds of cattle. Although we do not know whether Saul's intentions in sparing those innocent were entirely pure, we see at least that he acted according to the normal attitudes of a king concerned with his prestige, and of a man moved by religious scruples. He is generous toward Agag; he is also generous toward God, since he plans to offer Him sacrifices set aside for that purpose during the massacre (15:21). He is being told that the wish of the absolute stands higher than sacrifices. The demands of the absolute crush generosity, political and cultic scruples, and even the spontaneous reaction of a moral conscience. On that day Saul learns the lesson that the prophetic change goes so far as to unsettle the very foundations of his moral person. This change is being made without concern for human dispositions, and without justifying itself. Saul must bow. Thus his being is shattered. He becomes sick and will remain so to his death.

The tragedy of Saul is a limited case. For Saul is the only man who has been chosen by God without ever having met Him. He is engulfed by the history which God works out; he is a link in the chain of people whom God uses to talk to the world, but he himself has never heard God's word. If election is the criterion of prophecy, Saul is a prophet. But with him the prophetic experience is structly limited to that election and does not have the extension to which the election leads, the most important of which is the intimacy with God. One day Saul felt that he was being held by a new power. The road which should lead him to his father's donkeys led him somewhere else. But he has never discovered where that force came from. He was aware of being possessed, without knowing by whom. His prophecy is a spirit without words, but also without knowledge. In order to communicate with God, Saul needs the agency of Samuel, while in himself the election is silent. He carries it within himself like a lifeless load welded to his soul. Saul's morbid state is aggravated by the fact that he was a prophet without God. He was elected out of the blue sky—suddenly he held the election in his hand. He was given a message, and he had just enough time to become aware of it when the messenger disappeared without being seen, heard, or met again. This removal from God makes the message absolutely mysterious. Only Saul can decipher it, but he never succeeded in doing so, and this became the shock of his life.

Though this is an exceptional case, it is symptomatic for prophecy in general. Even those prophets whose election is not limited to one instant, but is extended into a prolonged intimacy with God, do not know the ultimate meaning of their message. Although God does not forget them, He does not support them sufficiently to justify them. The ultimate consequence of the change is loneliness. After the prophet has been transformed by prophecy, he lives in the absolute in the eyes of the people, and among men before God. He can be himself only by not being himself.

We want to follow up step by step the mechanism of that change, as seen in the example of Saul. Every prophet furnishes the illustration of one or the other of the aspects of such a transformation.

The break takes a spectacular form in the election of Elisha (I Kings 19:19-21.) The change of that peasant does not take place, as in the case of Saul, in connection with a journey. A journey is always the beginning of an adventure. It may seem natural that an unexpected event should occur on the way. But that the spirit takes hold of a man while he is at work, in the familiar frame of his daily activities—this must play havoc with a simple soul. At first Elisha does not understand anything about the meaning of Elijah's gesture, when he places his mantle over his shoulders, nor about the scope of that meaning when suddenly he grasps it. He would like to stress his family and peasant attachments, to remain the son of his parents in the tenderness of a last kiss, and to manifest his professional conscience by once more taking charge of the oxen in the stable. But the call is absolute.

"What have I done to you?" Elijah asks him. The acceptance or the refusal cannot be partial, but a totality must be chosen. By accepting the call, Elisha becomes an entirely different person. Either the awareness of Elijah's mantle on his shoulders does not mean anything, or else it crushes Elisha's person. He is no longer a son; he does not embrace his parents. He is no longer a peasant; he destroys his oxen together with his plow. Another Elisha will now be Elijah's companion.

Thus it is also another Abraham, another Moses, and another Amos whom the election introduces in history. To them the call means being sent forth. God says to them: "Go to the land which I shall show you."[64] "Go to Pharaoh!"[65] "Go to My people Israel!"[66] To go on one's way evidently means to renounce. To Abraham it is the break with his family, his native milieu, his civilization. To Moses and Amos it is, more simply, giving up their calling as shepherds. In all cases the choice is painful and total. Abraham knows that he will henceforth be a stranger and a nomad. Wandering is his life's commitment. In moving overtones he remembers this on different occasions, as for instance when he is forced to acquire a cave in order to bury his deceased wife, or when he does not want his son to return to Mesopotamia, not even to find a worthy wife there. Thus death and the future revive in Abraham the feeling of his having changed. Unlike the sedentary man he had been before, he does not own a sacred place which can be used for a grave but he must buy it; he does not have a wide choice when it comes to secure his son's future, but he must rely on the help of an intermediary, with all the risks which this entails. Likewise, when Amos recalls his earlier occupations, he does it in a moving way:

"I am neither a prophet nor the son of a prophet but I am an ox-driver and a dresser of sycomores. The Lord has taken me away from the flocks and has said to me: Go and prophesy to My people Israel." (7:14-15.)

In Amos' life there are two stages. In the first, nothing prepared him for prophecy. It would not have occurred to him to leave his oxen, his sheep, and his sycomores. The second stage is an entirely different one. In spite of his nostalgia for the peaceful times of the past, he is now totally a prophet, and no one would ever recognize in him the shepherd of old. He is himself surprised at this transformation, but he knows that it was unavoidable.

The account of Moses' first call could hardly have been told with greater simplicity. After many days of hesitation and discussion he is finally compelled to leave his flocks and to become a prophet.[67] But he did not understand how deeply he would be altered by the call. Still filled with concerns of his own, and viewing the prophetic condition through the aspect of his humble preoccupation, he starts out on the road like a good father, with his wife, his children, and his belongings. Only after a new, violent, obscure, and pathetic encounter does Moses understand that a prophetic march is unlike any other journey. Something separates him from now on from his family.[68] From that moment Moses really begins to take up his vocation, which all the more implies solitude and elevation.

One of the aspects of the change is that one has to go through paradoxes. First there is the social paradox: peasants or shepherds are called on to become prophets, simple people change to a complicated existence, and a normal situation is integrated into the field of the abnormal. But there are many shadings. Elisha and Amos were not at all prepared for prophecy, whereas Samuel and Jeremiah were predestined. As Levites and priests, both were accustomed to the sacred sphere. In order to be inspired they do not have to vanquish the unholy. But both were guided by a mysterious intention toward charisma, even before their birth.

Samuel's mother had sworn her son to become a Nazarite—he is "lent" to God.[69] Why then should God not choose him also as a prophet? In the case of Jeremiah, God Himself has sanctified him for prophecy from his mother's womb.[70] How then could Jeremiah escape his destiny? There is thus nothing surprising in the fact that both Samuel and Jeremiah were one day called to prophecy. But here too the surprising paradox of the election manifests itself. While God has time to wait for them, He takes hold of them in their early youth, when they are not prepared spiritually or intellectually. At the age when God surprises them, the prophet-children Samuel and Jeremiah run the risk of being considered overexcited or ridiculous. How can childhood and seriousness go together? Samuel takes God's voice for that of his teacher, and even the latter finds it difficult to imagine that Samuel should become a prophet.[71] Jeremiah cries out: "But I am only a child."[72] It does not matter. The call is compelling. Thus these physically and mentally weak children become the bearers of a tremendous message. The image would be grotesque but for its paradoxical importance. When the absolute wants to express itself, it needs a growing being. With a guilty people, children are the sole hope.

The first encounters of Isaiah and Ezekiel with God are also of a paradoxical nature. Isaiah is impure, and he lives in the midst of an impure people.[73] We must give that concept of impurity its Biblical sense—ritual as well as moral—and such a state was incompatible with receiving a divine revelation. In the sacred enclosure of the Temple Isaiah is surprised by God. Holiness chooses impurity in order to pave a way to man. In Ezekiel's experience we somehow have the same paradox.[74] That priest considers the foreign country to be impure. But in that impure country, on the banks of the river Kebar, in the midst of the exile, God appears to him. The term "in the midst of . . . ," which is also used in other passages,[75] adds a supplementary note. Both Isaiah and Ezekiel have become integrated into a community from which they do not distinguish themselves at all. Isaiah's lips are as impure as those of the people who surround him, just as Ezekiel is an exile in the midst of other exiles. But the election makes an end to that communion. Isaiah is the only one among the impure who is purified by a burning coal which an angel presses to his lips. Ezekiel is the only one among the exiles who is taken back to Jerusalem in a prophetic vision. Their paradoxical election is at the same time the most profound change of their very existence.

But if that change enriches Isaiah and Ezekiel—one passes from impurity to purity, and the other from exile to the return—it is almost always a harrowing experience.

When a prophecy is revealed, it wounds, and the first victim is the prophet himself. Before prophecy is spread abroad in order to irritate the world outside, it wears down the prophet's vitals. When little Samuel wakes up after his first prophetic dream, he is filled with terror. He does not dare to recount his dream. And when Eli insists, he hears him predict the fall of Shiloh. How well we can understand Samuel's anxiety! He is not only reticent out of pity for Eli, but his own fate is threatened by the message which he carries within himself. If Shiloh falls, so will the house that sheltered him, the roof which protects his youth, the sanctuary in which he has hoped to continue serving. The entire personal future of the young prophet is involved in that first awakening. Likewise, although the text is not as precise, Jeremiah's youthful prophecies must have concerned his village and his family at Anatoth, or else the fierce hatred of the people of Anatoth for Jeremiah would be unexplainable.[76] That child foretells his own destruction, and the same catastrophe will affect his relatives, friends, and his native village. As he was to say later in a tragic outcry, he was born for a curse. The womb in which he had been sanctified ought to have remained his tomb. He has left it only to injure the whole world and above all himself and those whom he loved.[77]

The break becomes evident from the first call, but it develops further. In Jeremiah's case it strikes his existence through and through. There are two Jeremiahs: one with his personal and natural interests, and the other, into which prophecy has changed him. The two are engaged in a merciless struggle, since they are antithetical. No one ever had a more sensitive nature than Jeremiah, no one was more outgoing or craving of love. Many times he mentions his father and his mother in an outburst of joy. He describes the welling emotion which the beloved or pitied child arouses in his parent's soul. He loves his people passionately, and no one understood better how to give lyrical expression to the theme of married love which unites God and Israel:

"Oh my mother, thou who has brought me forth . . ." (15:10)

" . . . the man who brought my father the good news of my birth, a message which made him happy." (20:15)

". . . She cries for her children and does not let herself be comforted for her lost children." (31:15)

". . . Is this a beloved child, a son to be fondled? The more I talk of him, the more shall I remember him; my heart yearns for him . . ." (31:20)

". . . I love thee, Israel, with an eternal love. . . ." (31:3)

". . . I remember the love of thy youth, the kindness of thy bridehood, when thou didst follow me in the desert. . . . (2:2)

It is against this man, whose natural sensitivity vibrates with all the undertones of love, that the other one arises. As a prophet, Jeremiah must condemn all he loves—his family, his friends, Jerusalem and her people, the object of his nostalgia and of his fervor. His love is taken out by its roots. Through his prophetic vocation Jeremiah is being removed from human love, from every earthly and human possibility for sympathy and affection. He has not known the sweetness of a sheltered and fondled childhood, and he will not know the feeling of friendship nor the trepidation of married love: "Thou shalt not take a wife, nor shalt thou have sons and daughters" (16:1). He will die a lonely death, without the comfort of tears. Wherever he goes, he stirs up mistrust and dissension. "All of them curse me" (15:10). As God had threatened from his first moment on, this sensitive child has become forever a fortified city, a pillar of iron, a brazen wall. But what a furious tempest rages within those fortifications! What a nostalgia of love, hurled against dark walls!

Isaiah is beset by pain of another kind. If Jeremiah must shed his love, Isaiah must shed his garments. For three years he must walk naked. His nakedness is a "sign" for Egypt and Ethiopia. It is the transformation of a man who had been known in Jerusalem for his decency and respectability. Had the purity of his married life not been a symbol in Jerusalem?[78] He and his wife and children are models of morality. Prophecy changes that modesty. In order to be a witness, Isaiah must exhibit himself. Prophecy assails his very nature. Ezekiel likewise is smitten at the most sensitive part of his conscience. That scrupulous priest has never soiled his body, has never allowed his lips

to taste anything impure. Now the prophetic demand tells
him to eat an impure cake, baked in excrements. Ezekiel
obeys the absolute order, but not without a rebellious cry
which weakens, at least partially, the harshness of the
divine demand.[79] It looks as if prophecy wanted—be it
only at certain moments and on a trial basis—to break
what is most personal in the prophet, and to change him
completely in relation to himself.

We are here certainly faced with a limited situation:
Not the prophet's particular psychology is involved but
what is most generally human in him. His natural morality is attacked by the absolute, and ethically this may be a
counterorder. Nobody would yield if he did not have the
certainty of a call by the absolute. To a certain degree this
is the case of Saul's encounter with Amalek, where a spontaneous and humanitarian feeling is thwarted by a call to
murder. The same holds true when Abraham is called
upon to sacrifice his only son.[80] Kierkegaard's analysis[81]
shows that the paradox of a change turns here into the
absurd. All human motives tell Abraham to disobey. But
he obeys, knowing well that his gesture does not make any
sense. But the most characteristic example is furnished by
Hosea at the beginning of his message:

"The beginning of God's word to Hosea, when the
Lord said to him: Go and get for yourself an unfaithful
woman that she may give you children of an unfaithful
woman, for the land has become unfaithful by forsaking
the Lord. So he went and took Gomer the daughter of
Diblaim. She conceived and bore a son . . . She conceived
again and bore a daughter . . . She conceived again and
bore a son . . ." (Hosea 1:2-3)

The prophetic awakening of the prophet is astonishing
to a degree that we can hardly believe that the prophet
put into practice what God had told him. And yet, nothing
allows us to be sure that Hosea's vocation was a purely
symbolic one. That marriage constitutes one of the high

points of prophecy. It indicates up to what unheard of point the prophets considered God's call to be absolute, and up to what point that absolute tore them out of normal dimensions. The scandal of the Word has here its fullest sense. For while Abraham was only put to the test, and his knife was stayed before it even touched Isaac, Hosea had to consummate his marriage with Gomer and to continue it until she had given him three children. It is not a scandal of a miracle within nature, nor is it the scandal of a social revolt, but here the scandal touches the human person in his instinctive morality and in his purity. It consists here in the fact that the source of all good, in the direction toward the good, forces man to do evil. The alteration is perfect. What Hosea would never have done without shame, without having the feeling of sinking in mire, he does here consciously and wide awake, in the service of God.

The Burden

But does he do it of his free will? We are allowed to doubt it. Decisions as grave as those of Hosea and Abraham, acts as spectacular as those of Isaiah and Ezekiel, sufferings as painful as those of Jeremiah and Samuel are not realized or accepted without resistance. The prophets themselves declare that they have been forced. Prophecy is a *burden*. Here we have the second aspect of pain.

As we have seen, a prophetic knowledge communicated by the spirit or the word implies violence and a confrontation. Between God and the prophet there is a fight and a holding on. But now we must stress that in that debate the Spirit and the Word are always victorious. For many years Jeremiah wandered through the streets of Jerusalem, a yoke on his neck.[82] Although that symbol surpasses the personal condition of the prophet—he is supposed to demonstrate the servitude of the nations under the scepter of Nebuchadnezzar—there is no more exact image for the description of the prophetic being—the prophet must bend his neck, he is a vanquished prisoner.

Jeremiah can distinguish clearly between the two instants of the revelation, the undecided fight, and the obedience following the victory of the absolute. He also knows that if the fight is exalting and can be compared to the violence of love, servitude is torture:

"O God, thou hast seduced me, and I was seduced, thou hast prevailed on me, and thou hast been victorious . . ."

When I said unto myself: I will not think of Him any more nor speak in His name, then it was in myself like a burning fire, contained in my bones; I tried to tame it but I could not. . . . (20:7, 9)

It is as if Isaiah asked for a fight. In connection with the theophany, there is, surprisingly, a divine monologue:

"I heard the Lord's voice say: Whom shall I send, and who will go for us?" (6:8)

Perhaps this was a conversation with angels; at any rate the question was not addressed to Isaiah. But his human reply interrupts, and he offers his services:

"Here I am, send me." (*Ibid.*)

But even if the acceptance was made voluntarily, the sequence of the vocation is no longer so. Isaiah, too, feels that he is being forced. God speaks to him and exhorts him "with a strong hand" (8:11). To Ezekiel, too, God's hand is a constraining one. It is evoked repeatedly, and represents a special category of the revelation besides the spirit and the word; it is the category of necessity. Through the spirit, Ezekiel *knows* God; through the word, he participates in God's history in the world. God's *hand forces* him to know and to participate, through clarity and the mystery, through language and silence, through motion and through paralysis. Ezekiel's entire personal attitude, which is sometimes so disturbing, at other times even morbid, is controlled by the *Hand*.

But the most characteristic expression for prophetic servitude is *massa, burden*. It is synonymous with *prophecy* and is used in that way by numerous prophets. A violent diatribe of Jeremiah (chapter 23) throws light on the primitive meaning of the "burden." Jeremiah rises against the false prophets, who prophesy without having been commissioned by God to do so, who steal the words which God has communicated to authentic prophets, and who imagine and fabricate visions and words. Under pain of curse, he forbids the use of the term *burden* as a description of their prophecy. Two conceptions of prophecy are contrasted in that scene. One, considered false by Jeremiah, arises out of man's free will—all he has to do is to consult his own heart, to let loose his imagination, to pilfer from his neighbor, to take hold of the spirit or the word, and then to announce a prophecy. The other, the authentic one, bases its very authenticity on the fact that it is a *burden,* a charge imposed from the outside, neither searched for nor desired but inflicted. In order to safeguard this criterion of authenticity Jeremiah forbids the armchair prophets to use the word "burden." Jeremiah knows that *the Word which God communicates to man is a burden,* but to apply that term to prophecies made up by men means to deprive the words of the living God of their very essence. It can be used only by a prophet who, like Jeremiah, knows his prophecy to be true *because* it is a burden.

It is impossible to get rid of that heavy burden. In every prophetic intervention there is a resoluteness. The criterion which Jeremiah chooses to distinguish true from false prophecy is not the only one considered in the Bible, but it gives the best account of the prophet's psychology and his metamoral situation. There is the criterion outlined by Jeremiah himself on another occasion; it distinguishes between the prophecy of misfortune, which is authentic because it implies a call to repentance, and the prophecy of good luck, which is false, because it is unfruitful from a moral point of view; then we have the opinion of Deuteronomy, which sees in loyalty to the Torah the proof for the truth of prophecy;[83] in addition to the divine character of prophecy which is attested by its transcending all morals, prophecy is shown to be true because it contains a dialectic between liberty and necessity. Prophecy proves that liberty remains a problem.[84]

The prophets have experienced this problem most painfully. Nothing is more instructive than an analysis of the efforts made by the prophets so as to preserve their liberty, and the difficulties they encountered in doing so. These efforts are of various degrees, and sometimes the first of them arises at the very moment of the first call, at the first blow to the prophet's personal freedom—he *rejects* the vocation.

The most characteristic scene is that of Moses' refusal.[85] He accepts his mission only after a long dialogue which lasted many days. The staging is grandiose. Before the miracle of the burning bush, which fascinates Moses, and whose secret he wishes to pierce, he stops, confounded to hear that what is revealed there concerns him. With an indefatigable patience he tries to plead his innocence. The simplicity of the dialogue is equaled only by the naïvité of the arguments with which Moses confronts his great Opponent. He does not try to find a basis for them, and there is no real dialectic but rather a series of objections, which in turn are all thrust aside, one by one, by God's reply, which, however, is not discussed either. Moses' last objection shows the real drama: "Send whom thou wilt." Like an animal trapped in a snare he would like to make his escape. He asks for nothing except the free gift of liberty. But God's wrath forces him to yield. At least, when talking to God, he has at first demonstrated his desire to remain free.

We find the same dialogue in the call of Jeremiah.[86]

That dialogue is shorter but more dramatic. Jeremiah's arguments, which are to a certain extent the same as those of Moses, are united into one outcry: "I am a child, I do not know how to talk, I am afraid." God forces him, not through His anger but through His hand. We have noticed that this is the symbol of the burden. God's hand touches Jeremiah's lips, and thus they are closed to refusal, open to prophecy.

But the lips are not closed forever, an inner debate goes on and reappears sometimes in moments of crisis during the prophetic career. Jeremiah confesses that he wishes at times to hold his message back and thus to show his freedom by refusing to let himself be forced to speak. As a touching detail, he does not dare to make that confession to God Himself but only to his own tortured soul, in a short monologue. Let us repeat therefore the verses (7ff.) of chapter 20, in which Jeremiah describes the seduction and the weight of the divine word: "O God, thou hast seduced me, and I was seduced, thou hast prevailed on me, and thou hast been victorious. All day long I am an object of laughter, everybody disgraces me. Every time that I begin talking I must protest and cry out loud about violence and oppression. For the Lord's word becomes in me a perpetual source of shame and insult. When I said to myself: I will not think of Him any more nor speak in His name, then it was in myself like a burning fire, contained in my bones. I tried to tame it, but I could not."

The first of these verses, which recalls the past and the first embrace, has a dialogical structure—the prophet addresses himself to God. But the following verses evoke God in the third person. In order to confide and to admit his temporary wish to escape God, Jeremiah hides. He talks but to himself, in a barely audible voice, perhaps in fear that God might hear his confession.

In similar circumstances other prophets do not hesitate

to use a dialogue. After having carried the burden of prophecy for a long time, they return to God and ask Him to remove it. Such returns are often the consequence of grave states of crisis following disappointments. Several times Moses takes up a dialogue as if to underline that his first refusal was justified:

"Why hast Thou sent me?" (Exodus 5:22)

"Erase my name from the book that Thou hast written." (*Ibid.*, 32:32)

"Why has Thou made Thy servant unhappy, and why have I not found favor in Thine eyes, and thou hast laid upon me the burden of this entire people. Am I then the father of this people or their mother, that Thou sayest unto me: Carry them in thy lap as a nurse carries an infant . . ." (Numbers 11:11f.)

In these verses there is not only a refusal to prophesy. We shall soon see that they conceal a real revolt. Nevertheless they indicate moments of weakness in Moses' activity, moments when he would have ardently wished to regain his liberty. Elijah, too, finds it necessary to complain to God. We do not know under what circumstances he had been elected. But following the scene on Mount Carmel, and when, hunted down by Jezebel, he must flee for his life, he addresses himself to his divine Opponent and tells Him that he is resigning. He concentrates his refusal in one single word: "Enough!" (1 Kings 19:4) This expresses all his weariness under the burden of prophecy.

Sometimes the dialogue is a silent one. This is certainly the case with Isaiah, who, unlike all others, claims to have been chosen, but who also had to refuse one day, as is evident from the fact that God had to compel him to continue (Isaiah 8:11). There are no words from either side but a silent confrontation, a brief encounter.

At other times again the fight is one-sided. God speaks, and the prophet indicates his refusal by keeping silent.

The first days of Ezekiel's vocation[87] constitute a long
debate between God and the prophet. God turns to the
spirit, the word, the hand; He inspires, persuades, and
commands. Faced with these means of persuasion, Ezekiel
remains passive. Only when the Spirit invades him completely, when the Word is eaten by him, when the Hand
is laid on his neck with force, does he go to the people to
whom God sends him. But after having arrived there, at
Tel Aviv, he goes into seclusion for seven days, in complete silence.[88] But why? Are not his spirit and his body
the carriers of a precise message, immediately meant for
the people who surround him? To hold back his message
—is that not a sin against his vocation, as God indeed
reminds him at the end of the seventh day?[89] But it is
just that reminder which makes Ezekiel a prophet. Before that time, he had refused. His obstinate silence toward God's violence, and his even more savage silence
before the people—those are the signs of his refusal.
During all these first days, Ezekiel walks in *bitterness*
and *anger*.[90] They are inarticulate, purely emotional, and
profoundly negative replies to God's calls.

Finally the refusal takes on an extreme form. Escape
is sought—not only from the vocation but from the dialogue with God. The uselessness of the dialogue is known
in advance, hence it is to be avoided through *flight*. As
soon as God has spoken to him, Jonah takes to flight. Here
is a prophet who has been enlightened by his own earlier
experiences or those of other prophets. God says to him:
"Arise and go to Nineveh." Jonah *rises and flees to
Tarshish*.[91] Here is a perfect contradiction, since Nineveh
is in the east, while Tarshish is in the west. The will to
escape the divine intention cannot be better expressed.
Tarshish is anyhow only a pretext. What Jonah is looking
for is the distance, or better, the removal. Ernst Simon
has shown well[92] what a remarkable progression there is
in that removal. At first Jonah flees in a boat which goes

out into the sea; then he descends into the hold of the ship; after that he goes to sleep, while everybody else prays excitedly; at last he wants to be thrown into the stormy sea. Instead of being put into chains by God, he wishes to die in the unchained elements of free nature.

The *refusal* is, however, only the first attempt to throw off the prophetic burden. The *revolt* is a more decisive one.

The refusal indicates a doubt which concerns only the prophet's person. Moses knows that God can choose a man to fulfill the precise plan for the liberation of Israel, but he thinks that He made a mistake in calling *him*. He has the feeling that he is not prepared for the task imposed upon him. This is also the meaning of Jeremiah's outcry: "I am only a child." And that of Elijah: "I am no better than my forefathers." This is a moral sentiment of a personal weakness which the Bible calls humility, *anavah*.[93] Sometimes the refusal is motivated by *fear,* the obsessing awareness of the obstacles and difficulties threatening the chosen one. When God says to him: "Fear not, I shall be with thee," he answers in fact with the anxiety that will appear again and again in the prophetic career, according to the circumstances. Besides the basic wish to be free, the refusal is also founded on the yearning to belong only to oneself, to do one's work in his own time, and not in the time of the absolute. The Biblical account attributes such a nostalgia to Jacob, that energetic patriarch who devotes himself to the God whom he has met at Beth El; and yet, on the eve of his meeting with Esau he has a moment of weakness. He wants to escape. He takes his wives and children across the river Jabbok, and he wants to follow them, when an angel waylays him and engages him in combat. In spite of himself, he becomes "Israel," the challenger of God.[94] He is refused the stay in his own personal time—he must penetrate God's time. But of whatever nature the moving

powers of the refusal may be, they always concern the
prophet himself. The *revolt* starts when the questioning
no longer concerns the chosen one but God.

The prophet has the painful feeling that God is not prepared for the fulfillment of His wish, that man is defeated
by the absurdity or the sudden halt of the divine intention.
He asks: "Why?" The question concerns the cause as well
as the goal of the divine action. It asks for the revelation
of a meaning, where reality does not furnish it. Not the
election is rejected but its paradox. The election is in vain,
and all its sufferings are futile, since they lead to a dead
end:

"Why hast thou made Thy servant unhappy? Why
hast thou sent me?" (Exodus 5:22)

Well, why has Moses been chosen? His first mission
to Pharaoh aggravates the situation of the Hebrews
instead of alleviating it. So far, they had only been mis-
treated, but now their very lives are at stake. Why must
Moses remain a prophet later on, with such a stiff-necked
people? He has promised to lead them to Canaan, but
they die in the wilderness. What a failure of the promise,
what an absurd enterprise!

"Enough!" (1 Kings 19:4) Elijah's outcry follows
the scene on Mount Carmel. For years on end, Ahab and
Jezebel have persecuted the servants of God. Many people have already died in battle, many prophets have succumbed to the sword. Only Elijah has escaped. Only he is
confronted with 850 prophets of the Baal and the Ashera
on Mount Carmel. The Lord has performed His miracle,
and the idol worshippers have found an inglorious end.
But neither the blood of the innocent and of the guilty,
nor the resounding miracle, suffice to convince Jezebel.
Elijah himself must die: "I have been zealous for thee,
O Lord God of hosts, for the children of Israel have
rejected Thy covenant, they have overthrown Thine
altars, and killed Thy prophets with the sword" (1 Kings

19:10). What else is needed for God's final victory? To what end that tragedy which makes so many people suffer, if the woman, the cause of the battle, remains unconvinced?

Jeremiah's revolt is more complicated. Since he has suffered more than others, and has been crushed and overwhelmed by the divine word according to his own expression (23:29), his questions are more numerous and more penetrating. First of all, they have to do—as with Moses and Elijah—with the disproportion between the means employed by God and the result to which they lead, the scandal of the divine staging, as we might call it. The redemption of Hanameel's field is one of those scenes, as contrived by God. As we have pointed out previously, this scene[95] is of prime importance for Jeremiah's prophecy. But Jeremiah realizes the whole artificiality and painful irony of this incident. God gives the actors a precise and limited role, and each of them recites the number of words needed for the success of the short interlude, and executes the few indispensable gestures. Hanameel must say: Buy my field. Jeremiah: I accept. The scribes must write down the transaction, and the witnesses must seal it. The setting, too, is furnished by God: the courtyard of a prison, in a besieged and starving city. Finally, the lesson of this enacted fable is also given by God: "Hope!" Although everything in and around the actors cries out in despair, they accept the lesson. But even before it becomes known to Jeremiah, and before he inscribes it into the very heart of his vibrant thought, he utters a majestic outcry. He fulfills his role in all its details, but then he stands up before God in a long prayer, a true defiance thrust at God, so that He should explain the unexplainable and stop playing games with the fate of human beings and start being serious about it.

"O Lord God, thou hast created the heaven and the earth with thy great strength and thine outstretched arm.

Nothing is too hard for thee. Thou extendest thy goodness to the thousandth generation, and thou visitest the
sins of the fathers to their children after them. Thou
great and mighty God, who art called the Lord of Hosts.
Great in thy plans, sovereign in their fulfillment, thine
eyes look upon all the paths of men, to reward them according to their ways and the merit of their works. For
Israel and others Thou hast sent to the land of Egypt
signs and wonders which are still remembered, and Thou
hast made thy name famous as is seen today. Thou hast
taken Thy people Israel out of Egypt with signs and
wonders, with a mighty hand and an outstretched arm, in
the midst of profound terror. Thou hast given to them
this land which Thou hadst promised to their fathers, a
land flowing with milk and honey. They entered it and
took possession of it; but they did not listen to thy voice
neither did they follow thy teaching, they refused to do
what Thou hast told them. Then Thou hast brought upon
them all this evil. Now the enemy is trying to take the
city by assault; it is already at the mercy of the Chaldeans who besiege it, and given over to the sword, the
famine, and the pestilence. What Thou hast foretold has
happened, and Thou art its witness. But Thou O Lord
hast said to me: buy thyself this field for money, and get
some witnesses—now that the city is handed over to the
Chaldeans!" (Jeremiah 32:16ff.)

But that serious appeal to God comes out of despair.
Then Jeremiah asks Job's question. He struggles with
God in two concise verses:

"Thou art too righteous, O Lord, that I should fight
with Thee. Yet will I talk to Thee of justice: Why does
the road of evil men prosper? Why do they live in security, all those who do perfidious things? Thou hast planted
them, and they take root; they grow and bring fruit . . ."
(Jeremiah 12:1f.)

In the scene of Hanameel, God answered Jeremiah's

prayer. But here, just as Job and the Psalmist had not received a reply, Jeremiah does not get one either. He seems to accuse God of forgetting the consequences of his actions. He planted the evildoers; why should it then surprise us that they take root, grow, and are fruitful? Their roots ought to have been taken out in time, or not have been planted in the first place. Is God thoughtless besides being ironical?

Finally, during this painful convulsion, Jeremiah asks himself whether God has not deceived him, whether his whole prophetic experience makes sense, and whether he is not the plaything of a painful illusion.

"Grasped by Thy hand, I have lived by myself, and Thou hast filled me with anger. Why is my suffering without an end, my wound poisoned, rejecting all remedy?

Art Thou to me a treacherous river, water which cannot be counted upon? . . . (*Ibid.* 15:17f.)

Job was afraid of being God's target. Jeremiah fears to be His plaything.

It is just such a fear which makes Jonah take flight. He, too, rebels against God's change of mind: "O Lord, is not that which I said when I was still in my land? That is why I made haste to flee to Tarshish. For I knew that Thou art a kind and merciful God and full of patience, changing Thy mind concerning evil!" (Jonah 4:2)

God's change of mind illustrates the futility of the prophetic vocation. They are examples of the whim in God's system when dealing with the world. Human effort is fruitless. God uses man as an instrument, as a plaything, without entrusting him with the secret of His intentions, without even telling him that there are any.

In the soul of the prophets the revolt releases a terrible confusion, a veritable nausea. Those prophets who have asked "Why?" have desperately yearned for death. They have gone through the nostalgia of getting rid of the weighty metaphysical appeal which carried them away to a nonexisting goal and did not take them out of the realm of the inexplicable.

"Erase my name from the book that Thou hast written. . . .

"If thou hast planned such an end for me, then let me rather die, if I have found favor in Thine eyes, and I shall not have to look any more upon this evil. . . . " (Moses in Exodus 32:32; Numbers 11:15)

"It is enough, O my God. Take my life away, for I am not better than my fathers . . . " (Elijah in 1 Kings 19:4)

"Cursed be the day that I was born! May the day that my mother brought me to the world not be blessed! Cursed be the man who brought to my father the good news of my birth and thus gave him great joy. May that man be like the cities which God hath destroyed in His anger. May he hear in the morning the cries of war, and the trumpets of battle at midnight!

"Why did He not let me die in the womb that carried me? My mother would then have been my tomb, and she would always have kept her fruit. Why did I have to leave the motherly womb to see misery and pain, and to live my days in contempt? . . . (Jeremiah 20:14ff)

"Perish the day that I was born, and the night in which it was announced that a boy had been conceived. May those constellations remain dark, may one wait in vain for light and never see the dawn, for the gates of the womb in which I was conceived were not shut up, and misery was not hidden from my looks. . . .

"Why did I not die from before birth, and why did I not breathe my last before leaving my mother's womb? If I only had remained unborn like the abortive child that one hides away, and like still born children who never saw the light of day. . . . " (Job 3)

"And now, O Lord, take my life from me, for I prefer death to life. . . .

"I treasure death more than life . . .

"I have a perfect right to be enraged, to the point that
I desire death. . . . (Jonah 4:3,8,9)

Those painful words express the weariness and disgust
when men were faced with a mystery beyond their understanding.

The March in the Night

Neither the refusal nor the rebellion liberates the
prophet. The more he tries to reject his vocation, the
more it takes hold of him. God's anger forces Moses to
accept his mission. The stormy sea and the "big fish"
lead Jonah forcefully back to his prophecy. Elijah is made
ready for new tasks. Isaiah and Ezekiel give in to God's
powerful Hand. Jeremiah remains a prisoner of the divine Word. No prophet has ever escaped God. Amos
analyzes the rigor of that necessity and gives us a logical
definition:[96] God and the prophet are linked to each other
like the lion and his prey, like the bird and its snare, like
the trumpet and war. When the lion roars, one is afraid,
and when God speaks, the prophet must answer. When
God and the prophet meet, they become inseparable.

The joint march, which is at first felt as a necessity,
soon sweeps the prophet off his feet. He no longer refuses but accepts in savage resignation, which may lead
him to martyrdom. A modern commentator believes he
has found in the Book of Hosea a hint of Moses' martyrdom—he is said to have died in the wilderness as a victim
of rebellion.[97] Although that exegesis is untenable, it is
not without sense, if we consider Moses' psychology.
According to a Jewish tradition Moses' substitute, Hur,
was killed in connection with the Golden Calf,[98] and
Isaiah died a martyr during Manasseh's rule.[99] The
prophets of the time of Elijah die by Jezebel's word.
Hanani and Michayu succumb in prison. Uriah is executed by Joachim. Jeremiah is repeatedly threatened
with death. Thus even death, which the prophets have

sought, does not liberate them. Neither Moses nor Elijah, Job, Jeremiah nor Jonah dies at the time when death would have meant liberation to him. Some of them do die as martyrs. God's prisoners, they die for His secret plans. Their death is not a deliverance but the final incident of their servitude.

The absolute cannot be translated in human terms; it cannot be explained at all. It is fulfilled. It seems that the prophet is not the organ of a self-revealing God but the instrument of a God Who is on the verge of hiding. Our analysis has led us to the recognition that God's movement toward the world is not an approach but a retreat. God takes the prophet's hand and leads him on that secret road which removes him. Prophecy does emerge from the absolute, but from an absolute which becomes darker and darker the more it comes into the open. It is a march with God, but toward the night of the unexplainable.

Sometimes, however, clarity arises in a lightning flash. God explains Himself. He justifies Himself and the prophet. Such a divine testimony is called *miracle* by the Bible. Although such miraculous moments are rare in the lives of the prophets, they do occur sometimes. At times, when the prophets did God's work in the world, they were relieved by God. God then entered the world, bringing along His own and the prophet's justice and innocence.

Sometimes that clarity arises slowly. Yesterday's darkness unveils itself today or tomorrow. This was notably the case with the prophecies of misfortune, the scandals and irritation of which lasted two centuries. At last the catastrophe was fulfilled, and all the prophecies were justified.

But in the very midst of the miracle and the confirmation there remains a darkness, a bitterness. One of the most dazzling miracles—the one on Mount Carmel, performed for Elijah's sake—fails to convince the one who was supposed to be shaken by it: Jezebel. The day following that miracle Elijah touches the nadir of his troubled restlessness. God has testified in vain. The confirmation does not heal the burning wounds of the attending prophets. Moses dies on the frontier of the Promised Land without seeing the fulfillment of the Word for which he has lived. Uriah is executed before the prophecies for whose sake he is put to death have been confirmed. Ezekiel does witness the confirmation, but without his wife, whom God has taken away as a symbol of suffering.[99]

Finally there are some who have seen neither miracle nor confirmation. Saul is sick to the end and dies with the whole bitterness of the mystery of his fate. But at least he knows that in one case he has disobeyed the absolute. But Jeremiah? None was a more loyal servant of the absolute than he. In the tragic moments of his existence God refuses to testify in his behalf and hands him over to persecution. The confirmation of his disastrous prophecies would have been complete, and he would have had the painful satisfaction of witnessing it, if the last incident of his life had not taken him to Egypt. Against his protests the Judeans who were maddened by the assassination of Gedalyah take him to Egypt,[100] and there he again becomes a prophet. His last prophecies[101] are addressed to those Judeans who have learned nothing from the catastrophe and have remained idol worshippers and blasphemers. As Jeremiah had done for forty years in Jerusalem, he foretells their sad end. However, he will not see the confirmation of that new prophecy. He dies with his thirst unquenched. Jeremiah is the prophet who walks with God, in the night, the silence, and the solitude, on a narrow path, at the foot of gigantic walls without windows, doors, or exit.

The Meaning

The Vision as a Symbol

But in the dark night Jeremiah *sees,* and his *vision* is *good.*

"The Lord addressed me thus: What seest thou, Jeremiah?

I replied: I see a branch of an almond tree.

Thou hast seen well, said the Lord to me, for I will hasten to fulfill My word." (Jeremiah 1:11f.)

All Jeremiah has seen is a branch of the almond tree, but by seeing it he has penetrated in its *meaning.* Through the reflection he reaches light. The prophetic vision unveils the essence of the things. Twenty times Jeremiah has seen the blossoms of an almond tree in his native region, and twenty times it has been the harbinger of spring. But now time becomes meaningful, whirling in blossoms which suddenly seem to be in a rush—the wood becoming a leaf, the leaf a flower, the flower a fruit, it is God's haste, which makes His word ripen. The almond tree itself as well as the word which expresses it, the element of which it is made and the place which it occupies, the moment when it appears and the growth which animates it—in short, all that designates the object for human understanding: language, matter, space, time, life— all become a *meaningful symbol.* Normal vision is *designation.* The prophetic vision is the *giving of a sense.* Out of the nomenclature according to human seeing, out of the catalogue of things, all of a sudden values arise. In the fields of Anatoth Jeremiah has seen twenty times how the peasant poked the cauldron to burn his straw. But now the cauldron surprises him because its opening faces north. Thus the direction of the cauldron stops being banal. Time takes on a meaning. It trembles already at the disaster which the Chaldeans will bring from the north:

"What seest thou?

"I see a boiling cauldron facing north.

"And the Lord said to me: From the north disaster will come upon all the inhabitants of the earth." (Jeremiah 1:13)

How many times has Jeremiah passed by the potter, who turned his vessels in the streets of Jerusalem! He is a humble artisan, busy with his work, perhaps sometimes impatiently working, and he breaks the clay when it does not obey its master's orders. Suddenly Jeremiah sees. The potter's finger stands out and has unheard-of proportions. It is now God's finger, and its gesture of impatience is God's impatience, the clay is Israel, humanity, all rebels, and God breaks them and throws them out like so much waste.

At the basis of the prophetic vision is certainly the Hebrew concept of the concrete. Tresmontant is right in insisting on the *meaning* of tangible things in the Biblical cosmos. Tangible things have by nature a meaning which does not have to be added from the outside. Tresmontant writes: "The meaning of the tangible explains itself by the fact that it has been created by a word; it is itself a language, the substantial manifestation of a creative word. . . . The tangible elements mean something. All creation is like an organ being played with words. The Biblical writers . . . play this symbolic instrument with surprising coherence. One might say that of all them use the same instrument, the same registers, the same key, and the variations are played according to a code, a counterpoint, which keeps the original meaning of the element."[102] From this we derive a permanent meaning for the symbolism of the Biblical elements, a possibility of expressing the immanent things through the *mashal*, the *parable*.

But the vision of the prophets is not just a parable. It is not an account made of elements whose meaning is

clear but is an understanding of the meaning. If we were
to hold on to the musical metaphor we would say that on
the elementary instrument the parable plays, and the vision deciphers. The unveiled "cipher" may differ from the
known meaning—the main thing is that it is *right*. The
vision includes thus a variety of meanings, and for this
reason it is surprising. The note one hears is not the
expected one. It is different from, and sometimes contrary
to, the one that has resounded so often when one looked
forward to the precise touch on the instrument. There are
changes and paradoxes in the vision; the harmony of
things reveals itself in being disharmonious. But the
great importance of the vision lies in the fact that it proclaims that changes, paradoxes, disharmonies are *right*.
The vision brings the things to light and at the same time
shows their unity; it is the harmonizing force of the disorder which it provokes; it cures by wounding; it is the
light through secrets.

Therefore the vision at first presents a difficult and
painful stage, namely, that of unveiling. Then follows a
stage of clarity and joy—judgment. The dialogues between God and Jeremiah, Amos, and Zechariah throw
light on the path of the vision. The prophet must begin
by discovering a new relationship between the things
themselves: almond tree—haste; the potter's finger—
God's finger. These are meanings which the objects did
not always have in themselves but which have just now
been put into them. These meanings are above suspicion.
The opening of a pot facing north gets its meaning by its
direction. The object of this place, the *here*, is the true
sign. At some other place the cauldron may have a different meaning. Likewise, Amos sees God create locusts. It
is not the locusts that are significant but the fact that they
are being created,[103] their instantaneous presence, *now*.
The vision discovers the *here* and the *now* of the element.
This difficulty causes hesitation in the prophets. The dia-

logues that have to do with the visions are not practical exercises in "seeing right." God assists the prophet in decoding: "What seest thou?" Often the prophet lacks intelligence. "What is this, O Lord?" asks Zechariah.[104] Ezekiel understands only much later that the *creatures* he had seen on the banks of the river Kebar in Babylonia were angels of the Temple at Jerusalem.[105]

The phase of decoding leads to that of judgment. "Thou hast seen well."[106] When all is said and done, the vision is always "good," for this refers to exact vision as well as to the content of the prophecy. When God created the world, He too had a *vision,* and that vision was "good."[107] In spite of all its disharmonies, contradictions, separations and multiplicities, the world offered a right and good vision. The prophetic vision includes that optimistic aspect. When the vision shatters the usual dimensions of the world, when it confuses normal nomenclatures, it restores the correctness and the goodness of the world. The prophet's vision grants him a justification of his vocation, an assurance of being in accord with God's truth, a "sign." The Bible calls such a verified vision *oth* or *mofeth.*

But the word *oth* sometimes stands also for "miracle," and we must beware of confounding the two meanings. Through the miracle the absolute penetrates the world and justifies itself through its self-revelation. The sign is but an allusion of the absolute, but a *certain* allusion. A miraculous situation includes the absolute, while a meaningful situation apprehends it—it does not state anything about the absolute, except that it is close and real. We have said that the prophets were acquainted with miracles, although only rarely, and some witnessed none at all. But the sign was given to the prophets in their visions. The apprehension of the absolute, the unshakable feeling of the closeness of a removed God, of the presence of a concealed God, of the truth of the paradox, of the har-

mony of the contradictions—all this characterizes prophecy and is essential to it. But the *vision* comes from the
outside. Its sign is outside the prophet, who beholds it
without becoming part of it. A new and even more essential aspect of prophecy arises when the sign manifests itself in the prophet's life, which means that the prophet
himself, in his personality and existence, becomes a
"sign," when a *living* prophecy becomes the token of the
absolute.

Isaiah and Ezekiel apply the terms *oth* and *mofeth* to
themselves. They know that they have a meaning, that
their vocation is not for nothing, and they say so.[108] Other
prophets, too, have the experience of a meaning, even if
the term "sign" does not appear in that connection. Thus
Jeremiah's neck, bending under its yoke, is such a sign.
So are Ezekiel's paralysis and silence, and Isaiah's nakedness. The wounding of the anonymous prophet mentioned
in the Book of Kings[109] is a sign. The food given to Elijah
in his misery by most miserable creatures, a widow and a
raven, are signs.[110] The shade given to Jonah, and then
taken away from him, is a sign.[111]

Through this inner meaning the prophetic scandal
passes from the area of psychology to that of metaphysics. The prophet's suffering does not remain a personal
accident but is inherent in the destiny of a man allied
with God. The change, the burden, freedom denied, martyrdom—those are not experiences which attack the prophetic individual, surprise him, and place him outside a
fate which is common to all men, but they are situations
through which he becomes a man, by freeing himself from
the human illusions of liberty, autonomy, and eternity, by
presenting a harsh reality but also the exalting splendor
of human servitude.

Man becomes another entity, he does not experience
himself any longer. His *here* and his *now* are not the ultimate limits of his existence. He finds himself by looking

THE PROPHETIC EXISTENCE

for himself elsewhere. The prophet is a man who discovers himself as being different. It does not matter that this makes him suffer, since it makes him aware of whatever he did not know about himself, and since by impoverishing him and wounding him in whatever he had been, it enriches him and restores him in whatever he had never been and ought always to have been.

Man is not at liberty to withdraw from God. The call of the absolute triumphs always. Man's way is hemmed in by God. What an illusion to believe oneself free, just because the road is long, the landscape wide, and God hides in darkness or distance. The awareness of God's omnipresence gives the prophetic burden an eminently positive meaning. When Amos describes human destiny, he compares it to that of "a man who flees the lion and is faced with a bear; he enters his house, leans against a wall, and is stung by a serpent . . . " (Amos 5:19)

Man is handed over to God:"If they try to hide in the underworld, from there My hand will seize them; let them go up to heaven, I shall make them come down; let them hide on top of the Carmel, there I shall seek them out and take them; if they hide before Me on the bottom of the sea, there will I command a serpent to sting them . . . " (Amos 9:2f.)

The prophet is a man who knows himself to be surrounded by God, and that neither space nor time are ever without God. It does not matter whether he is seized in terror or in joy. In his fate feelings do not count but realities. The burden of the prophets signifies fullness with God.

Martyrdom, too, is a reality. It is man's insistence on being different, on being together with God. In martyrdom no mystery concerning another world is being revealed, nor is death being explained. But human history receives a meaning. Martyrdom is the negation of the absurd. Everything receives a meaning through the ultimate testimony of man who accepts that meaning to the very limit. Everything is orientated in relation to that testimony. Everything becomes *sanctified* through it. Jewish tradition calls the *sanctification of God* the martyrdom, which has found its first historical examples in the lives of the prophets.

Prophetic Prayer

Jeremiah *sees* and Jeremiah *prays*. At the height of his suffering, when, in the episode of buying the field, God's seriousness is at stake, he prays. This is the very moment when he and his partners feel that they are deprived of all liberty and initiative, when they only play the roles which God has given them, and which to them have neither rhyme nor reason. Here prophecy and prayer are contrasted in a particular way. The former seems to be merely mechanical, almost a ritual. Were it not for the primary fact of the inspiration and the vocation, due to which the actors have been brought together against their own will, it would remain an empty liturgy, the different parts of which are executed with a slavish and cold heart. On the other hand, Jeremiah puts the whole warmth of his exacerbated soul into the prayer. Here he does not say what he must but what he wishes. Prayer is here the spontaneity which faces the obligation of the prophecy.

But there is no other prophetic prayer than that. Whenever we find a prayer in the mouth of a prophet, it has this character of entire liberty. It is neither praise nor gratitude, for praise and gratitude are based on positive feelings concerning God's majesty or goodness. But the prayer of the prophets bursts forth out of man's anxiety before the inexplicable. It is not founded on an affirmation but on a question. It is often termed a *tefillah,* which is not really a prayer but comes close to a debate.[112] Prophetic prayer is created by man. It does not repeat what it has seen or heard. It introduces a new word in the world. The prayer of the prophets is man's *davar* side by side with the one of God.

It is indeed only in the face-to-face that prayer arises, when the prophet feels that he is in touch with God, although he is separated from Him; when, through the meaning of the vision and the knowledge of the ruach, he becomes aware of facing a Partner who does not give Himself entirely but keeps a remainder of His mystery for Himself. Prayer dwells on the border of that remainder. When it is reabsorbed, and God is seen in all His clarity, the prophet no longer has a prayer, but remains silent. Job is the best example. He prays when he faces the inexplicable. His dialectic is a never-wearying prayer, supported by a harassing and unresolved question which torments his flesh and soul. But when his divine Partner appears at last and justifies Himself, Job becomes silent: "He puts his hand before his mouth" (40:4). Prophetic prayer is the question which man asks God. It disappears when God replies. It has sense only before God's silence or, which is the same in the realm of the absolute, before God's question. The prophet's prayer arises when God is not the Being Who in His self-revelation answers all questions, solves all problems, and through His very existence grants the entire world laws as well as peace and a perfect clarification; but when, on the contrary, He lifts mankind to His own transfigured inaccessability, as if He had to understand the world in order to understand Himself. The prophet's prayer is the human word which God needs.

The Biblical system of the Word is constructed on prophetic prayer. There is in the Bible a confrontation of God and man which we have called dialogue, but this is not simply a transmission of the Word but an authentic dialogue, wherein the Word of the one is as impatiently looked forward to as the Word of the other. The astounding meaning of the prophetic prayer is that God's

Word is neither egoistic nor jealous. It seeks the human Word. The divine monologue wishes to be interrupted. Isaiah understands this immediately when he answers the question which God had addressed to Himself.[113]

In certain Biblical pages we find God's naïve desire to be heard and to see His own anxiety somehow shared. "Should I hide from Abraham what I am going to do? ... God does not do anything without revealing His secret to His servants, the prophets." We have shown above[114] that there is something eminently prophetic in this concept which makes of the prophet an instrument of the absolute. However, God is not looking for an instrument but for a partner. The dialogue between God and Abraham helps God understand His own justice, which was not entirely known to God. Abraham has talked for a long time, and his Word has indeed helped to clarify the notion of justice. But the clarity of justice is not yet complete. At a certain moment Abraham has stopped talking. He has interrupted the dialogue. Some of the mystery hides justice. The clarification would have gone further if Abraham had not stopped talking. The dialogues between God and the prophets are variations of this effort at elucidation. It is not a question of justice any longer but of whatever is problematic in the history of human beings. God reveals Himself, but what is this sending forth of the *spirit* and the *word* if not the sign of a wish?

"Where art thou?" God asks Adam this naïve question,[115] not because Adam has gone astray but because God has lost him. God does not find Adam, whose Word is indispensable to Him. Sin does not break man but the Throne.[116]

Faced with such a break, man may well ask himself: "Where is God?"[117] Jeremiah takes the priests to task for not asking that question, for settling for an illusory cosmic peace, when peace is supposed to be reconstructed on the ruins of the world. Jeremiah prays because he senses that God is not entirely in the prophecy which He sends to him, and that the prophecy is not an end in itself but rather a path in the ruins, a call in the split. Jeremiah's prayer does not arise out of God's presence but out of His distance, and it is this prayer which brings God back. Just as Abraham's prayer has clarified justice, Jeremiah's prayer has clarified God's presence. But just as Abraham's prayer—in coming to a stop—has left part of justice in the field of mystery, so has Jeremiah's interrupted prayer left some of God's presence entrusted to the mystery. The individual dialogue is necessarily limited. The prophet can only hear part of the question God addresses to him. But his intuition helps him to apprehend the entire meaning, since his own existence is integrated with that of the Biblical people. Prophetic prayer comes closer to its full meaning the more it stops being the Word of a man and becomes the Word of Israel.

The March in the Light

In every individual experience the great prophetic attempt to know God through the *ruach* and to realize Him through the *davar* leads to some difficulties. No prophecy has ever been fully achieved, and the prophetic prayer elucidates only a fragment of God's question to man. Sooner or later, in the prophet's lifetime or at the moment of his death, night becomes victorious over the temporary clarity, the Spirit disappears, the Word becomes silent.

Has that silence ever had an absolute meaning? Has the Word been shut up with the last prophet, and does the end of the prophetic canon in the Bible prove that incompleteness? Did the prophetic line become extinct without any harm to the divine-human relations? Post-Biblical man has often asked this question, but the answers given are of very different kinds.

All admit that the Biblical prophets had an apprehension of a luminous future, which they called Israel. Many texts testify to the prophets' belief in a prophetic existence for Israel. This existence implies a change, for Israel is holy, devoted to God, set apart, different and unique, and accepts that change as the unavoidable condition of their election:

"Israel is holy, devoted to God ... (Jeremiah 2:3)

They live by themselves, and cannot be counted among the nations ... (Numbers 23:9)

Their existence means servitude and a scandal, for the election seizes Israel just as it surprises the prophet, in a plan secretly determined, and which fastens them tightly to their vocation:

"The Lord hath called me from the womb, before my birth He has proclaimed my name. . . . He hath said: Thou art my servant, Israel, in whom I glorify . . . " (Isaiah 49:1ff)

This is a meaningful existence, since the change and the servitude set Israel aside by making of them a symbol, the "sign" of the divine history in the world. Israel is the world's axis, nerve, center, and heart. Jeremiah 25 and Isaiah 53 show[118] that such recent terms[119] may well be used without adulterating prophetic thinking. In taking up an idea which our analysis of the prophetic experience has yielded, we might say that to the prophets Israel is the vision of the world. When the Spirit blows over Israel, the entire world arises pathetically and notices the passing of God. When God looks at Israel be it in anger or in love, the world loses its anonymity, the clouds disperse, everybody comes running, all with their own individuality, color, stamp, and fate.

It is thus not surprising that when the prophets changed the provisional knowledge which they shared into an absolute intuition, they affirmed the eternity of the vision of Israel. Israel is inscribed in the world like a law, the law of the heavens and the stars and the earth (Isaiah 30:26; Jeremiah 31:34ff).

Although all post-Biblical interpreters agree on the existence of that vision in the Bible, they interpret it in different ways. Some of them are interested in the divine history without, however, being involved by it. To them, Biblical prophecy is a phase in the spiritual history of humanity, but although they recognize the density of that phase, they consider it utterly completed, and the prophetic vision of Israel is but one of the unrealized dreams of the past. Others are profoundly disturbed by the divine history—Christians, Moslems—and to these Biblical prophecy is ancient history, but it is brought to life again by a new revelation which had been introduced by Biblical prophecy. Accordingly, the prophetic vocation of Israel is realized in that new revelation, by being incarnated in the final and supreme Prophet, in his Spirit and in his Body. Others, finally—the Jews—see in Biblical prophecy a question which divine history asks them even today. To them Biblical prophecy is a trust which concerns them immediately and continually, since they have never ceased being Israel. It seems to them that the chain of the generations is what Isaiah had in mind when he prophesied:

"Thus saith the Lord: This is My covenant with them: My spirit which is upon thee and the Words which I have put in thy mouth will not leave thy mouth or that of thy children or thy children's children for evermore. . . . " (59:21)

They are thus convinced that the Spirit and the Word have not disappeared with the prophets but that they go on uninterruptedly all through the history of the people of Israel. This is a history which the prophets could not grasp entirely, which they could not probe in its universality, but which was made irrevocable by its secret character. To that history they entrusted the fulfillment of their own unfulfilled vocation.

According to the Jewish conviction Israel is neither a myth nor a God but the people loyal to Biblical time. It is the people on whom the prophets had already based the entire responsibility for the covenant, and around whose history they wove the history of all, even their own. Because—different opinions of the commentators notwithstanding—there is in the Bible a continual communion between the prophets and their people. We have seen that the prophets accepted the dimensions of Biblical time; how they worked out a thought which included all the frames of Biblical thinking; how all the different psychological experiences were tied in with the problems of Biblical man. It is also present in the very heart of the most expressive form of that thought and of those experiences—in the symbolism of married love between God and Israel.

That symbolism did not only exist in the prophets' thought but in their very lives. The happy union of Isaiah and his wife, the fulfillment of their love which they find in their children is the sign of the fruitful love between God and Israel (8:18). Hosea's unfortunate love, the low station of the spouse he chooses, and the birth of the illegitimate children—those are signs of the failure of the love. Jeremiah's celibacy is the sign for the break in the love. The death of Ezekiel's wife is a sign of the continuity of the love through suffering and removal. To be themselves the signs of the married love between God and Israel—this is the most essential security the prophets obtained. Israel's history is thus that of the prophets, and to separate their history from that of Israel would mean to wound them in the deepest recesses of their souls. Perhaps the *shining* meaning of prophecy, the one which throws light on its essence beyond the canonical limits of the Bible, resides in that existential intimacy between the personal life of the prophets and the destiny of the people of Israel.

Notes

1. I Kings 18:13.
2. *Ibid.*, 18.
3. *Ibid.*, 22.
4. II Chronicles 16:10.
5. *Ibid.*, 24:17ff.
6. See Babylonian Talmud Yebamoth 49b, and *The Ascension of Isaiah*, London 1900.
7. Jeremiah 26:20ff.
8. *Ibid.*, verse 24.
9. Amos 7:10ff.
10. I Kings 11:29ff.
11. *Ibid.*, 19:16; II Kings 9:1f.
12. Micah 3:5, 11.
13. Jeremiah 20.
14. *Ibid.*, 28.
15. *Ibid.*, 38:6.
16. *Ibid.*, 26.
17. II Kings 22:3.
18. *Ibid.*, 25:22; Jeremiah 40:5.
19. Jeremiah 27:16; 38:7.
20. *Ibid.*, 29:25.
21. Ezekiel 2:3, 7f; 3:7, 9 and *passim.*
22. *Ibid.*, 33:32f.
23. Hosea 11:1.
24. Ezekiel 16: 1ff.
25. Hosea 14:4.
26. Jeremiah 2:2.
27. Hosea 1–3.
28. Jeremiah 3:1ff; Ezekiel 16.
29. Lamentations 1:1.
30. I Samuel 12:12.
31. *Ibid.*, 8:7.
32. Ezekiel 20:33.
33. See Martin Buber: *Koenigtum Gottes,* 3rd ed. 1956. M. Frankfort: *La royauté et les dieux,* pp. 426ff. André Néher: *Existence Juive,* Paris, 1962, pp. 80ff.

34. Ezekiel 37, where v. 25 corrects v. 24: David will not be king any more but a *nassi;* see also 46:2f.
35. Isaiah 11:1.
36. Jeremiah 33:15.
37. This is the general trend in Wellhausen's classical theory developed in his *Prolegomena zur Geschichte Israels.*
38. Babylonian Talmud Berachoth 14b. Babylonian Talmud Sotah 22b.
39. I Samuel 2:12f; 3:11f.
40. Amos 7:13.
41. Amos 4:1ff. See my commentary in *Amos, contribution à l'étude du prophétisme* pp. 82f and 85f.
42. Jeremiah 7; Ezekiel 8.
43. Jeremiah 7:4.
44. Amos 2:7f. Hosea 4:6ff.
45. Amos 2:6.
46. Micah 3:5, 11.
47. Jeremiah 2:8.
48. Ezra 5:1f.
49. Isaiah 6.
50. *Ibid.,* 1.
51. Ezekiel 43:18f.
52. Jeremiah 33.
53. Isaiah 66.
54. Ezekiel 1:24, 33.
55. *Ibid.,* 10:18 and 43:4.
56. *Ibid.,* 24:15ff.
57. Proverbs 11:14.
58. Amos 3:7.
59. See my *Notes sur Qohelet,* Paris, 1951, and my essay on Job in *Judaism* XIII, 1 (Winter 1963).
60. Amos 5:10, 13.
61. Isaiah 57:21; Ezekiel 13:10, 16; Jeremiah 28:9.
62. This has been dealt with by Darmesteter in *Les prophètes d'Israel,* Paris, 1892.
63. I Samuel 9. See my *Existence juive,* pp. 47ff.
64. Genesis 12:1.
65. Exodus 3:10.
66. Amos 7:15.
67. Exodus 3.
68. *Ibid.,* 4:18ff.
69. I Samuel 1:28.
70. Jeremiah 1:5.
71. *Ibid..* 3:1ff.

72. Jeremiah 1:6.
73. Isaiah 6:5.
74. Ezekiel 1:1ff.
75. Isaiah 6:5 and Ezekiel 1:1.
76. Jeremiah 11:21ff.
77. *Ibid.*, 15:10 and 20:14.
78. Isaiah 20.
79. *Ibid.*, 8:18.
80. Genesis 22.
81. Kierkegaard: *Fear and Trembling.*
82. Jeremiah 27:2 and 28:10.
83. Deuteronomy 13:2ff, 18, 20.
84. See my *Amos*, p. 158.
85. Exodus 3 and 4.
86. Jeremiah 1.
87. Ezekiel 1, 2, and 3.
88. Ezekiel 3:15.
89. *Ibid.*, 3:16ff.
90. *Ibid.*, 3:14.
91. Jonah 1:2f.
92. See Ernst Simon: *Bruecken*, Heidelberg, 1965, pp. 437ff.
93. "Anava" is explicitly mentioned as a dominant feature of Moses' character. See Numbers 12:3.
94. Genesis 32:23ff. See also Richard and André Néher: *Transcendance et Immanence*, Lyon, 1946, p. 16. See also my *L'existence juive*, pp. 11ff.
95. Jeremiah 32. See also my *Jeremiah*, pp. 208ff.
96. Amos 3:3ff.
97. Sellin: *Moses und seine Bedeutung fuer die israelitsch-juedische Religions-geschichte*, 1922. Sellin's theses have been taken up by S. Freud in his *Moses and Monotheism*, tr. Katherine Jones. New York, 1939.
98. Babylonian Talmud Sanhedrin 7a. Midrash Rabba Shmoth 41:7.
99. Ezekiel 25:15ff.
100. Jeremiah 43:5f.
101. *Ibid.*, 8ff. and chapter 44.
102. Claude Tresmontant: *Essai sur la pensée hebraique*, pp. 56 and 58.
103. Amos 7:1. This is the actual meaning of the root *y-z-r*.
104. Zachariah 4:4.
105. Ezekiel 10:20.
106. Jeremiah 1:12.
107. Genesis 1:31.
108. Isaiah 8:18; Ezekiel 24:24, 27.
109. I Kings 20:35ff.
110. *Ibid.*, 17:6, 9.

111. Jonah 4:6ff.

112. The root of *tfillah*, prayer, is *p-l-l*, which means "to judge."

113. Isaiah 6:8.

114. Concerning this entire problem see A. J. Heschel: *God in Search of Man*, Philadelphia, 1955, and A. Néhér: *Le Puits de l'Exil—La théologic dialectique du Maharal de Prague*, Paris, 1966, pp. 193ff.

115. Genesis 3:9.

116. God's Throne is reached through evil. Through the evil incarnated in Amalek the "throne is divided." See Midrash Tanchuma on Deuteronomy 25:19.

117. Jeremiah 2:6.

118. Whether the Suffering Servant stands for a people or for a man, it is certain that he is called Israel. See Isaiah 49:3.

119. Following Isaiah 53, the medieval Jewish philosopher Judah Hallevi uses the image of the heart. which Jacob Gordin in the twentieth century changes to nerve, axis or center. (See *Encyclopedia Judaica* s.v. Judah Hallevi.)

Index

351